Texas Blossoms

Food, Flowers
&
Friendship

Introduction by Liz Carpenter

Another Cookbook by the Richardson Woman's Club
Richardson, Texas

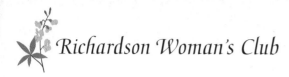

Richardson Woman's Club

Proceeds from the sale of *Texas Blossoms* will be used for service projects and philanthropies sponsored by the Richardson Woman's Club, Inc.

Texas Brazos-Republic Trails

Front Cover:

Cattle graze peacefully among the "bluebonnets" set amid rolling pastures of the Texas Brazos-Republic Trails in Washington County.

Photography by Richard Reynolds

Back Cover:

Up close is a single "bluebonnet", the state flower of Texas, also called buffalo clover, wolf flower, and el conejo (the rabbit). The bluebonnet was adopted as the state flower, on request of the Society of Colonial Dames in Texas, by the Twenty-seventh Legislature.

Photograph provided by Lady Bird Johnson Wildflower Center

Graphic Art by Michael L. Ringham, B.E.D., M.S. Visual Sciences

ISBN 0-9609416-1-4
Richardson Woman's Club, Inc.
Library of Congress Control Number: 2002093409

First Printing   December 2002   10,000 copies
Second Printing   December 2006   5,000 copies

WIMMER
COOKBOOKS

A CONSOLIDATED GRAPHICS COMPANY

800.548.2537   wimmerco.com

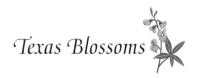

Introduction by Liz Carpenter

Lady Bird Johnson would be the first to tell you that she plants better than she cooks. But that doesn't prevent her from supplying choice recipes tested and enjoyed by some of the choosier diners of our country — Spiced Tea and Pedernales River Chili are two favorites. What makes the new cookbook of the Richardson Woman's Club so enticing is a whole variety of recipes from all parts of Texas. The title "Texas Blossoms" is no exaggeration. Photographs from the Lady Bird Johnson Wildflower Research Center and many others illustrate what picturesque landscapes are ours — from West Texas to the Gulf Coast. Texas land tends to shape its occupants with their own characteristics as different as the terrain of barren plains or piney forests. Historians claim that Texas is 11,000 years old. My own people came here in 1829 when Texas was still a part of Mexico. Space was great and people were few. You needed friends and you knew it. Yes, friendship became a habit. If the cattle stampeded, you needed a friend to help turn the herd. If the oil rig blew down, you needed friends to help you right it. So we assume friendship. We give it and mostly we get it. But whether you were born here or newly arrived, Texas let's you belong to it. We pride ourselves on our friendship as well as our differences. The variety of land, of tastes and the 5,000 wildflowers which now can be found somewhere in our vast countrysides are a joy we want to share. That's what this book is all about — sharing! Taste Texas with all its flavors. And toast the lady who has brought us together under the bounty of blossoms.

Liz Carpenter is a true Texas treasure. She has spent a lifetime as a communicator, reporter, author and speaker. Her most notable achievement was as press secretary for Lady Bird Johnson and chief of staff for the LBJ administration. As a speechwriter, she is the author of one of the most memorable speeches of the sixties — a 58-word, seven-sentence text that Lyndon Johnson delivered after the death of President John F. Kennedy.

LBJ Ranch

Mrs. Lyndon B. Johnson's Recipe for Spiced Tea

I like to serve this to guests on a cold winter's day here at the Ranch – just as I did at the White House.

~ Lady Bird Johnson

6 teaspoons tea (or 8 teabags)
2 cups boiling water

Pour water over tea and let cool. Strain and add:

1 small can frozen lemon juice
1 small can frozen orange juice
1½ cups sugar
2 quarts water
1 stick of cinnamon

Simmer mixture for 20 minutes. If too strong, add water.
Add extra sugar to taste. This recipe makes 16 to 20 cups.

Texas
Blossoms

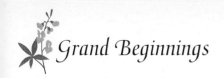

A Texas Blossoms Menu for a

Holiday Open House

Bacon and Swiss Dip
Holiday Pine Cones
Polly Dupont Meatballs
Holiday Ham Spread
Salmon Log
Get Your Goat Mushrooms
Christmas Olive Appetizers
Heavenly Hot Pecans
Hot Asparagus Canapé
Rye Bread Party Snacks
Bacon Cheese Tasties
Friendship Punch
Winter Warmer
Big-Batch Fudge
Candied Fruit Slices

Avocado-Feta Salsa

1 large avocado, peeled, pitted and diced	½ tablespoon chopped fresh oregano
2 plum tomatoes, diced	1 tablespoon olive oil
¼ cup chopped red onions	½ tablespoon red wine vinegar
1 garlic clove, minced	2 ounces crumbled feta cheese
1 tablespoon chopped fresh parsley	

Combine all ingredients; toss and serve immediately with chips. To make ahead, combine all ingredients except the avocado and chill. At serving time add avocado.

Gazpacho Dip

Must Be Chilled

3   tablespoons vegetable oil
1½ tablespoons cider vinegar
1   teaspoon salt
1   teaspoon garlic salt
¼   teaspoon pepper

1   (4-ounce) can chopped ripe olives with liquid
1   (4½-ounce) can chopped green chiles with liquid
2-3 tomatoes, finely chopped
4-5 green onions, finely chopped

Blend oil and vinegar. Add salt, garlic salt and pepper. Stir. Mix with olives and liquid, green chiles and liquid, tomatoes and onions. Chill several hours for flavors to mix. Serve cold with tortilla chips.

Variation: Add 3 or 4 peeled, pitted and diced ripe avocados at serving time.

"Gazpacho Dip" was one of the favorite recipes from
our first cookbook, *The Texas Experience*. It was also reprinted
in a *Southern Living* magazine article featuring our cookbook as
a member of the Community Cookbook Hall of Fame.

Olé Salsa

Must Be Made Ahead

1   (8-ounce) bag frozen corn, thawed and rinsed
1   (8-ounce) bottle Wish-Bone Italian dressing
1   (4½-ounce) can chopped green chiles, drained
1   (8-ounce) can ripe olives, drained, and diced

3   medium ripe avocados, peeled, pitted and diced
4   green onions, sliced
½   cup chopped fresh cilantro
3-4 small or 2 large tomatoes, chopped
1½ cups mixed shredded colby and Monterey Jack cheese

Combine all ingredients in a medium bowl. Cover and chill for at least 5 hours. Serve with tortilla chips.

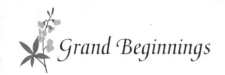

Black Bean Salsa

Must Be Chilled

1 ripe avocado, peeled, pitted and diced	2-3 tablespoons olive oil
3-4 tablespoons lime juice	½ teaspoon ground cumin
1 poblano pepper, diced	½ cup fresh, chopped cilantro or parsley
½ red bell pepper, diced	2 cups canned black beans, drained and rinsed
½ habanero or 2 jalapeño peppers, seeded and diced	½ cup cooked corn kernels
½ red onion, diced	Salt and pepper to taste

Combine diced avocados with lime juice in a medium bowl. Add all the remaining ingredients. Cover and chill at least 2 hours. Taste and adjust seasoning. Serve with tortilla chips. Serves 8 to 12 as a dip.

Hint: Always use caution when handling peppers. You may wish to wear rubber gloves.

Great served as a side dish with steak.
Drain and place on lettuce leaf.

Prairie Fire

4 (15-ounce) cans red kidney beans	2 tablespoons minced onions
8 tablespoons margarine	2 garlic cloves, minced
2 cups shredded provolone cheese	½ teaspoon salt
¼ cup finely chopped jalapeños	

Drain beans and reserve ⅔ cup liquid. Mash beans. In a saucepan combine beans, reserved liquid, margarine, cheese, jalapeños, onions, garlic and salt. Heat and stir until hot. Transfer to chafing dish or crock pot. Serve with corn chips. Makes 6 cups.

Salsa de Tomate
Must Be Chilled

4 large firm tomatoes, peeled and chopped
1 cup finely chopped onions
1 cup finely chopped green bell peppers
2-4 large fresh jalapeños, seeded and minced
1 teaspoon salt, optional
¼ teaspoon cayenne pepper

2-3 tablespoons chopped cilantro
½ teaspoon dried oregano, crumbled
½ teaspoon ground coriander, optional
2 tablespoons lime juice
2 tablespoons balsamic vinegar
1 (8-ounce) can tomato sauce
2 tablespoons vegetable oil

Combine all ingredients. Chill for several hours. Serve with your favorite corn chips or vegetables. Makes 3¾ cups.

Great served as a side dish with baked chicken or roast pork.

Cowboy Caviar
Must Be Chilled

1 (15-ounce) can black beans, drained and rinsed
1 (10-ounce) can diced tomatoes and green chiles, drained
1 garlic clove, minced
1 small onion, finely chopped
2 tablespoons vegetable oil
2 tablespoons fresh lime juice

¼ teaspoon salt
¼ teaspoon ground cumin
1 (8-ounce) package cream cheese, softened
3 green onions, chopped
1 tomato, chopped
Chopped cilantro to taste

In a medium bowl, combine black beans, tomatoes and green chiles, garlic, onions, oil, lime juice, salt and cumin. Cover and refrigerate 2 hours. Spread softened cream cheese onto a serving platter. Spoon bean mixture evenly over cream cheese. Spread chopped green onions, tomatoes and cilantro over top.

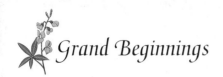

Bacon and Swiss Dip

Dip:

1	(8-ounce) package cream cheese	2	tablespoons sliced green onions
½	cup mayonnaise	8	slices bacon, cooked and crumbled
4	ounces shredded Swiss cheese		
		½	cup buttery cracker crumbs

Pita Chips:

Pita rounds	¼	cup sesame seeds, toasted
Butter		

Dip:

Microwave cream cheese on medium for 30 seconds. In a medium bowl, mix cream cheese, mayonnaise, Swiss cheese and green onions until well blended. Spoon into a 2½-cup glass casserole or 9-inch glass pie plate. Microwave on high for 4 minutes or until thoroughly heated, turning dish every 2 minutes. Combine bacon and cracker crumbs. Sprinkle over top.

Pita Chips:

Cut each bread round in half and then each half in sixths. Split each triangle in half at the seam. Spread rough side of each triangle with butter; sprinkle with sesame seeds. Place triangles, seed side up, in single layer on baking sheet. Bake in a preheated 350 degree oven for 8 minutes or until crisp. Best if served immediately. Serve with dip.

Camembert Cheese Dip

Must Be Chilled

3-4 wedges Camembert cheese
3 (3-ounce) packages cream
    cheese, softened
½ cup light cream

Dash salt
Chopped walnuts
Assorted fruits

Scrape the Camembert cheese slightly to remove part of the rind. In a small bowl, combine the cheeses. Add the cream and salt. Blend until smooth and creamy. Chill. Serve in a small bowl garnished with chopped walnuts. Serve with bunches of red grapes, sliced pears, melon sticks and sliced apples.

Gulf Coast Crab and Asparagus Dip

½ cup sour cream
1 (8-ounce) package cream
    cheese, softened
1 (10½-ounce) can asparagus
    spears, drained and chopped
½ cup freshly grated Parmesan
    cheese

2 tablespoons sliced green onions
1 teaspoon prepared horseradish
1 teaspoon Dijon mustard
1 (6-ounce) can crabmeat, drained
⅓ cup sliced almonds

In a medium bowl, combine sour cream, cream cheese and asparagus and blend well. Add Parmesan cheese, green onions, horseradish, mustard and crabmeat and mix well. Spread evenly in an ungreased 1-quart baking dish. Sprinkle with almonds. Bake in a preheated 350 degree oven for 20 to 25 minutes or until thoroughly heated. Serve warm with assorted crackers or fresh vegetables.

Variation: Add one more can of asparagus and serve as a side dish.

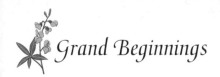

Holiday Pine Cones

Must Be Made Ahead

3 (8-ounce) packages cream cheese, softened	1 (5-ounce) jar Roka blue cheese, at room temperature
2 (5-ounce) jars Old English cheese, at room temperature	3 tablespoons red wine vinegar
	1 teaspoon garlic salt
	Pecan halves

In a large bowl, blend cheeses, vinegar and garlic salt. Refrigerate for 8 hours. Divide into 3 portions and shape into pine cones. Starting at the top, layer pecan halves around the entire pine cone by sticking the end of the pecan slightly into the cheese to make it resemble a pine cone. Garnish with holiday greens and serve with crackers. May be frozen. Makes 3 pine cones.

House Special Cheese Ball

Must Be Chilled

1 (5-ounce) jar Old English cheese	1 tablespoon chives or green onions, chopped finely
1 (4-ounce) package crumbled blue cheese	⅔ cup finely chopped pecans, divided
2 (3-ounce) packages cream cheese	¼ cup finely chopped fresh parsley, divided
¼ teaspoon Accent	
½ teaspoon Worcestershire sauce	
Tabasco sauce, optional	

Soften cheeses. Mix cheeses with Accent, Worcestershire sauce, Tabasco sauce, chives and half the pecans and half the parsley. Shape into a ball. Chill until firm. Mix the remaining pecans and parsley together and roll ball in mixture. Wrap in plastic wrap and chill. Serve with crackers. Makes 10 to 12 servings.

Favorite Cheese Ball

Must Be Made Ahead

1   (16-ounce) package margarine, softened

4   (8-ounce) packages cream cheese, softened

1   (4½-ounce) can chopped ripe olives, drained

4   ounces crumbled blue cheese, softened

6-8 green onion tops, chopped

2   (2-ounce) jars diced pimientos, drained

2   cups chopped pecans, toasted

In a large bowl, mix all ingredients except pecans thoroughly. Chill overnight. Divide into four portions. Shape into balls and roll in chopped pecans. Makes 4 cheese balls.

Curried Chicken Cheese Ball

Must Be Made Ahead

1   cup seedless green grape halves, divided

2   (8-ounce) packages cream cheese, softened

2   (6-ounce) cans chicken, drained

4   green onions, finely chopped

1   tablespoon sour cream

1   teaspoon curry powder

1   teaspoon Lawry's seasoned salt

Red bell pepper, diced

Reserving a few grapes for garnish, combine grapes, cream cheese, chicken, green onions, sour cream, curry powder and seasoned salt in a large bowl. Stir until well blended. Divide mixture in half and shape each half into a ball. Cover with plastic wrap and chill 8 hours. Garnish with grapes, red pepper and curry powder. Serve with crackers or bread. Makes 2 cheese balls.

Variation: Reserve grapes. Beat all ingredients in an electric mixer until smooth and creamy. Refrigerate several hours and return to room temperature. Stir in finely chopped grapes and serve as a dip.

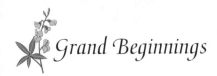

Brawny Braunschweiger Roll

Must Be Chilled

1 (16-ounce) package unsmoked braunschweiger at room temperature
1 (8-ounce) package cream cheese, softened
1 (2-ounce) bottle prepared horseradish, drained

1 tablespoon dry mustard
1 tablespoon Worcestershire sauce
2 tablespoons Beau Monde
Cayenne pepper, to taste
Tabasco sauce, to taste
Chopped parsley

Mix braunschweiger, cream cheese, horseradish, mustard, Worcestershire sauce, Beau Monde, cayenne and Tabasco sauce in a medium bowl. Shape into a roll and sprinkle with parsley. Chill. Serve with unsalted crackers or toast. Serves 25 to 50.

Raspberry-Cheese Loaf

Must Be Made Ahead

1 (8-ounce) package shredded Cheddar cheese
1 (8-ounce) package shredded American cheese
2 green onions, finely chopped
1 cup finely chopped pecans
⅔ cup mayonnaise
¼ teaspoon garlic salt

¼ teaspoon pepper
1 pound bacon, fried extra crisp and crumbled
Dash red pepper flakes, optional
McCormick salad supreme seasoning
Raspberry preserves

Mix together cheeses, onions, pecans, mayonnaise, garlic salt, pepper, bacon and pepper flakes in a medium bowl. Shape into a loaf. Sprinkle with McCormick seasoning. Cover and chill at least one hour. When ready to serve, pour raspberry preserves over the top. Serve with crackers.

Peppy Pepperoni Ball

Must Be Made Ahead

1 (8-ounce) package cream cheese, softened
½ cup sour cream
4 tablespoons margarine, softened
1 teaspoon Worcestershire sauce
1 teaspoon Tabasco sauce
1 (8-ounce) package pepperoni, finely ground
Red pepper flakes to taste, optional

In a medium bowl, beat cream cheese, sour cream, margarine, Worcestershire sauce and Tabasco sauce until fluffy. Blend in pepperoni and red pepper flakes. Shape into ball and chill. Serve with crackers.

Beefy Cheese Log

Must Be Made Ahead

1 (8-ounce) package cream cheese, softened
1 (2½-ounce) package thin-sliced corned beef, chopped
3 green onions, chopped
1 teaspoon Accent
1 teaspoon Worcestershire sauce
Chopped pecans

Place cream cheese in a medium bowl. Add corned beef, onions, Accent and Worcestershire sauce and mix well. Shape into a log and roll in wax paper. Chill until firm. Remove from paper and roll in chopped pecans covering log completely. Wrap in aluminum foil and refrigerate until ready to serve. Serve with crackers.

Double this recipe. It doesn't last long!

Texas Beer Cheese Spread

Must Be Chilled

½ (8-ounce) package cream cheese, softened

1 (10-ounce) package sharp Cheddar cheese, shredded

1 garlic clove, minced

1 tablespoon Worcestershire sauce

½ teaspoon dry mustard

¼ teaspoon cayenne pepper

¼ cup beer (more for thinner spread)

In a large electric mixer bowl, beat cheeses together. Add garlic, Worcestershire sauce, dry mustard and cayenne. Gradually add beer, beating until blended. Cover and chill for an hour. Makes 2½ cups.

Spicy Hot Pimiento Cheese Spread

Best Made Ahead

2 cups finely grated Cheddar cheese

2 cups finely grated Monterey Jack cheese

⅔ cup finely chopped onion

¼-½ cup seeded, rinsed and minced jalapeños

3 garlic cloves, minced

1 (7-ounce) jar diced pimientos

¼ cup chopped cilantro, optional

¾-1 cup mayonnaise

In a medium bowl, blend together cheeses, onions, jalapeños, garlic, pimientos and cilantro. Add enough mayonnaise to make spreading consistency. Serve with large or round corn chips. Makes about 3 cups.

Hint: Taste canned or fresh jalapeños before deciding on amount to use. "Heat" varies tremendously.

Variation: Add ¼ to ½ cup sour cream and use as a dip.

Boursin Cheese Spread

Must Be Chilled

8 ounces whipped butter, softened
2 (8-ounce) packages cream cheese, softened
1-2 garlic cloves, crushed
½ teaspoon dried oregano, crumbled
¼ teaspoon dried dill weed
¼ teaspoon dried basil, crumbled
¼ teaspoon dried marjoram, crumbled
¼ teaspoon dried thyme, crumbled

Blend all ingredients together in a medium bowl. Chill until ready to serve.

Ranch Baked Cheese

1½ cups whole pecans halves
1 tablespoon butter
3 (8-ounce) packages cream cheese, softened
6 tablespoons milk
3 (2.5-ounce) packages sliced beef, chopped
¾ cup finely chopped green bell peppers
6 tablespoons dried minced onions
1½ teaspoons garlic salt
¾ teaspoon pepper
1½ cups sour cream

In a small saucepan over medium heat carefully sauté pecans in butter for about 3 minutes stirring constantly. Drain on paper towels and set aside. Combine cream cheese and milk. Stir in sliced beef, green peppers, onions, garlic salt and pepper. Fold in sour cream and blend well. Put into a 13x9x2-inch baking dish and bake in a preheated 350 degree oven for 20 minutes. After baking, top with pecans and serve with crackers. Serves 30 to 40.

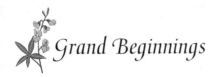

Elegant Cheese and Apples

Must Be Made Ahead

4 ounces Camembert cheese (including rind), cut up	2 tablespoons milk
1 cup shredded Swiss cheese	2 tablespoons sour cream
4 ounces blue cheese, crumbled	1¼ cups chopped pecans
3 (8-ounce) packages cream cheese, softened, divided	Chopped fresh parsley
	6-8 green apples
	Lemon lime soft drink

Let Camembert, Swiss and blue cheeses stand at room temperature 30 minutes. In large mixing bowl, combine these cheeses with 2 packages of cream cheese; set aside. Line a 9-inch pie plate with foil, plastic wrap or cheese cloth. Combine milk, sour cream and the remaining package of cream cheese. Spread in pie plate on top of the foil. Press pecans gently into the cheese. Spoon the cheese mixture over nuts, spreading to the pie plate edges. Cover tightly with plastic wrap. Refrigerate at least 2 to 3 days before serving. It's best if kept for a week. To serve, remove plastic wrap from top of cheese. Turn out onto serving dish. Peel off the foil. Sprinkle with chopped parsley or additional chopped pecans. Slice unpeeled apples into thin wedges. Lay these in a 13x9x2-inch pan into which you have poured enough lemon lime soft drink to cover the bottom of the pan. Pour additional liquid over top of the apples when you have one full layer in the pan. Repeat with all slices. Allow to soak at least 10 to 15 minutes. Remove and let drain. (This retards discoloration without changing the taste as lemons do.) Arrange apples around cheese and serve with crackers. Serves 20 to 25.

Cold appetizers are good served directly from the refrigerator and have a convenient make ahead quality. They are usually equally good at room temperature, making them a good choice to sit out for awhile on a buffet.

Nachos Grande

1	pound lean ground beef	1	(4½-ounce) can chopped green chiles
1	large onion, chopped		
1	teaspoon Lawry's seasoned salt	1	cup grated Cheddar cheese
½	teaspoon ground cumin	¾	cup chunky picante sauce
2	(16-ounce) cans refried beans		Large tortilla chips
1	(1¼-ounce) package Lawry's taco seasoning mix	1	cup sliced ripe olives
		1	cup guacamole
2	cups grated Monterey Jack cheese	½	cup sour cream
		¼	cup chopped green onions

Brown meat and onions; drain well and add seasoned salt and cumin. Combine beans, taco seasoning mix and Monterey Jack cheese and mix well. Spread beans in a shallow baking dish. Cover with meat mixture. Sprinkle green chiles over meat; top with Cheddar cheese and picante sauce. Bake, uncovered, in a pre-heated 400 degree oven for 20 to 25 minutes or until thoroughly heated. Tuck tortilla chips around edge of dish and garnish with olives, guacamole, sour cream and onions. Serve with tortilla chips. Serves 10 to 12.

Rustler's Chicken Liver Pâté

Must Be Chilled

8	tablespoons butter, divided	⅛	teaspoon pepper
1	pound chicken livers	2	tablespoons brandy, optional
1	small onion, chopped		Thin crackers
⅛	teaspoon salt		Chopped onions

Melt 2 tablespoons butter in skillet, over medium low heat. Add livers, onions, salt and pepper. Cover and cook 5 minutes. Liver should be firm and pink inside. Cool. Put in blender and blend until smooth. Melt the remaining butter and add it with the brandy to the liver mixture and chill. Spread on thin crackers when ready to serve. Garnish with chopped onions.

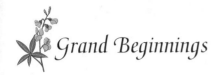

Holiday Ham Spread

Must Be Chilled

4 cups finely chopped ham
2 (8-ounce) packages cream
   cheese, softened, divided
¾ cup mayonnaise, divided

½ cup chopped green onions
   (about 2 bunches)
¼ cup sweet pickle relish

Combine ham, 4 ounces cream cheese, ½ cup mayonnaise, green onions and relish in a medium bowl. Mix well and chill. Combine the remaining 12 ounces of cream cheese and the remaining ¼ cup mayonnaise and mix well. Spoon ham mixture onto a serving plate and shape into desired form (Christmas tree, wreath or heart). Spread cream cheese mixture on top and sides as if frosting a cake. Decorate as desired. Serves 25.

Salmon Log

Must Be Chilled

1 (15-ounce) can red salmon
1 (8-ounce) package cream
   cheese, softened
1 tablespoon lemon juice
2 teaspoons grated onions
1 teaspoon prepared horseradish

¼ teaspoon salt
¼ teaspoon liquid smoke
½ cup chopped pecans
3 tablespoons finely chopped
   parsley

Drain and flake salmon, removing skin and bones. Combine salmon with cream cheese, lemon juice, onions, horseradish, salt, liquid smoke and pecans. Mix thoroughly. Chill several hours. Shape mixture into a log and roll in parsley. Serve with crackers. Serves 25.

Texas Oil Well Butter

Must Be Chilled

2	sticks unsalted butter	2	ounces caviar
1	tablespoon lemon juice	1	hard-cooked egg, very finely chopped

Melt butter and stir with lemon juice and caviar in a small bowl. Chill. Serve softened on unsalted crackers topped with egg.

Easy and elegant.

Delicious Apple Spread

Must Be Chilled

1	(8-ounce) package cream cheese, softened	¼	cup sugar
1	cup grated sharp Cheddar cheese, softened	1	cup chopped unpeeled Red Delicious apple
¼	cup mayonnaise	½	cup chopped celery
		1	cup chopped pecans

Combine cheeses, mayonnaise and sugar in a small bowl. Add apples, celery and pecans. Chill. Serve with wheat crackers.

Cowgirls' Delight

Must Be Chilled

12 ounces cream cheese, softened	¼ cup boiling water
½ cup butter, softened	¼ teaspoon grated lemon zest
½ cup sour cream	½ cup golden raisins
½ cup sugar	1 cup slivered almonds, toasted
1 envelope unflavored gelatin	Cinnamon graham crackers

In a large mixer bowl, blend cream cheese, butter and sour cream. Mix in sugar. Dissolve gelatin in water. Stir into cream cheese mixture. Fold in lemon zest, raisins and almonds. Place in a greased 1-quart mold and refrigerate until set. Serve with cinnamon graham crackers. Serves 20.

Polly DuPont Meatballs

2 pounds ground chuck	1 chili sauce bottle of water
1 (2-ounce) package onion soup mix	½ cup brown sugar
1 cup breadcrumbs	1 (16-ounce) can sauerkraut, drained
2 eggs, slightly beaten	1 (15-ounce) can whole cranberry sauce
1 (12-ounce) jar chili sauce	

Combine ground chuck with onion soup mix, breadcrumbs and eggs. Shape into small balls and place in a 12x8x2-inch glass dish. Combine chili sauce, water, brown sugar, sauerkraut and cranberry sauce. Pour over meatballs; but do not stir. Bake in a preheated 325 degree oven for 2 hours. Serves 20.

Polly DuPont is a Richardson gift shop that serves these meatballs at their open house. They decorate our Clubhouse dining room with their crystal and china for our annual Tour of Homes.

Tangy Meatballs

1	pound ground beef	1	(12-ounce) jar grape or currant jelly
1	egg, beaten		
	Salt and pepper to taste	1	(12-ounce) jar chili sauce

Combine beef, egg, salt and pepper. Mix well. Shape into small balls. Sauté in a medium skillet until brown. Keep warm until ready to use. Combine jelly and chili sauce in a chafing dish. Add meatballs and keep warm over low heat. Additional seasonings may be added to meatballs if desired. Serves 12.

Hint: Instead of sautéing, bake the meatballs on a broiler pan in a preheated 325 degree oven for 8 to 10 minutes. Larger meatballs will need to cook longer. The broiler pan drains much of the fat away.

Sweet and Sour Sausage Balls

1	pound sausage	1½	cups ketchup
1	pound hot sausage	6	tablespoons brown sugar
2	eggs, slightly beaten	¼	cup red wine vinegar
¾	cup Italian breadcrumbs	¼	cup soy sauce
	Vegetable oil		

Combine sausages, eggs and breadcrumbs in a medium bowl. Shape into small balls. In a large skillet, sauté in oil until brown. Drain. In a large pot, combine ketchup, brown sugar, vinegar and soy sauce. Add sausage balls and simmer for 30 minutes. Serve hot. May be frozen. Serves 25 to 30.

Spicy Steak Sticks

Must Be Made Ahead

1 cup medium picante sauce	¼ teaspoon seasoned salt
¼ cup canola oil	4 garlic cloves, minced
2 teaspoons lemon pepper	1½ pounds sirloin steak, cut into ¾-inch cubes

Mix together picante sauce, oil, lemon pepper, seasoned salt and garlic in a large resealable bag. Add meat cubes and marinate in refrigerator for 2 to 6 hours. Place 2 cubes of beef on a 4-inch wooden skewer. Repeat until all are used. Grill over medium coals 5 to 7 minutes, turning occasionally. Makes approximately 32 appetizer servings.

Christmas Olive Appetizers

½-1 (2.6-ounce) jar sesame seed	3 (8-ounce) packages cream cheese
1 (13-ounce) jar giant pimiento stuffed olives	

Put sesame seeds in a jelly-roll pan in a preheated 325 degree oven for 15 minutes or until lightly toasted. Cool. Drain the olives and pat them dry, making sure there is no liquid in the olive. Chill until they are very cold. Wrap each olive in a cream cheese jacket and roll in sesame seeds. Chill until firm. When ready to serve, cut each olive in half and serve on a bed of lettuce with the colorful red, green, and white sides up.

This recipe is too easy to believe and oh so delicious!

Armadillo Eggs

Must Be Made Ahead

2 cups large, whole green or ripe olives, drained and liquid reserved

½ cup olive liquid

½ cup extra virgin olive oil

½ cup beer

½ cup white vinegar

2 garlic cloves, minced

2 cayenne peppers

1 bay leaf

¾ teaspoon Gebhardt chili powder

½ teaspoon cumin seeds, toasted and ground

Place the olives in a medium bowl. Shake the remaining ingredients in a jar with a tight fitting lid and pour the marinade over the olives. Cover, refrigerate and let mixture marinate for at least 2 days (longer, if you can), stirring occasionally. Drain and serve.

Unlike most cowboys, the olives get better with age.

Get Your Goat Mushrooms

12 medium fresh mushrooms

1 tablespoon unsalted butter

¼ cup finely chopped onions

4 ounces crumbled goat cheese

1 teaspoon lemon juice

¼ teaspoon salt

¼ teaspoon dried dill weed

3 tablespoons olive oil

Remove stems from mushrooms and chop them finely, reserving the caps. In a small skillet, melt the butter over low heat and sauté the onions until soft. Add mushroom stems and cook until liquid evaporates. Remove from heat and add cheese, lemon juice, salt and dill; mixing well. Brush the mushroom caps with oil and fill with the stuffing. Place mushrooms on a lightly greased baking sheet and drizzle with the remaining oil. Bake in a preheated 425 degree oven for 10 minutes until lightly browned. Serves 4 to 6.

Mushrooms Rosemary

Must Be Chilled

18 mushrooms, 2-inches in diameter	2 (3-ounce) packages cream cheese, softened
4 slices bacon	1-1½ teaspoons dried rosemary, crumbled
1 tablespoon minced garlic	
¼ cup chopped olives	Olive oil

Wash and stem mushrooms. Mince stems and set aside. In a large skillet, cook bacon until crisp. Drain and pat dry on paper towel. Crumble into small pieces. Reserve 1 tablespoon of bacon drippings from pan. Sauté mushroom stems, garlic and olives in the bacon drippings. Add bacon, cream cheese and rosemary. Brush rounded ends of mushrooms with olive oil and place on a jelly-roll pan. Stuff mushrooms with cheese mixture. Cover and chill about 2 hours. Bake in a preheated 350 degree oven for about 15 minutes or until mushrooms are tender.

Texas Wagon Wheels

1 pound hot sausage	2 (8-ounce) cans crescent rolls
1 (8-ounce) package cream cheese	1 egg white, slightly beaten
1 (4-ounce) can mushroom stems and pieces, drained, optional	Poppy seed, optional

In a medium skillet, lightly brown sausage. Drain. While sausage is still hot, add cream cheese and stir until melted and creamy. Add mushrooms and cool completely. Separate crescent rolls into 2 rectangles, pressing perforations together. Divide the sausage mixture and form a log of sausage mixture lengthwise down center of each rectangle. Fold over the long sides of pastry to cover sausage log. Repeat. Place each log seam side down on ungreased baking sheet and brush them with egg white and sprinkle with poppy seeds. Bake in a preheated 350 degree oven for 20 minutes or until crust is golden. When completely cooled, slice in 1½-inch pieces. May be made ahead, frozen and reheated.

Atsie Catsie

2 pounds grated sharp Cheddar
   cheese
4 (4½-ounce) cans chopped green
   chiles

18 eggs, barely stirred
1½ teaspoons salt

Spread cheese on a 15x10x1-inch jelly-roll pan. Cover with green chiles. Pour eggs on top, add salt and slightly mix all together with a fork. Bake in a pre-heated 350 degree oven for 30 to 35 minutes. Cut in small squares to serve.

Apricot Sorpresa

Must Be Chilled

50 medium pecan halves
50 fresh cilantro leaves without
   stems

3 (6-ounce) packages whole,
   Mediterranean sun-dried
   apricots
1 (8-ounce) package mascarpone
   cheese, softened

Toast pecan halves in a single layer on cookie sheet in a preheated 350 degree oven for 4 to 5 minutes. Watch to prevent burning. Cool. Rinse cilantro. Cut 50 leaves. Place on damp paper towel and cover with another damp paper towel. Open apricots along one edge. Spoon ½ to 1 teaspoon mascarpone cheese onto one side of opened apricot. Press cilantro leaf into cheese, near fold, so that some of the leaf extends outside the edge of the apricot. Press pecan half onto cheese. Close side of apricot. Refrigerate in a covered container until ready to use.

Hint: Mediterranean sun-dried apricots are moist, whole and usually slit on one side. They are recommended instead of California sun-dried apricots. Three packages of apricots are specified because some in the package are too small to open.

"Sorpresa" means surprise in Spanish and Italian.

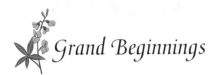

Blue Cheese Deviled Eggs

Must Be Chilled

8	hard-cooked eggs, peeled	¼	cup mayonnaise
6	tablespoons blue cheese, crumbled		Lemon juice to taste
			Salt and pepper to taste
1	(6-ounce) roll sharp Cheddar cheese		

Slice eggs lengthwise and carefully remove yolks. In a medium bowl, mash the yolks and add the cheeses, mayonnaise, lemon juice, salt and pepper. Spoon into egg whites. Cover and chill.

Cheesy Artichoke Appetizer

2	(8-ounce) cans Crescent dinner rolls	1	(7-ounce) can chopped green chiles, drained and patted dry
1	cup grated mozzarella cheese	3	tablespoons grated onions
1	cup grated Cheddar cheese	¾	cup chopped green or ripe olives
3	cups dry grated Parmesan cheese	1	cup mayonnaise
			Dash Tabasco sauce
3	cups canned artichoke hearts, drained and patted dry, chopped		Dash Worcestershire sauce
		1	(2-ounce) jar diced pimientos

Unroll dough and press into the bottom and up sides of a 15x10x1-inch jelly-roll pan, sealing the perforations. Bake in a preheated 375 degree oven for 20 minutes or until lightly browned. In a large bowl, combine the cheeses, artichoke hearts, green chiles, onions, olives, mayonnaise, Tabasco sauce and Worcestershire sauce. Spread the mixture on top of the dough. Return to oven for 20 minutes or until bubbly. Remove from the oven and let stand for 5 minutes before cutting into bite-size pieces. Sprinkle with additional Parmesan and garnish with a slice of pimiento. Makes 36 squares. May be frozen after cutting into bite-size pieces.

Mamacita's Deviled Eggs

6   hard-cooked eggs, peeled
1   tablespoon diced green onions
1   tablespoon chopped fresh cilantro
1   small serrano or jalapeño pepper, seeded and finely chopped

¼   cup mayonnaise
1   teaspoon prepared mustard
½   teaspoon salt
¼   cup (1-ounce) shredded Cheddar cheese
Chili powder

Cut eggs in half lengthwise; carefully remove yolks. Mash the yolks in a small bowl. Add the green onions, cilantro, pepper, mayonnaise and salt. Spoon into egg whites; sprinkle with cheese and chili powder. Cover and chill.

Cowboy Spurs

½   pound hot sausage
½   pound grated Monterey Jack cheese
1½ cups buttermilk biscuit baking mix
15 canned whole jalapeños

½   pound Monterey Jack cheese with jalapeños, cubed
1   (16-ounce) package Shake 'n Bake for Pork
2   eggs, beaten

Mix sausage and grated cheese. Add biscuit mix ½ cup at a time until thoroughly mixed. Knead several times and set aside. While wearing rubber gloves, slit and seed jalapeños. Stuff each pepper with a cube of cheese and pinch pepper closed around the cheese. Divide the cheese and sausage mixture into 15 balls and pat each into a flat pancake about ¼-inch thick. Place the cheese stuffed pepper into the middle of each pancake and completely cover the pepper with the dough, being sure that all edges are well sealed. Roll back and forth in your hands to form a smooth ball. Roll each ball in Shake 'n Bake until coated. Dip each ball in beaten eggs and then Shake 'n Bake again. Bake in a preheated 300 degree oven. They will crust nicely when slightly cooled. Serve slightly warm. Makes 15 balls.

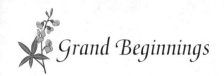

Four Way Appetizer Tarts

Tart Shells:
1   crust from 1 (15-ounce)
     package refrigerated pie crust

Basic Egg Mixture:
2   eggs, beaten
⅓   cup milk

Chicken Divan Filling:
½   cup finely chopped broccoli
⅓   cup finely chopped chicken
¾   tablespoon dried dill weed

Sliced ripe olives
Sour cream
Fresh dill

Hunan Shrimp Filling:
1   (4¼-ounce) can shrimp, drained
2   tablespoons chopped green onions
2   teaspoons soy sauce
¼   teaspoon cayenne pepper

1   teaspoon garlic powder
Sour cream
Small shrimp
Chopped chives

Jalapeño Cheese Filling:
½   cup shredded Monterey Jack
     cheese with jalapeños
⅓   cup green bell peppers or
     canned chopped green chiles

2   tablespoons chopped pimientos
Diced green bell peppers
Sliced pimientos

Spinach Filling:
½   cup fresh spinach, washed,
     drained and finely chopped
3   tablespoons grated Parmesan
     cheese

2   tablespoons pine nuts or walnuts
2   garlic cloves, minced
Additional nuts

Tart Shell:

On a lightly floured surface, roll pie crust into a 16-inch circle. Using a 3-inch biscuit cutter, cut into 18 rounds. Fit rounds into mini-muffin pans. Fill each pastry cup with about 1 tablespoon of filling combined with egg mixture. Bake in a preheated 375 degree oven for about 15 minutes or until the centers appear set and pastry is lightly brown. Cool in pan for 5 minutes. Remove from pan. May be made ahead, chilled or frozen. To reheat, arrange tarts on ungreased baking sheet, bake uncovered in a preheated 350 degree oven until warm for 8 minutes if the tarts were chilled or 20 minutes if the tarts are frozen.

Four Way Appetizer Tarts continued

Chicken Divan Filling:
Combine broccoli, chicken and dill with the basic egg-milk mixture. Garnish with a sliced ripe olive, topped with sour cream and fresh dill. Makes 18.

Hunan Shrimp Filling:
Combine shrimp, green onions, soy sauce, red pepper and garlic powder with the basic egg-milk mixture. Garnish with sour cream, small shrimp and chives. Makes 18.

Jalapeño Cheese Filling:
Combine cheese, green bell peppers or green chiles and pimientos with basic egg-milk mixture. Garnish with green bell peppers and pimientos. Makes 18.

Spinach Filling:
Combine spinach, cheese, nuts and garlic with basic egg-milk mixture. Makes 18.

Hint: Ingredients are for each filling of 18 tarts. Increase the amount of eggs, milk and pie crust according to how many kinds of tarts you are making.

Salmon Puffs

1 (15½-ounce) can red salmon, drained, liquid reserved	1 egg, beaten
1 tablespoon lemon juice	½ teaspoon salt
2 tablespoons chopped onions	¼ teaspoon pepper
½ cup flour	1 heaping teaspoon baking powder
	Vegetable oil

Remove excess skin and bones from salmon and flake apart in a medium bowl. Add lemon juice, onions, flour, egg, salt and pepper. Mix well. Add baking powder to ¼ cup reserved liquid. Beat with a fork until foamy. Add liquid mixture to salmon and mix well. Drop by well rounded teaspoons into hot oil. Fry until brown and crispy.

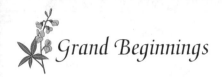

Mushroom Empanadas

Filling:

3	tablespoons butter	½	teaspoon salt
8	ounces fresh mushrooms, finely chopped	⅛	teaspoon freshly ground pepper
1	large onion, finely chopped	1	tablespoon flour
⅛	teaspoon dried thyme, crumbled	¼	cup sour cream
		1	tablespoon sherry

Cream Cheese Pastry:

½	pound butter	1¾	cups flour
1	(8-ounce) package cream cheese	½	teaspoon salt

Filling:

In a medium skillet, melt butter and sauté mushrooms and onions. Add thyme, salt, pepper and flour. Blend in well. Add sour cream and sherry and cook until mixture thickens.

Cream Cheese Pastry:

Mix together butter, cream cheese, flour and salt. Chill. Roll on a floured surface to ⅛-inch thickness. Cut pastry with a 2½-inch biscuit cutter. Place 1 teaspoon of filling on each round and fold pastry into a half moon. Mash edges with a fork to seal and prick tops. Bake in a preheated 425 degree oven for 15 to 20 minutes.

Hint: If the empanadas are not to be served immediately, freeze them uncooked. Follow baking directions when ready to serve. They should be served piping hot.

Pecan-Cheese Crispies

2	cups shredded sharp Cheddar cheese	1	cup flour
1	cup butter or margarine, softened	1	cup self-rising flour
¼	teaspoon Tabasco sauce	2	cups crispy rice cereal
½	teaspoon dry mustard	60	pecan halves

Combine cheese and butter and beat well with electric mixer until blended. Add Tabasco sauce and mustard. Gradually add flours until blended. Stir in cereal. Shape dough into 1-inch balls. Place on ungreased baking sheets and flatten with a fork (making a crisscross design). Press a pecan half in center of each. Bake in a preheated 350 degree oven for 12 to 14 minutes. Makes 5 dozen. Crispies may be frozen. To serve, thaw at room temperature for 1 hour and bake.

Feta-Sesame Wafers

Must Be Made Ahead

⅓	cup sesame seed	4	tablespoons butter, softened
2	(4-ounce) packages crumbled feta cheese	1⅓	cups flour
		¼	teaspoon cayenne pepper

In a non-stick skillet, toast sesame seeds over low heat until you can smell the seeds. Do not brown. Cool on a paper towel. Beat cheese and butter with an electric mixer until fluffy. Add flour, sesame seeds and cayenne. Divide dough and form into 9-inch logs. Cover the logs with a cylinder of wax paper and twist the ends to make the logs more even. Refrigerate 2 hours. Slice into ¼-inch slices and put on ungreased baking sheets 1-inch apart. Bake in a preheated 350 degree oven for 13 to 15 minutes or until lightly brown. Cool on racks. Makes 6 dozen.

Hint: These bake better on a double thickness cookie sheet. If you are using a standard cookie sheet, rotate the cookie sheet halfway through the baking time.

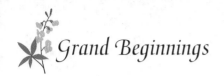

Cocktail Sticks

Must Be Frozen

1	loaf thin sliced bread	1	medium onion, finely chopped
½	pound grated sharp Cheddar cheese	2	ounces slivered almonds
		1	cup mayonnaise
6	slices crisply fried bacon, crumbled	2	teaspoons Worcestershire sauce

Cut each bread slice into thirds. In a small bowl, mix together cheese, bacon, onions, almonds, mayonnaise and Worcestershire sauce. Spread on bread fingers. Place on baking sheet and freeze. Put frozen slices in plastic bags and store in freezer. Bake frozen in a preheated 400 degree oven for 10 minutes. Makes 69 pieces.

Hint: Make sandwiches before cutting into thirds. You may also trim the crusts then if you like.

Hot Asparagus Canapés

Must Be Frozen

25	slices thin white bread	1	egg
3	ounces blue cheese	1	(10½-ounce) can asparagus spears
8	ounces cream cheese, softened		Melted butter, do not substitute

Trim crusts from bread and flatten with rolling pin. In a small bowl, blend cheeses and egg. Spread evenly to edges of bread. Roll an asparagus spear in each slice of bread. Dip rolls in melted butter. Place on a baking sheet and freeze. When ready to serve, bake frozen in a preheated 400 degree oven for 15 minutes. Slice each roll into 3 pieces. Makes 75 canapés.

Cheese and Onion Thins

1   cup mayonnaise
½   (2-ounce) package onion soup
    mix

1   (5.29-ounce) package
    Norwegian Kavlicrisp crackers
    Grated Parmesan cheese

Mix mayonnaise with 1 envelope of soup mix. Spread thinly on each cracker. Place on baking sheet, sprinkle with cheese. Bake in a preheated 400 degree oven until bubbly. Cool. May be frozen until ready to use.

Italian Canapés

8   ounces grated sharp Cheddar
    cheese
½   cup chopped ripe olives
1   cup mayonnaise

¼   cup finely grated onions
    Pinch Italian seasoning
    English muffins

In a small bowl, mix cheese, olives, mayonnaise, onions and Italian seasoning. Spread on split English muffins. Cut each half in half. Brown under broiler.

Rye Bread Party Snacks

¾   cups mayonnaise
½   cup grated fresh Parmesan cheese
1   small bunch green onions,
    minced

1   (4½-ounce) can chopped ripe
    olives, drained
1   teaspoon curry powder
3   loaves sliced party rye bread

In a small bowl, mix mayonnaise, cheese, onions, olives and curry powder. Spread evenly on bread slices. Place under broiler for 2 to 3 minutes until warm and cheese melts. Serve immediately. Serves 20.

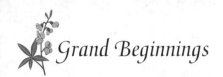

Artichoke Crostini

1 baguette	2 garlic cloves, minced
1 cup mayonnaise	Chopped green onions, optional
1 cup grated Parmesan cheese	Chopped tomatoes, optional
1 (14-ounce) can artichoke hearts, drained and chopped	Crumbled bacon, optional
1 (4½-ounce) can chopped green chiles, drained	

Slice baguette into ¼ to ½-inch slices. Place on a baking sheet lined with aluminum foil. Bake in a preheated 400 degree oven for 5 minutes or until lightly browned. In a medium bowl, combine mayonnaise, cheese, artichoke hearts, green chiles and garlic; spread on bread slices. Return to 400 degree oven for 5 minutes or until cheese melts. Garnish with onions, tomatoes and bacon, as desired.

Bacon-Cheese Tasties

4 ounces bacon, crisply fried and finely chopped	½ cup mayonnaise
3 cups (12-ounces) shredded provolone cheese	2½ tablespoons finely minced onions
	12 English muffins, split

In a medium bowl, combine bacon, cheese, mayonnaise and onions. Spread about 2 tablespoons on each half of English muffin. Place on an ungreased baking sheet. Bake in a preheated 325 degree oven for 13 to 15 minutes or until cheese mixture is melted and edges of muffins are lightly browned. Cut into thirds. Serve immediately. Makes 72 pieces.

T Bar S Ranch Toast Shingles

Must Be Frozen

1 pound Italian breakfast sausage	½ teaspoon garlic powder
1 pound hot sausage	Dried oregano, crumbled, to taste
1 pound Velveeta cheese, cubed	Dash cayenne pepper
1 teaspoon Worcestershire sauce	1-1½ loaves party rye bread

In a large skillet, brown sausages and drain. Add chunks of cheese and stir until melted. Add Worcestershire sauce, garlic powder, oregano and cayenne. Spread 1 heaping tablespoon of sausage mixture on each slice of rye bread. Place on baking sheet. Freeze. When frozen, transfer to plastic bags. To serve, bake frozen in a preheated 350 degree oven for 20 minutes until browned on top.

Crispy Cheese Pita Wedges

8 tablespoons butter	2 cups grated 2 percent sharp Cheddar cheese
1 small garlic clove, finely minced	
½ teaspoon Worcestershire sauce	1 cup freshly grated Parmesan cheese
¾ teaspoon paprika	
¼ teaspoon cayenne pepper	6 large pita breads

In a small mixer bowl, combine butter, garlic, Worcestershire sauce, paprika and cayenne. Cream about 1 minute. Add cheeses and cream until fluffy. Split the pita in half horizontally and spread with cheese mixture. Cut bread into 6 triangles with a serrated knife. Bake in a preheated 350 degree oven for 10 to 12 minutes. Serve warm. The cheese mixture may be made ahead and then brought to room temperature before spreading. Makes 36 pieces.

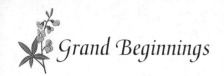

Marvelous Mozzarella Canapés

4 ounces cream cheese, softened	⅓ cup finely grated mozzarella cheese
¼ cup mayonnaise	
1 tablespoon lemon juice	1 egg, beaten
Several dashes Tabasco sauce	12 slices very thin sliced bread
1 cup chopped ripe olives	Butter, softened

In a small bowl, combine cream cheese, mayonnaise, lemon juice, Tabasco sauce, olives, mozzarella cheese and egg. Blend well. Remove crusts from bread and cut each slice into quarters. Spread each bread quarter with butter and then cheese mixture. Place on a baking sheet and broil 3 to 5 minutes. Serve immediately. Makes 48 bite-size pieces.

Greek Cheese and Spinach Pastry

1 egg	½ cup Parmesan cheese
1 (8-ounce) package cream cheese, softened	3 tablespoons finely chopped spinach, squeezed dry
1 cup shredded mozzarella or feta cheese	Phyllo dough, thawed
	Melted butter

In a small bowl, mix together the egg, cheeses and spinach. Set aside. Cut dough into 2½-inch squares and dip 4 or 5 squares at a time in butter and stuff into mini-muffin pans. Keep extra dough covered with a damp cloth to prevent the dough from drying out. Spoon a large teaspoon of cheese mixture into muffin cup. Top with another layer of phyllo squares dipped in butter. Bake in a preheated 350 degree oven for 15 to 20 minutes until lightly browned. Serve hot. Makes 48.

Mushroom Croustades

36 slices thin wheat bread, cut into 3-inch rounds	½ teaspoon salt
¼ cup butter	⅛ teaspoon cayenne pepper
⅓ cup finely chopped green onions	1 pound sausage, browned and drained
8 ounces fresh mushrooms, finely chopped	1 cup whipping cream
2 tablespoons flour	2 teaspoons fresh lemon juice
1 tablespoon minced fresh parsley	3 tablespoons freshly grated Parmesan cheese

Carefully fit bread into lightly greased mini-muffin tins, pressing gently into sides to form cups. Bake in a preheated 400 degree oven for 8 to 10 minutes or until firm to touch. In a large skillet, melt butter over medium heat. Add green onions and sauté 3 to 4 minutes. Stir in mushrooms and cook, stirring frequently for 10 to 15 minutes or until most of the liquid is evaporated. Stir in flour, parsley, salt and cayenne until well blended. Add sausage and cream and bring to a low boil. Reduce heat to low and simmer until mixture thickens, about 10 minutes. Stir in lemon juice and remove from heat. Let cool slightly. Spoon filling evenly into bread cups. Sprinkle cheese over tops. Bake in a preheated 350 degree oven for 8 to 10 minutes or until cheese melts. Serve warm. Makes 36 croustades.

Hint: Croustades may be frozen before they are baked.

Because most hot appetizers will be cooked at the last minute, they require prior planning and coordinating, especially for a large crowd. The best ones to use are made ahead and baked straight from the freezer.

Ham and Cheese Stuffed Puffs

Puffs:

1 cup water	1 cup flour
½ cup margarine	4 eggs

Filling:

8 ounces deviled ham	1 tablespoon prepared horseradish
1 (8-ounce) package cream cheese, softened	3 tablespoons sweet pickle relish

Puffs:

Heat water and margarine to a rolling boil in a medium saucepan. Add flour to boiling mixture. Remove from heat and stir until it forms a ball. Beat in eggs all at once until mixture is smooth. Drop by rounded teaspoons onto an ungreased baking sheet. Bake in a preheated 400 degree oven for 25 minutes or until puffed golden brown and dry. Remove puffs onto a wire rack and cool away from drafts. Cut each puff in half.

Filling:

Mix together deviled ham, cream cheese, horseradish and relish until blended. Spread 1 teaspoon of filling on bottom half of puffs. Replace top half and serve. Makes 50 puffs.

Savory Puffs Filling

16 hard-cooked eggs, minced	4 teaspoons minced onions
12 slices crisply cooked bacon, crumbled	4 teaspoons Worcestershire sauce
	1 cup mayonnaise
4 teaspoons prepared horseradish	1-2 teaspoons salt

In a large bowl, combine all ingredients and chill. Serve on crackers or tiny savory puffs made from the previous recipe. Makes 4 cups.

Crab Bundles

1 (3-ounce) package cream cheese with chives, softened	2-3 dashes Tabasco sauce
¼ cup finely chopped onions	1 (6-ounce) package frozen crabmeat, cooked, drained and flaked
¼ cup finely shredded carrots	
2 tablespoons finely chopped red bell peppers	9 sheets frozen phyllo dough, thawed
½ teaspoon Worcestershire sauce	½ cup margarine or butter, melted

In a medium bowl, combine cream cheese with chives, onions, carrots, bell peppers, Worcestershire sauce and Tabasco sauce. Stir in crabmeat. Lightly brush 1 sheet of phyllo at a time with some of the margarine or butter. Place another sheet of phyllo dough on top of the first sheet and brush with some of the margarine or butter. Repeat with a third layer. (Cover remaining phyllo dough with a damp cloth to prevent drying.) Cut the stack of dough into twelve 4-inch squares. Place a rounded teaspoon of filling in the center of each square. For each bundle, bring the four corners together, pinch and twist slightly. Repeat with the remaining dough to make a total of 36 bundles. Arrange on an ungreased parchment or foil lined baking sheet. Bake uncovered in a preheated 375 degree oven for 12 to 15 minutes or until golden. Serve warm. Makes 36.

Bull's Eyes

1 (8-ounce) package cream cheese, softened	1 (8-ounce) container sour cream
1 (4½-ounce) can chopped green chiles, drained	4 green onions, finely chopped
1 (4-ounce) can sliced ripe olives, drained	Large flour tortillas

In a medium bowl, combine cream cheese, green chiles, olives, sour cream and onions. Spread mixture on tortillas and roll up. Wrap in foil and refrigerate until firm. Cut into ½-inch slices and serve.

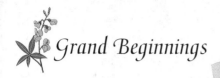

Heavenly Hot Pecans

2	tablespoons butter	½	teaspoon salt
1	cup large pecan halves	3	dashes Tabasco sauce
2	teaspoons soy sauce		

Melt butter in a shallow pan. Spread pecans evenly in 1 layer over butter. Bake in a preheated 300 degree oven for 30 minutes, stirring often. Remove from oven. Mix soy sauce, salt and Tabasco sauce in a small bowl. Pour over toasted nuts, stirring well to coat. Spread the nuts on a double layer of paper towels to cool. Pack them in an airtight container.

Sherried Walnuts

Great For The Holidays

2	cups brown sugar	¼	teaspoon salt
½	cup corn syrup	2-3	cups sugar
¼	cup sherry	2-3	cups walnut halves

In a small bowl, mix together the brown sugar, corn syrup, sherry and salt. Set aside. Pour sugar in a large bowl. Place walnuts in the brown sugar mixture and coat evenly. (If brown sugar mixture becomes runny, just add more brown sugar until it becomes thicker.) Then roll in the white sugar. Lay each walnut half on wax paper to dry. Turn to dry on other side of walnut. They stay nice and crisp if left out in an open bowl.

Hint: Be sure to use a top quality California sherry in this recipe.

Bloody Marys for Brunch

1	(46-ounce) can tomato juice	½	teaspoon cracked pepper
1½-2 cups vodka		1	teaspoon salt
⅛	cup Worcestershire sauce	1	teaspoon celery salt
⅓	cup lemon juice	Celery ribs	
½	teaspoon Tabasco sauce, or to taste		

Combine tomato juice, vodka, Worcestershire sauce, lemon juice, Tabasco sauce, cracked pepper, salt and celery salt. Serve over lots of ice. Garnish each drink with a rib of celery. Serves 12.

Mango Margaritas

1	(26-ounce) jar sliced mangoes with liquid	1	cup gold tequila
Sugar		½	cup Triple Sec or Cointreau
1	(6-ounce) can frozen limeade concentrate, thawed, undiluted	¼	cup Grand Marnier
		Crushed ice	

Spoon 3 tablespoons mango liquid into a saucer; pour mangoes and remaining liquid into container of an electric blender. Place sugar in another saucer. Dip rims of glasses into mango liquid and then sugar. Set aside. Add limeade concentrate, gold tequila, Triple Sec and Grand Marnier to blender container; process until smooth, stopping once to scrape down the sides. Pour half of the mixture into a small pitcher and set aside. Add ice to remaining mixture in blender to bring it to the 5-cup level. Process until slushy, stopping once to scrape down the sides. Pour into prepared glasses; repeat with remaining mango mixture and ice. Serve immediately. Makes 10 cups.

Hint: Use colored decorator sugar for the rims of the glasses.

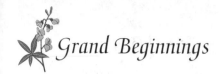

Sparkling Strawberry Mimosas

2½ cups orange juice, chilled

1 (10-ounce) package frozen strawberries, partially thawed

1 (750-milliliter) bottle dry champagne, chilled

1 cup whole fresh strawberries

Additional whole fresh strawberries, optional

Fresh mint sprigs, optional

Combine orange juice and frozen strawberries in blender. Process until pureed. Pour into a pitcher. Add champagne and stir gently. Add 1 cup whole fresh strawberries. Pour in frosted champagne glasses and float a fresh strawberry and mint sprig on top as garnish, if desired. Serve immediately. Makes 8 cups.

Hill Country Peach Fuzzies

Great On A Hot Summer Day

2 ripe medium peaches, peeled and pitted

6 ounces fresh orange juice

6 ounces vodka

2 ounces peach brandy

8 ice cubes

Put all ingredients into a blender. Blend until the mixture is slushy. Pour it into tall glasses and serve immediately. Serves 4.

Brownsville Border Buttermilk

1 (10-ounce) container of frozen orange juice concentrate

8 ounces rum

1 cup ice

Put all ingredients in blender and blend until slushy. Serve immediately. Serves 4.

This is a drink served in the Rio Grande Valley
at brunches in place of or along with Bloody Marys.

Sangría Blanco

Must Be Chilled

2	oranges, sliced and seeded	2	(3-inch) cinnamon sticks
1	lemon, sliced and seeded	2	(750-milliliter) bottles Chablis, chilled
1	lime, sliced and seeded		
⅔	cup brandy	1	quart club soda, chilled
½	cup sugar		

Combine oranges, lemon, lime, brandy, sugar and cinnamon sticks in a large pitcher. Cover and chill at least 4 hours, stirring occasionally. Remove and discard cinnamon sticks. Add Chablis and stir well. Cover and chill at least 2 hours. Stir in club soda and serve over ice. Makes 2 quarts.

Hint: If making this in large quantities you may want to reduce the amount of fruit.

Sangrita y Tequila

Must Be Made Ahead

8	ounces tomato juice	Dash cayenne pepper or few drops Tabasco sauce
8	teaspoons fresh orange juice	
8	teaspoons fresh lime juice	Tequila
4	teaspoons grated onion	

Combine tomato juice, orange juice, lime juice, onion and cayenne pepper or Tabasco sauce. Chill the mixture at least 1 hour to blend the flavors. Pour the drink into the smallest glass you own and serve it with shots of high quality tequila. Leftover sangrita, refrigerated, can be kept for at least a week.

In Mexico, tequila is often sipped and chased
with an accompanying glass of spicy sangrita.

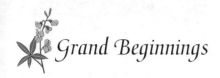

Texas Medicinal

⅓ cup bourbon	⅔ cup boiling water
1 teaspoon honey or to taste	1 cinnamon stick
1 teaspoon lemon juice	

Pour the bourbon into a glass. Add the honey and lemon juice. Put a spoon into glass so it won't break as you add the boiling water. Stir with cinnamon stick. Sip. Go to bed early.

This is a tried and true remedy for curing a severe cold or a broken heart.

Poor Charlie

1½ ounces vodka	2 ounces Fresca
3-4 ounces orange juice	

Combine ingredients and serve over ice. Serves 1.

Great for brunches, luncheons or midnight breakfasts.

Kahlúa

1 (2-ounce) jar instant coffee	1 vanilla bean
4 cups sugar	2 cups brandy
2 cups boiling water	

Mix coffee with sugar. Dissolve in boiling water and let cool. Slit vanilla bean and cut into very small pieces. Combine with coffee and add brandy. Pour into a bottle or large jar with tight fitting lid. Tighten cap and let stand for 30 days.

Variation: For crème de cacao, substitute 2 ounces cocoa for coffee.

Homemade Irish Liqueur

1¾ cups Irish whiskey, brandy, rum, bourbon, Scotch or rye

1 (14-ounce) can sweetened condensed milk

1 cup whipping or light cream

4 eggs

2 tablespoons chocolate flavored syrup

2 teaspoons instant coffee

1 teaspoon vanilla extract

½ teaspoon almond extract

Combine all ingredients in a blender container and blend until smooth. Serve over ice. Store tightly covered in refrigerator up to 1 month. Stir before serving. Makes 5 cups.

Apricot Punch

Must Be Frozen

2 (6-ounce) packages apricot or peach gelatin

1 cup boiling water

3 cups warm water

1 (12-ounce) can frozen lemonade concentrate

1 (46-ounce) can apricot nectar

1 (46-ounce) can pineapple juice

½ gallon cold water

4 (1-liter) bottles ginger ale

1 (750-milliliter) bottle wine, optional

Dissolve gelatin in boiling water. Add warm water, lemonade, apricot nectar and pineapple juice. Mix. Add cold water. Freeze in 4 equal size containers. Stir several times while it is freezing. Thaw when ready to serve and add 1 bottle ginger ale per container. Serves 40. If you want to use wine, reduce the water to 1 quart. Add wine with ginger ale at serving time.

To prevent punch from becoming diluted, prepare an ice mold or block from fresh fruit and fruit juice, or freeze a large cluster of grapes to use as a garnish and "ice".

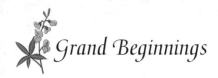
Banana Frozen Punch

Must Be Frozen

2 cups sugar
6 cups water
1 (46-ounce) can pineapple juice
2 (12-ounce) cans frozen orange juice concentrate, thawed

1 (12-ounce) can frozen lemonade concentrate, thawed
5 bananas, peeled and mashed
3 (2-liter) bottles Sprite
Fresh mint for garnish

Mix sugar, water, pineapple juice, orange juice, lemonade and bananas. Freeze. Take out of freezer about 4 hours before serving. Add Sprite just before serving. Garnish with mint if desired. Serves 60.

Frozen Margarita Punch

Must Be Frozen

4 (12-ounce) cans frozen limeade concentrate, thawed
3 quarts water
3 cups Triple Sec

3 cups tequila
2 (2-liter) bottles 7Up
Strawberries, optional
Lime slices, seeded, optional

Combine limeade, water, Triple Sec and tequila. Freeze 8 hours or more stirring twice during freezing process. Remove from freezer 30 minutes before serving. Break into chunks; add 7Up and stir until mixture is slushy. Makes 2½ gallons. Float strawberries and lime slices, as garnish.

Calculate how much beverage you'll need by the size
of your punch cups. Most cups hold about 4 ounces.

Friendship Punch

Must Be Made Ahead

1 (20-ounce) container unsweetened frozen strawberries, thawed

3 (6-ounce) cans frozen lemonade, thawed

1 (1-liter) bottle ginger ale or lemon-lime soda

Fresh mint

1 (750-milliliter) bottle white wine, optional

Fresh strawberries for ice ring

Combine strawberries and lemonade. Chill until ready to serve. Add ginger ale just before serving. Serve over an ice ring made with fresh strawberries. Garnish with sprigs of fresh mint. Makes 1½ gallons, without the wine.

This recipe was given to me by my aunt whose husband
was President of a small college. She said she used it many times
for teas, open house, senior banquets, etc. with or without wine
depending on the group she was serving.

Winter Warmer

1 (64-ounce) bottle apple juice

2¼ cups pineapple juice

2 cups orange juice

1 cup lemon juice

½ cup sugar

1 teaspoon whole cloves

1 stick cinnamon

Orange slices, studded with whole cloves

Orange slices for garnish

Combine all ingredients (except garnish) in a Dutch oven and bring to a boil. Cover, reduce heat and simmer 30 minutes. Uncover and simmer 30 minutes. Cool slightly. Strain and discard spices. Serve hot. Garnish with orange slices. Makes 2¾ quarts.

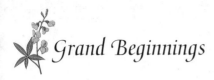

Richardson Woman's Club Coffee Punch

1	(2-ounce) jar instant coffee	1	(1-liter) bottle ginger ale
2	quarts hot water	1	pint heavy cream
2	cups sugar	½	gallon French vanilla ice cream
2	quarts half-and-half		

Dissolve instant coffee in hot water. Cool. Add sugar and half-and-half; mix well. At serving time, add ginger ale, cream and ice cream. Stir to mix. Makes 60 (4-ounce) servings.

Hint: Heavy cream contains 36 to 40 percent milk fat. It's available at specialty and gourmet markets. The best substitute is whipping cream.

An RWC Favorite. The New Member Tea, held the first
Thursday afternoon in September, is a special event of the
Richardson Woman's Club. Several of the recipes are traditional and
this punch has been a favorite for 47 years. This recipe is included
in our other best-selling cookbook, *The Texas Experience*, which
is a selection of the Community Cookbook Hall of Fame.

Vienna Coffee

3	cups very strong, hot coffee	4	whole allspice
2	cinnamon sticks		Whipped cream
4	whole cloves		Ground nutmeg

Pour hot coffee over cinnamon sticks, whole cloves and allspice. Let stand over lowest heat for 10 to 15 minutes. Strain and pour into wine glasses. Top with whipped cream and sprinkle with nutmeg. Serve with sugar or add ½ teaspoon sugar to coffee before whipped cream. You may wish to sweeten the whipped cream. Serves 6.

Espresso Coffee Bar

Coffee:
Espresso grinds for regular drip-pot coffee makers, brewed or regular coffee brewed strong

Toppings:
Grated semi-sweet chocolate   Whipped cream

Spices and Seasonings:

Shaker of sugar	Shaker of ground allspice
Brown sugar	Shaker of ground nutmeg
Grated orange zest	Lemon slices
Instant cocoa mix	Powdered chocolate
Cinnamon sticks	Chocolate curls
Whole allspice	Cream

Mocha Coffee:
Coffee and instant cocoa mix topped with whipped cream

Cappuccino:
Coffee, cream, ground nutmeg and sugar stirred with a cinnamon stick.

Mexican Coffee:
Coffee and powdered chocolate topped with whipped cream and chocolate curls and stirred with a cinnamon stick.

Spiced Coffee:
Coffee, brown sugar and a dash of allspice topped with orange zest and stirred with a cinnamon stick.

Demitasse:
Half a cup of coffee with a twist of lemon.

Write out recipes for each kind of espresso and let guests make their own.

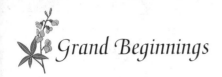

Grand Marnier Cappuccino

¼   cup evaporated skimmed milk
3   cups strong hot brewed coffee

2   tablespoons Grand Marnier or other orange-flavored liqueur

Grated semi-sweet chocolate, optional

Place milk in a small narrow glass or steel bowl; freeze 30 minutes or until small crystals form around the top. Beat milk at high speed in an electric mixer 5 minutes or until stiff peaks form. Combine coffee and Grand Marnier. Divide coffee mixture among 4 coffee cups. Top each with whipped milk. Sprinkle with grated chocolate, if desired. Serve immediately. Serves 4.

Variation: For Kahlúa Cappuccino, substitute 2 tablespoons Kahlúa or other coffee-flavored liqueur for orange-flavored liqueur.

Variation: For Crème De Menthe Cappuccino, substitute 2 tablespoons white crème de menthe liqueur for orange-flavored liqueur.

Mexican Coffee

½   cup ground dark roast coffee
1   tablespoon ground cinnamon
¼   teaspoon ground nutmeg
5   cups water
¼   cup firmly packed dark brown sugar

⅓   cup chocolate syrup
1   cup milk
1   teaspoon vanilla extract
Sweetened whipped cream
Ground cinnamon, optional

Place coffee in coffee filter or basket; add cinnamon and nutmeg. Add water to coffee maker and brew according to manufacturer's directions. Combine brown sugar, chocolate syrup and milk in a large saucepan. Cook over low heat, stirring constantly, until sugar dissolves. Stir in coffee mixture and vanilla extract. Serve immediately with a dollop of whipped cream. Sprinkle with cinnamon if desired. Makes 6½ cups.

Café Au Lait Mix

1½ cups instant non-dairy creamer
¼ cup packed brown sugar

¼ cup instant coffee crystals
Dash salt

Thoroughly mix all ingredients together. Store in airtight container. When ready to serve, mix ¼ cup mix with ⅔ cup boiling water.

Mexican Hot Chocolate

2 tablespoons hard cinnamon candies
1½ cups milk
1½ cups whipping cream

½ cup semi-sweet chocolate chips
1 tablespoon instant coffee
Candy cane for garnish

Blend cinnamon candies on medium speed in blender until powdered. Heat milk and whipping cream. Add to blender container along with chocolate and coffee. Blend on high until frothy or 20 seconds. Add candy cane to each mug. Serves 4 to 6.

Sugar-Free Hot Chocolate Mix

3 cups powdered nonfat milk
3 tablespoons cocoa

1½ teaspoons sugar substitute
Instant non-dairy creamer, optional

Mix together powdered milk, cocoa and sugar substitute. Store in an airtight container. When ready to serve, mix ⅓ cup mix with 1 cup hot water. Add instant non-dairy creamer for richer flavor. Makes 9 to 10 servings.

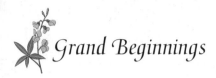
Grand Beginnings

Instant Hot Chocolate Mix

1   (25.6-ounce) box instant dry
      milk powder
1   (16-ounce) box powdered sugar

1   (16-ounce) box instant
      chocolate flavored drink mix
1   (16-ounce) jar non-dairy creamer
      Miniature marshmallows, optional

Mix together the dry milk powder, powdered sugar, chocolate drink mix and non-dairy creamer. Store in airtight container. Use 2 to 4 tablespoons of mix for each cup of hot water. Top with marshmallows, if desired.

Hint: Great to give as gifts for the holidays. Just place in individual airtight containers and decorate.

Variation: Velvet Hot Chocolate: Add 2 teaspoons amaretto and ⅛ teaspoon rum extract to each serving.

Variation: Mocha Chocolate: Add 1½ teaspoons instant coffee granules and ⅛ teaspoon vanilla extract to each serving.

For tea concentrate for a function, bring 1 quart of water to a
boil and pour over ⅔ cup of loose tea. Cover and let stand for
5 to 10 minutes. Stir, then strain into a warmed teapot. If using tea bags,
bring 1 quart of water to a boil and pour over 10 individual serving tea bags
that have been placed in a warmed teapot. Cover and let stand for
5 to 10 minutes and then remove tea bags. Makes concentrate for
25 people. To use the concentrate, pour about 1 inch of the tea concentrate
into the teacup. Add water that has been boiled just prior to the function
and placed in warmed pitchers for pouring. Silver pitchers or coffee pots
work very well. It is best to have a specific person assigned to pour the tea
who has had the proportions of tea to water explained to them.
Milk is offered along with lemon and sugar.

Spiced Tea Mix

2 cups orange breakfast drink powder	2 (2-quart) packages sweetened lemonade mix
1 cup instant tea	1 tablespoon ground cinnamon
2 cups sugar	1 teaspoon ground cloves
	1 teaspoon ground nutmeg

Combine all ingredients. Store in airtight jars. Use 1 tablespoon for each mug of boiling water. Makes 192 servings.

A great gift item.

Almond Tea

3 small tea bags	10 tablespoons lemon juice
6 cups water, divided	1 tablespoon almond extract
1 cup sugar	1 teaspoon vanilla extract

Boil 2 cups of water and steep the tea bags for 10 minutes. Combine 4 cups water and sugar in a sauce pan and boil 5 minutes. Combine sugar water with the tea and add lemon juice, almond and vanilla extracts. Serve over ice. Serves 6.

Iced Lemon Tea

1 quart water	1 quart cool tea
2 cups sugar	½ teaspoon almond extract
Grated zest of 1 lemon	1 teaspoon vanilla extract
1 cup lemon juice	

Boil water, sugar and zest together for 5 minutes. Add lemon juice, tea, almond and vanilla extracts. Cool and serve over ice. Serves 6.

Excellent cool drink for hot days. It can be stored in refrigerator.

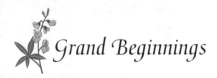

O'Suzanna's Summer Tea

Must Be Made Ahead

2	quarts water, divided
2	family size peach tea bags
½	cup sugar, optional
1	(12-ounce) can frozen lemonade concentrate, thawed

1	(32-ounce) bottle ginger ale or cherry 7Up

Lemon, lime or mint, optional

Bring 1 quart water to boil and pour over tea bags. Let steep as recommended on package. (If using sugar, add next.) Add lemonade and 1 quart cold water. Chill. Just before serving add ginger ale or 7Up. Can be served with lemon, lime or mint. Makes 18 (6-ounce) glasses.

Peaches and Cream Sipper

1	(16-ounce) package frozen unsweetened peaches, slightly thawed
1	(6-ounce) can frozen apple juice concentrate
1	(8-ounce) carton vanilla low-fat yogurt

⅓	cup instant nonfat dry milk powder
¼	cup water
⅛	teaspoon vanilla extract

Ice cubes

Fresh strawberries, optional

Combine peaches, apple juice, yogurt, dry milk, water and vanilla extract in container of a blender and blend until smooth. Gradually add enough ice to measure 4 cups in blender; blend until smooth. Pour mixture into glasses. Garnish each serving with a fresh strawberry, if desired. Makes 4 cups.

Hint: Be sure your dry milk is fresh. You can omit the dry milk, but the drink won't be as creamy.

Variation: Add 1 tablespoon peach Schnapps for each 6-ounce serving and 1 teaspoon ground cinnamon to each blender. Sprinkle nutmeg on top of each drink.

Iced Apple Tea

3   cups boiling water
4   cinnamon-apple tea bags
1   tablespoon sugar

1   (6-ounce) can frozen apple juice
    concentrate, thawed
2   cups cold water
    Cinnamon sticks, optional

Pour boiling water over tea bags; cover and steep 5 minutes. Remove and discard bags. Stir in sugar, juice concentrate and cold water. Serve over ice. Serve with cinnamon sticks. Makes 5 cups.

Breakfast Smoothie

6   ice cubes
½   cup low-fat vanilla or plain yogurt
½   cup orange juice or milk
½   banana

½   mango or 1 peach
4-5 fresh pineapple chunks
5-6 fresh strawberries
1   tablespoon honey, optional

Put all ingredients in a blender and turn off and on until well blended and the ice is slivered. Vary the fruits according to what you have on hand. Makes 2 (8-ounce) glasses.

Hint: Freeze all fruits except strawberries. It makes them sweeter and is a wonderful way to use extra bananas. (Bananas blend better when cut in fourths.)

Strawberry Cooler

1   cup skim milk
1   cup plain low-fat yogurt
2   tablespoons sugar

2   tablespoons vanilla extract
2   cups whole strawberries

Combine milk, yogurt, sugar and vanilla extract in blender and process until smooth. Gradually add strawberries. Process until smooth and slightly thickened. Taste for sweetness. Makes 3¾ cups.

Variation: Use frozen unsweetened strawberries or use regular frozen strawberries and omit sugar.

Great Starters

North Texas is characteristically a fertile blackland prairie unlike any other place in the world except for a small area in Australia. Our North Texas city of Richardson's annual spring-time display of enchanting beauties in Breckenridge Park includes these vibrant poppies and cornflowers.

Photography by John Guthrie

North
Texas

Chilled Peach Soup

Must Be Chilled

12 peaches, peeled and sliced	½ cup orange juice
1 cup sugar	½ cup sherry
½ cup lemon juice	4 cups sour cream

Mix peaches and sugar in blender until smooth. Add juices, sherry, and sour cream; blend well. Chill several hours or overnight before serving. Serves 8.

Strawberry Soup

4 cups frozen strawberries, thawed	½ cup cold water
1 cup sugar	1 cup claret
1 cup sour cream	

Puree the strawberries through a fine sieve. Mix the puree with sugar and sour cream. Add the water and claret. Heat this mixture very slowly over low heat, stirring constantly. Do not boil. May be served hot or cold. Serves 6 to 8.

Spanish settlers brought peaches to Texas in the sixteenth century, when they planted trees at the missions. Today, the state is one of the leading peach producers in the country, harvesting about twenty million pounds of fruit annually. The annual *"Peach Festival"* is celebrated in the town of Fairfield in Freestone County during the Fourth of July Celebration.

Asparagus-Tomato Soup

1½ cups (about ¾ pound) asparagus, cooked and chopped
3 (14½-ounce) cans chicken broth
1 medium onion, chopped
1 carrot, chopped
Dash pepper
2 teaspoons chopped parsley

1 teaspoon salt
½ teaspoon dried thyme, crumbled
1 bay leaf
½ teaspoon dried basil, crumbled
1 (28-ounce) can tomatoes with basil, chopped
2 tablespoons flour
2 tablespoons butter, melted

Combine asparagus, broth, onions, carrots, pepper, parsley, salt, thyme, bay leaf, basil and tomatoes. Cover and simmer 30 to 35 minutes. Remove the bay leaf. Put half of the vegetables in blender and blend. Return vegetables to soup mixture. Combine flour and butter; add to soup and cook 10 to 15 minutes longer. Serves 8.

Bean Soup Pronto

¾-1 cup chopped onions
1 tablespoon vegetable oil
1 (4½-ounce) can chopped green chiles, drained
1 (16-ounce) can refried beans
2 cups chicken broth
Salt and pepper to taste

Tabasco sauce, optional
2 tablespoons chopped fresh cilantro
5-6 tablespoons grated Monterey Jack cheese
5-6 tablespoons sour cream

Place onions and oil in a large skillet over medium high heat and cook until onions are soft, but not brown. Add green chiles, refried beans and chicken broth to onions. Cook and stir until soup is heated and no lumps remain. Season with salt and pepper. Add Tabasco sauce to taste. Stir in cilantro just before serving. Top with grated cheese and sour cream. Serves 6.

Hint: For a quick meal, keep these ingredients in your pantry.

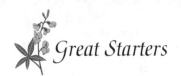

Spicy Black Bean Soup

1	tablespoon vegetable oil	2	tablespoons finely chopped fresh cilantro
1	red or green bell pepper, chopped	1	tablespoon lemon juice
¾	cup chopped onions	1	teaspoon dried oregano, crumbled
¾	cup chopped carrots		
2	garlic cloves, chopped	½	teaspoon dried thyme, crumbled
1	(14½-ounce) can reduced sodium chicken broth	¼	teaspoon crushed red pepper
		¼	fresh jalapeño, finely chopped
1½	cups water	⅛	teaspoon white pepper
2	(15-ounce) cans black beans, drained and rinsed		Sour cream, optional
			Dash nutmeg, optional

Put oil in 2-quart saucepan, cook bell peppers, onions, carrots and garlic covered, over medium heat for 5 minutes or until tender. Remove from heat. Stir in broth, water, beans, cilantro, lemon juice, oregano, thyme, red pepper, jalapeños and white pepper. Place ½ mixture in blender and blend briefly until smooth. Remove and add the remaining soup mixture repeating the same process. Put entire mixture back on the heat, bring to boil and simmer for 10 minutes covered for well done vegetables. Serve with dollop of sour cream, topped with sprinkle of nutmeg. Serves 4.

Sizzlin'-Shiverin' Broccoli Soup

1	(10-ounce) package frozen chopped broccoli	1	cup sour cream
1	medium onion, chopped	1	(10¾-ounce) can cream of mushroom soup, undiluted
¼	teaspoon ground nutmeg	2	tablespoons butter or margarine, melted
1	cup chicken broth		

Cook the broccoli, onions, nutmeg and broth for 6 minutes. Place in a blender or food processor and add the sour cream, mushroom soup and butter. Blend on high for 20 seconds. Return to heat if it is to be served hot. It's good served cold, too! Serves 6.

Black-Eyed Pea Soup

Yummy!

1	(14½-ounce) can beef broth	1	cup chopped bell peppers
2	(14½-ounce) cans chopped tomatoes	3	cups diced, cooked ham
		6	slices jalapeños
3	(15-ounce) cans black-eyed peas	1	(16-ounce) package frozen sliced okra
2	cups chopped celery		
2	cups chopped onions	1	cup whole kernel corn

Place broth, tomatoes, peas, celery, onions, bell peppers, ham and jalapeños in 6-quart soup pot and cook for 1 hour on medium or low heat. Add okra and corn and cook for 30 minutes longer. Serves 8 to 10.

Hint: You can use the canned black-eyed peas with jalapeños and eliminate the slices of jalapeño. It's a spicy soup, but delicious.

Cream of Broccoli Soup

3	carrots, chopped	1	(10-ounce) package frozen chopped broccoli
3-4	ribs celery, chopped		
1	bunch of green onions, chopped	1	(8-ounce) container sour cream
6	tablespoons margarine	8	ounces Cheddar cheese, shredded
3	(14½-ounce) cans chicken broth		
3	(10¾-ounce) cans cream of potato soup, undiluted		Dash Tabasco sauce

Sauté carrots, celery and green onions in margarine for 15 minutes. Add broth, potato soup and broccoli. Simmer 30 minutes. Just before serving add sour cream, cheese and Tabasco sauce. Serves 8 to 10.

An RWC Favorite, we've served this in the Tea Room twice.

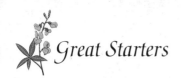

Cold Velvety Cucumber-Avocado Soup
Must Be Chilled

8 small fresh cucumbers, peeled and chopped	1 cup sour cream
1 avocado, peeled and pitted	½ cup half-and-half
3 green onions with tops, sliced	2 tablespoons fresh lemon juice
1 tablespoon minced fresh dill or ½ teaspoon dried	Salt, pepper and celery salt to taste
1 (10½-ounce) can chicken broth	2 dashes Worcestershire sauce

Combine ingredients in blender. Chill at least 1 to 2 hours. Garnish with slice of cucumber and sprig of dill. Serves 4 to 6.

The word "soup" is supposed to come from
the sound of people slurping liquid from a spoon.

Easy Potato Soup

1 (24-ounce) package frozen diced hash brown potatoes	2 cups water
1 cup chopped onions	2 (10½-ounce) cans cream of celery soup, undiluted
½ teaspoon salt	2 cups milk
⅛ teaspoon pepper	Shredded Cheddar cheese, optional
1 (14½-ounce) can chicken broth	

Combine potatoes, onions, salt, pepper, broth and water in Dutch oven and bring to boil. Cover, reduce heat and simmer 30 minutes. Stir soup and milk together until smooth. Add to vegetables and heat thoroughly. Garnish with cheese. Serves 8.

Easy French Onion Soup

3	medium onions, thinly sliced	1	teaspoon salt
3	tablespoons butter	⅛	teaspoon pepper
2	(10½-ounce) cans beef broth	6	slices toasted French bread
1½	cups water	1½	cups shredded Swiss cheese

Put onions and butter in a 3-quart casserole dish. Cover and microwave 10 minutes on high, stirring after 5 minutes. Add broth, water, salt and pepper. Cover and microwave on high 8 to 10 minutes. Spoon soup into 6 individual bowls and top each with 1 slice toasted bread and ¼ cup cheese. Microwave up to 3 bowls at a time, allowing ¾ to 1 minute per serving. Serves 6.

Baked Potato Soup

Rich and Scrumptious!

6-8 slices bacon, fried crisply, drippings reserved
1 cup diced yellow onions
½ cup flour
6 cups chicken stock, heated
4 cups diced, peeled baked potatoes
2 cups heavy cream or milk
¼ cup chopped parsley

1½ teaspoons granulated garlic
1½ teaspoons dried basil, crumbled
Salt and pepper to taste
1½ teaspoons Tabasco sauce
1 cup grated Cheddar cheese
¼ cup diced green onions, white part only
Chopped parsley, optional

Chop bacon and reserve. Cook onions in remaining drippings over medium high heat until transparent, about 3 minutes. Add flour, stirring to prevent lumps and cook for 3 to 5 minutes until mixture just begins to turn golden. Add chicken stock gradually, whisking to prevent lumps until liquid thickens. Reduce heat to simmer and add potatoes, cream, most of the bacon (reserving some for garnish), parsley, garlic, basil, salt, pepper and Tabasco sauce. Simmer for 10 minutes; do not allow to boil. Add most of the grated cheese (reserving some for garnish) and green onions; heat until cheese melts. Garnish each serving as desired with additional chopped bacon, grated cheese and chopped parsley. Serves 8.

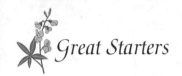

Caribbean Tomato Soup

1	(14½-ounce) can tomatoes with liquid	1	cup canned unsweetened coconut milk
1	(10¾-ounce) can low-sodium tomato soup, undiluted	¼	teaspoon Tabasco sauce
2	tablespoons grated fresh ginger	2	tablespoons lime juice
		⅛	teaspoon salt

In a food processor or blender, puree the canned tomatoes with the tomato soup and ginger until smooth. Pour into a medium saucepan. Stir in coconut milk, Tabasco sauce, lime juice and salt. Cook over low heat and stir until heated through. Serve hot. Serves 4.

Snappy Tomato Bouillon
Can Be Chilled

1	(46-ounce) can tomato juice, divided	3	teaspoons instant beef bouillon
1	celery rib with leaves, chopped	1	teaspoon sugar
1	tablespoon chopped green onions	½	teaspoon salt
2	tablespoons chopped parsley	⅛	teaspoon pepper
		2-3	drops Tabasco sauce
		8-12	lemon slices for garnish

Pour 2 cups tomato juice into a small saucepan. Add celery with leaves, onions, parsley, bouillon, sugar, salt, pepper and Tabasco sauce. Bring to a boil; simmer 5 minutes over medium heat. Pour into blender or food processor. Process until nearly smooth; strain. In a large pitcher, combine strained juice and remaining tomato juice. Refrigerate until cold, 1 to 2 hours. Pour into 8 (6-ounce) glasses or 12 (4-ounce) glasses. Garnish each with 1 lemon slice. You can serve this hot or cold. Serves 8 to 10.

Cauliflower and Ham Chowder

2	cups sliced cauliflower florets	¼	cup water
1	(14½-ounce) can chicken broth	2	tablespoons cornstarch
1	cup light cream or half-and-half	⅛	teaspoon white pepper
1	(10¾-ounce) can cream of potato soup, undiluted	2	cups diced, cooked ham

In large saucepan cook cauliflower, covered, in chicken broth until almost tender, about 10 minutes. Do not drain. In a mixing bowl gradually stir cream into potato soup. Mix water, cornstarch and pepper. Stir into potato soup; pour over cauliflower and cook until thickened and bubbly, stirring frequently. Add ham and simmer 10 minutes, stirring occasionally. Serves 5 to 6.

Clam Chowder

3	slices bacon, cut into 1-inch pieces	1	large potato, cubed
1	onion, minced	1	(10¾-ounce) can cream of celery soup, undiluted
1	(6½-ounce) can minced clams, drained, and liquid reserved	1½	cups milk
			Dash pepper

Cook bacon until crisp. Drain and discard all but 2 tablespoons bacon drippings. Crumble the bacon and reserve a few pieces of bacon for garnish. Sauté onions in bacon drippings 4 to 5 minutes. Add clam liquid and potatoes. Mix well. Cover and cook over low heat until potatoes are cooked, about 15 minutes. Add bacon, clams, soup, milk and pepper. Mix well. Cook over low heat until heated. Garnish with remaining bacon and serve. Serves 6.

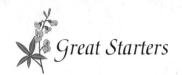

Hearty Corn Chowder

2   slices bacon, fried crisply and
    crumbled
2   tablespoons reserved bacon
    drippings
1   onion, chopped
¼   cup chopped celery
½   bay leaf, crumbled
1   tablespoon flour

2   cups water
1½ cups diced, peeled potatoes
1   (8-ounce) can cream style corn
1   cup evaporated milk
Salt and freshly ground pepper to
    taste
Chopped parsley for garnish

Heat reserved bacon drippings in a heavy saucepan. Add onions, celery and bay leaf and sauté about 5 minutes. Blend in flour. Stir in water; add potatoes and bring to boil. Simmer covered about 15 minutes. Add corn and milk and heat well. Season to taste with salt and pepper. Garnish with crumbled bacon and parsley. Serves 2 as a main course.

Chicken Gumbo

½   cup finely chopped onions
4   tablespoons margarine
2   (14½-ounce) cans chicken broth
½   green bell pepper, chopped
1   (10-ounce) package sliced
    frozen okra
1   cooked chicken, skinned and cut
    in pieces

2   teaspoons salt
¼   teaspoon pepper
2   cups diced canned tomatoes
1   (14¾-ounce) can cream style
    corn
½   cup uncooked rice
Tabasco sauce to taste, optional

Sauté onions in margarine for 5 minutes. Add chicken broth, bell peppers, okra, chicken, salt, pepper, tomatoes, corn, rice and Tabasco sauce. Simmer for 40 minutes. Serves 6.

Italian Wedding Soup

Meatballs:

1	pound ground beef	2	teaspoons dried oregano, crumbled
1	pound ground sausage		
2	eggs	1	teaspoon dried rosemary, crumbled
1	cup soft breadcrumbs		
		1	garlic clove, crushed
			Olive oil

Soup:

2	(14½-ounce) cans chicken broth	1	cup fresh spinach leaves, torn into pieces
2	broth cans water		
2	cups small cubes cooked chicken	1	large onion, sliced finely
		2	eggs, slightly beaten
1	(5-ounce) package vermicelli		Parmesan cheese, freshly grated

Meatballs:

In a large bowl combine beef, sausage, eggs, breadcrumbs, oregano, rosemary and garlic. Shape mixture into bite-size meatballs. Slowly and evenly brown the meatballs in olive oil until cooked.

Soup:

In a large saucepan combine the chicken broth and water. Bring to a boil. Add chicken, vermicelli, meatballs, spinach and onions. Simmer, uncovered, until the vermicelli is tender. Drop in the eggs, stirring only until the eggs are cooked. Sprinkle individual portions with Parmesan cheese. Serves 10.

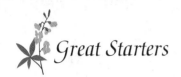

Chicken Tortilla Soup

3½ cups water

2 chicken breasts halves with skin and bone

5 whole peppercorns

½ celery rib with leaves

⅛ small onion

1 carrot

1 teaspoon salt

2-3 sprigs fresh cilantro

1 small onion, chopped finely

2 garlic cloves, minced

1 (4½-ounce) can chopped green chiles

2 tablespoons vegetable oil

1 (14½-ounce) can beef broth

3 cups chicken broth, reserved from chicken

1 (10-ounce) can tomatoes with green chiles

2 cups tomato juice

2 teaspoons Worcestershire sauce

1 teaspoon ground cumin

1 teaspoon chili powder

Salt and pepper to taste

2 tablespoons chopped fresh cilantro

Grated Monterey Jack cheese

Tortilla chips

In water cook the chicken breasts with peppercorns, celery, ⅛ small onion, carrot, 1 teaspoon salt and sprigs of cilantro until tender, about 30 to 45 minutes. Cool chicken and shred. Strain broth and reserve for soup. Discard vegetables. Using a large soup pot, sauté chopped onions, garlic and green chiles in oil over medium heat until soft, not brown. Add the beef broth, reserved chicken broth, tomatoes and green chiles, tomato juice, Worcestershire sauce, cumin, chili powder and salt and pepper to taste. Simmer 30 minutes and add chicken and chopped cilantro. Serve with cheese and tortilla chips on top. Serves 8.

An RWC Favorite served at the Tea Room.

Sopa de Tortilla

1	cup chopped onions	6	cups chicken or turkey broth
1	teaspoon olive oil	1	(10-ounce) package frozen corn
1	(4½-ounce) can chopped green chiles	2	cups cooked chicken cut in ½-inch cubes
1	(1.5-ounce) package taco seasoning	⅓	cup chopped fresh cilantro
		4	ounces tortilla chips
1	(14½-ounce) can tomatoes with liquid	½	cup grated Monterey Jack cheese

In a 5-quart sauce pan sauté onions in oil 3 to 4 minutes. Stir in chiles and taco seasoning. Cook 1 minute and add tomatoes and liquid. Stir in broth. Bring to a boil. Add corn and chicken and reduce heat to low. Simmer 5 minutes and add cilantro. Spoon into bowls. Add tortilla chips and top with cheese. Serves 6 to 8.

I have made a lot of different tortilla soups
and this is the fastest and best of all.

Bean Counter Soup

1	(28-ounce) package 15 bean soup mix	½	cup lemon juice
2	(14½-ounce) cans Mexican style tomatoes		2-3 pounds boneless, skinless chicken breasts, cubed and browned
1	(15-ounce) can whole kernel corn, drained	1	onion, chopped
2	(1.5-ounce) packages taco seasoning		Sour cream

Rinse beans and soak overnight. Drain beans and cover with water. Add tomatoes, corn, taco seasoning, lemon juice, chicken and onions. Simmer 1 hour or until beans are tender. Put in bowls and top with sour cream. Serves 12.

Rio Grande Soup

2 (14½-ounce) cans stewed Mexican style tomatoes with liquid
1 (14½-ounce) can chicken broth
½ pound smoked turkey, cubed
1 large green bell pepper, diced
1 (8-ounce) can whole kernel corn, drained
¾ cup picante sauce

1 (2¼-ounce) can sliced ripe olives, drained
1½ teaspoons ground cumin
1 teaspoon dried basil, crumbled
1 garlic clove, crushed
½ cup sliced green onions
Sour cream
Shredded Monterey Jack cheese
Chopped cilantro

In a large saucepan combine tomatoes, broth, turkey, pepper, corn, picante sauce, olives, cumin, basil and garlic. Simmer 10 minutes, uncovered. Add onions and simmer 5 minutes more. Garnish with sour cream, cheese and cilantro. Serves 6.

She-Crab Soup

¼ pound butter
4 tablespoons flour
4 cups milk
2 cups crabmeat
Few drops onion juice

½ teaspoon Worcestershire sauce
Dash ground mace
Salt and pepper to taste
½ cup whipping cream, whipped
Dry sherry

Melt butter and blend in flour. Add milk, crabmeat, onion juice, Worcestershire sauce, mace, salt and pepper. Cook slowly 20 minutes over hot water. Whip cream and set aside. Warm sherry. Pour ½ tablespoon sherry into individual soup bowls and add soup. Top each bowl of soup with a serving of whipped cream. Serve hot. Serves 4.

Hint: If crab roe is available with the fresh crab, include it with the crabmeat.

Double Delight Blueberry Salad

Must Be Chilled

Salad:

2   (3-ounce) packages blueberry, cherry or raspberry gelatin

2   cups boiling water

1   (16-ounce) can of blueberries or 1 (16-ounce) package of frozen blueberries, drained and liquid reserved

1   (20-ounce) can crushed pineapple, drained

½   cup chopped pecans

Topping:

1   (8-ounce) package cream cheese

1   cup sour cream

½   cup sugar

½   teaspoon vanilla extract

Salad:

In a 13x9x2-inch dish dissolve gelatin in boiling water. Stir until completely dissolved. Use the blueberry juice plus enough cold water to make 2 cups of liquid and stir into dissolved gelatin. Stir the blueberries, pineapple and pecans into the gelatin. Refrigerate until set. Serves 9 to 12.

Topping:

Mix all ingredients and spread on gelatin before serving.

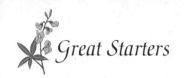

Cherry-Pineapple Salad

Must Be Chilled

1 (8-ounce) package cream cheese
Cream, optional
1 (20-ounce) can crushed pineapple
1 cup maraschino cherries, sliced or halved, drained, liquid reserved

1 cup sugar
4 tablespoons mayonnaise
2 envelopes unflavored gelatin
Cherry liquid plus cold water to make 1 cup
1 pint whipping cream

Soften cream cheese with a little cream. Add fruits, sugar and mayonnaise, and set aside. In top of double boiler soak gelatin in juice and water about 5 minutes. Then dissolve over hot, not boiling water. Add to fruit mixture. Whip cream and fold into other ingredients. Put in mold and refrigerate. Serves 6.

Molded Lime Salad

Must Be Chilled

1 (3-ounce) package lime gelatin
1½ cups boiling water
½ teaspoon lemon pre-sweetened powdered drink mix
1 (16-ounce) carton cottage cheese
1 (3-ounce) package cream cheese

1 cup chopped walnuts
1 cup mayonnaise
½ teaspoon grated onion
1 cup peeled, chopped cucumber
¼ teaspoon salt
1 teaspoon lemon juice or vinegar

Make gelatin according to package directions using boiling water and cool until syrupy. Combine powdered drink mix, cottage cheese, cream cheese, walnuts, mayonnaise, onion, cucumber, salt and lemon juice and add to gelatin mixture. Pour into ring mold and chill. Serves 8.

Gulf Coast Crab Louie Salad

Must Be Chilled

2	envelopes unflavored gelatin	1	tablespoon fresh lemon juice
1	cup water, divided	½	teaspoon salt
⅔	cup chili sauce	2	hard-cooked eggs, finely chopped
½	cup rosé wine		
½	cup sour cream	1	pound fresh or frozen crab chunks
½	cup mayonnaise		
½	cup tomato juice		Lettuce
1	tablespoon grated, minced onion		Spiced peaches, optional
			Stuffed olive, optional

Soften gelatin in ½ cup cold water. Heat chili sauce, remaining water and softened gelatin. Add wine, sour cream, mayonnaise, tomato juice, onions, lemon juice and salt. Chill until partly set, about 2 hours. Fold eggs and crab into mixture. Pour ingredients into a 6-cup mold. Chill until set. Serve unmolded on a bed of lettuce with spiced peaches around the shape.

Hint: A fish shaped mold makes a pretty presentation. Use a slice of stuffed olive for the eye.

Pear Salad

Must Be Chilled

2	(3-ounce) packages lemon gelatin	Orange juice, optional
1	(29-ounce) can pears, drained and liquid reserved	1 (8-ounce) package cream cheese
		1 (8-ounce) tub frozen whipped topping, thawed

Dissolve gelatin in 2 cups hot pear juice or a combination of pear and orange juice. Cool until mixture starts to get thick. Puree pears in blender. Add gelatin mixture, cream cheese and whipped topping. Blend well. Chill in 13x9x2-inch dish for at least 2 hours. Serves 9 to 12.

Hint: You'll need 2 cans of pears to yield 2 cups of pear juice.

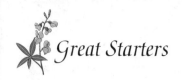

Cranberry Mousse

Must Be Chilled

1 (20-ounce) can crushed pineapple, drained, and liquid reserved	2-3 tablespoons fresh lemon juice
1 (6-ounce) package raspberry gelatin	1 teaspoon fresh grated lemon zest
1 cup water	¼ teaspoon ground nutmeg
1 (16-ounce) can cranberry sauce	2 cups sour cream
	½ cup chopped pecans, optional

Add pineapple juice to gelatin in 2-quart saucepan. Stir in water. Heat to boiling, stirring, to dissolve gelatin. Remove from heat. Blend in cranberry sauce. Add lemon juice, zest and nutmeg. Chill until it thickens slightly. Blend sour cream into gelatin. Fold in pineapple and pecans. Pour into 2-quart mold. Chill. Serves 8 to 10.

Spiced Peach Salad

Must Be Chilled

4 oranges	1 (6-ounce) package lemon gelatin
1 (22-ounce) jar pickled or spiced peaches, drained and liquid reserved	1 cup boiling water
1 (16½-ounce) can pitted, sweet Royal Ann cherries, drained and liquid reserved	1 cup chopped pecans
	Lettuce leaves

Peel and section oranges over bowl, reserving any juice. Chop orange sections; reserve. Remove pits from peaches; chop peaches and cherries and reserve. Combine reserved fruit juices and add enough water to make 3 cups liquid. Set aside. Combine lemon gelatin and boiling water, stirring until gelatin dissolves, about 2 minutes. Add oranges and juice mixture and chill until syrupy. Fold peaches, cherries and pecans into gelatin mixture. Spoon mixture into a lightly oiled 7-cup mold. Cover and chill until firm. Unmold gelatin salad onto a lettuce-lined plate for serving. Serves 14 to 16.

Mango Mousse

Must Be Chilled

Mousse:

1 (14¾-ounce) can mangoes with liquid

1 (8-ounce) package cream cheese, regular or low-fat

2 (3-ounce) packages orange gelatin

1 (3-ounce) package lemon gelatin

2 cups boiling water

Topping:

1 cup sour cream

1-2 tablespoons honey

Mousse:

Blend mangoes and liquid and cream cheese until smooth. Dissolve gelatins in boiling water. Add blended fruit and cheese. Mix using a blender or food processor. Chill until set in a 1½-quart mold or oblong dish. Serves 12.

Topping:

Blend sour cream and honey together. Drop a dollop on individual servings.

Hint: You can use 3 fresh mangoes, peeled and diced instead of the canned ones.

Variation: Use apricots instead of mangoes, but use only about ¼ cup liquid.

An RWC Favorite, we served this pretty,
delicious salad in the Tea Room.

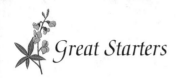

Mandarin Orange Salad

Must Be Chilled

Salad:

2 (3-ounce) packages orange gelatin

2 cups boiling water

1 (6-ounce) can frozen orange juice concentrate, undiluted

1 (10-ounce) can Mandarin orange segments

1 (15½-ounce) can crushed pineapple with liquid

Topping:

1 (3-ounce) package instant lemon pudding

2 cups cold milk

1 cup frozen whipped topping, thawed

Grated Cheddar cheese as desired

Salad:

Dissolve gelatin in boiling water and immediately add frozen orange juice concentrate. Add Mandarin oranges and pineapple. Put in 13x9x2-inch dish and chill until well set.

Topping:

Mix pudding and milk according to package directions. Add whipped topping. Spread on top. Sprinkle with cheese and chill. Serves 12 to 16.

Undressed Salad

6 cherry tomatoes, halved

1 medium avocado, peeled, pitted and diced

1 small cantaloupe peeled, seeded and diced

2 teaspoons fresh lemon juice

Salt and pepper to taste

Mix all ingredients. Serves 2.

Tangy Tomato Aspic

Must Be Chilled

1 (3-ounce) package lemon gelatin	½ teaspoon salt
1¼ cups hot water	Dash Tabasco sauce
1 (8-ounce) can tomato sauce	Dash black pepper
1½ tablespoons white vinegar	Dash ground cloves
¾ tablespoon onion juice from grated onion (about 1 medium onion)	Dash cayenne pepper
	Dash horseradish, to taste

Dissolve gelatin in hot water. Blend in tomato sauce, vinegar, onion juice, salt, Tabasco sauce, pepper, cloves, cayenne and horseradish. Pour into 6 individual molds or 1-quart ring mold or small 10x10x2-inch dish. Chill until firm.

Hint: This is good made with sugar-free lemon gelatin.

This is such an RWC Favorite, we've served
it at the Bridge Festival twice.

Frosted Cranberry Salad

Must Be Frozen

1 (16-ounce) can whole cranberry sauce	1 (3-ounce) container whipped cream cheese
3 tablespoons lemon juice	¼ cup mayonnaise
½ pint heavy cream, whipped	¼ cup powdered sugar, sifted
	1 cup pecans, chopped

Crush cranberries with a fork. Add lemon juice and pour into loaf pan. Combine whipped cream, cream cheese, mayonnaise, powdered sugar and pecans. Spread over cranberries and freeze. Remove from freezer 10 minutes before serving. Slice and serve on a bed of greens. Cranberry mixture can be poured into small paper cups and topped with cream cheese mixture for individual servings. Just peel away the paper cup and serve. Serves 8.

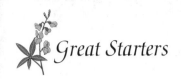

Favorite Frozen Fruit Salad

Must Be Frozen

5 bananas, chopped	1 (15¼-ounce) can pineapple tidbits
2½ tablespoons lemon juice	
1 cup sugar	½ cup finely chopped pecans
1 (16-ounce) jar maraschino cherries, drained, chopped	1 (12-ounce) tub frozen whipped topping, thawed
	1 pint sour cream

Mix all ingredients in a large bowl and pour into a buttered 3-quart casserole or 13x9x2-inch dish. Freeze 24 hours. Thaw 30 minutes before cutting into squares. Store again in freezer until serving time. Serves 24.

Spiced Fruit Salad

Must Be Made Ahead

1 (20-ounce) can pineapple chunks, drained and liquid reserved	½ cup orange juice
	1 scant cup sugar
1 (15¼-ounce) can pineapple tidbits, drained and liquid reserved	1 (3-ounce) package cherry gelatin
	½ cup cider vinegar
1 (29-ounce) can sliced pears, drained and ½ liquid reserved	2 whole cinnamon sticks
	6 whole cloves
1 (29-ounce) can sliced peaches, drained and ½ liquid reserved	

Mix all juices with sugar, gelatin, vinegar and spices. Simmer 30 minutes. Remove cinnamon sticks and cloves. Mix with fruit. Keeps 1 week, refrigerated. Serves 16 to 20.

An RWC Favorite, served at the Tea Room.

Old-Fashioned Salad

Must Be Chilled

2 (11-ounce) cans Mandarin orange segments, drained

1 (15¼-ounce) can pineapple tidbits, drained

1 cup angel flake coconut

2 cups miniature marshmallows

2 cups sour cream

Mix ingredients together and chill before serving. Serves 6 to 8.

Señora's Fruit Salad

Cooked Fruit Dressing:

2 tablespoons butter

1 tablespoon flour

½ cup pineapple juice

½ cup maraschino cherry juice

Dash salt

½ teaspoon prepared mustard

Juice of 1 lemon

1 egg yolk

Salad:

1 apple, unpeeled, diced

1 banana, peeled and sliced

½ cup chopped pecans

¼ cup maraschino cherries, drained and liquid reserved

1 cup pineapple chunks, drained and liquid reserved

Grapes

Cooked Fruit Dressing:

Cook butter and flour until bubbly. Slowly add pineapple and cherry juices. Add salt, mustard and lemon juice. Cook until thick. Remove from heat. Add egg yolk. Beat with a fork until smooth. Cover and let cool. Pour cooled dressing over salad. Serves 4 to 6.

Salad:

Combine all ingredients and serve with salad dressing.

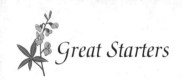
Puddin' Fruit

Must Be Chilled

2 (11-ounce) cans Mandarin orange segments, drained and liquid reserved

1 (20-ounce) can pineapple tidbits, drained and liquid reserved

2 (3½-ounce) boxes vanilla pudding, not instant

2 (15-ounce) cans sliced peaches, drained

1 (6-ounce) jar maraschino cherries, drained, rinsed and halved

5 chilled bananas

Add enough pineapple juice to the orange juice to make 2 cups and bring to a boil. Add pudding, stirring constantly and cook until it begins to thicken (about 1 minute). Cool. Mix together pudding, oranges, pineapple, peaches and maraschino cherries in large bowl. Cover and chill. Just before serving, peel and slice bananas and fold into mixture. Serve 8 to 12.

Great for brunch.

Beeville, seat of Bee County, is all abuzz in March when the Texas Wildflowers are blooming. Southern Living *magazine featured US Highway 181, Farm Road 797 and Farm Road 1349 as the places to see them in the Texas Gulf Coast region. Your special gift there is a kaleidoscope of color including wine cups, yellow blossomed prickly pear cactus, purple thistle, pretty pink primrose, gentle Queen Anne's lace, white plains larkspur and scarlet Indian paint brush.*

Orange Salad with Yogurt Dressing

Must Be Chilled

Salad:

6	seedless oranges, peeled and sectioned

3-4 tablespoons finely chopped fresh mint

Yogurt Dressing:

1   (8-ounce) carton plain yogurt

1   teaspoon finely grated orange zest

2   tablespoons orange juice

2   teaspoons honey

4   bananas

Salad:

Combine the oranges and mint. Cover and chill 2 to 24 hours. Serves 8.

Yogurt Dressing:

Combine yogurt, orange zest, orange juice and honey. Cover and chill 2 to 24 hours. Peel and slice the bananas and add to dressing no more than one hour before serving. Serve the dressing over the oranges.

Great for brunch.

Fiesta Time Tossed Salad

1   head lettuce, washed and drained

½   medium onion, finely chopped

1   (15-ounce) can chilled Ranch Style beans, drained and rinsed

2   tomatoes, diced

1   pound shredded sharp Cheddar cheese

1   cup crushed Fritos corn chips

¾   (8-ounce) bottle Kraft Catalina dressing, chilled

Tear lettuce into bite-size pieces. Place in a large serving bowl. Add onions, beans and tomatoes. Cover and chill. When ready to serve, add cheese, Fritos and dressing. Toss gently. Serves 4 to 6.

Citrus Crunch Salad

¼   teaspoon salt

5   tablespoons sugar, divided

¼   cup vegetable oil

2   tablespoons vinegar

¼   tablespoon chopped parsley

Dash Tabasco sauce

Dash pepper

½   cup sliced almonds

1   head romaine lettuce

1   (11-ounce) can Mandarin
     orange segments

Combine salt, 2 tablespoons sugar, oil, vinegar, parsley, Tabasco sauce and pepper and stir until salt and sugar are dissolved. Sauté almonds in the remaining 3 tablespoons sugar until caramelized. Cool. Tear lettuce into bite-size pieces. Drain oranges. Toss all gently in a large salad bowl. Serves 6.

This is a great salad to take to potluck dinners. Everything can be prepared ahead of time and combined at the last minute.

Grecian Salad

Salad:

1   head romaine lettuce, rinsed
     and torn into bite-size pieces

1   (4-ounce) package feta cheese,
     crumbled

¾   cup seedless green grape halves

½   cup pine nuts, toasted

Salad Dressing:

½   cup olive oil

¼   cup white wine vinegar

¼   teaspoon pepper

Dash salt

Salad:

Combine lettuce, feta cheese, grape halves and toasted pine nuts in a large bowl; set aside.

Salad Dressing:

Combine olive oil, vinegar and seasonings in a jar; cover tightly and shake vigorously. Pour over salad and toss gently. Serves 6 to 8.

Asian Inspired Tossed Salad

Sweet and Sour Dressing:

½ cup vegetable or safflower oil

½ cup sugar

¼ cup red wine vinegar

1 tablespoon soy sauce

Salt and pepper to taste

Salad:

1 (3-ounce) package Ramen noodles, uncooked, broken up in package

4 tablespoons unsalted butter

2 tablespoons water

1 cup chopped walnuts

1 bunch broccoli, coarsely chopped

1 head romaine lettuce, washed, broken into bite-size pieces

1 small red onion, chopped

1 cup sweet and sour dressing

Sweet and Sour Dressing:

Blend all ingredients.

Salad:

Discard flavor package with the noodles and brown noodles in butter. Add water and cook until the noodles have absorbed the water. Cool noodles on paper towels. Combine noodles and walnuts with broccoli, lettuce and onions. Pour dressing over salad and toss to coat well. Serves 8.

Variation: Sauté sliced shitake mushrooms and toss with salad. Top with black sesame seeds. Replace walnuts with toasted pine nuts.

An RWC favorite we discovered during testing.

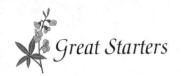

Mexican Salad with Avocado Dressing

Must Be Chilled

Avocado Dressing:

1 avocado, peeled, pitted and mashed	½ teaspoon ground cumin
¾ cup sour cream	¼ teaspoon salt
1½ tablespoons lime juice	¼ teaspoon cayenne pepper
2 garlic cloves, crushed	2 tablespoons vegetable oil

Salad:

3 tomatoes, cut into wedges	6 cups shredded iceberg lettuce
¾ cup sliced ripe olives	3 tablespoons chopped cilantro
1 small purple onion, sliced into rings	

Avocado Dressing:

Combine avocado, sour cream, lime juice, garlic, cumin, salt and pepper in a mixing bowl; beat at medium speed with an electric mixer until smooth. Add oil, 1 tablespoon at a time, beating until blended. Cover and chill at least 3 hours. Serves 8.

Salad:

Arrange tomatoes, olives and onions on shredded lettuce. Sprinkle with cilantro. Serve with dressing.

The annual *"Tomato Festival"* is held the third weekend in September in Jacksonville. The tomato was first grown in Central America by the Aztec Indians. The Spaniards brought it to Texas in the 1500's.

Mock Caesar Salad

Must Be Chilled

Dressing:

Juice of 1 lemon
3   garlic cloves, crushed
¾   cup vegetable oil
1   teaspoon sugar

½   teaspoon dried tarragon, crumbled
Salt and pepper to taste

Salad:

2   heads romaine lettuce, washed and drained
¼   pound bacon, fried and crumbled
⅔   cup sliced almonds, toasted

2   cups cherry tomatoes, halved
1   cup grated Swiss cheese
⅓   cup grated Parmesan cheese

Dressing:

Combine dressing ingredients and refrigerate for at least 3 hours.

Salad:

Tear lettuce into bite-size pieces. Add bacon, almonds, tomatoes and cheeses. Toss with dressing just before serving. Serves 10 to 12.

Variation: Top with slices of grilled chicken.

An RWC Favorite served at the
Bridge Festival and the Tea Room.

93

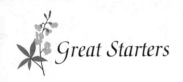

Deluxe Salad

Dressing:

½	cup sugar	3	tablespoons grated onion
2	teaspoons celery seed	⅓	cup vinegar
1	teaspoon dry mustard	1	cup vegetable oil
1	teaspoon salt		

Salad:

4	cups leaf lettuce torn in bite-size pieces	½	cup chopped celery
1	cup green and red grape halves	½	cup toasted walnuts
1	large Granny Smith apple, chopped	⅓	cup crumbled blue cheese

Dressing:

Whisk sugar, celery seed, mustard, salt, onion and vinegar. When everything is well mixed, slowly whisk in the oil.

Salad:

Combine lettuce, grapes, apple, celery, walnuts and blue cheese. Toss with dressing. Serves 8.

Variation: Increase walnuts to 1 cup and add 2 to 3 cups diced chicken for a main dish.

Spinach Salad with Prosciutto Dressing

Prosciutto Dressing:

6 tablespoons olive oil

¼ cup chopped prosciutto
(about 1½-ounces)

2 tablespoons minced garlic

6 tablespoons dry white wine

6 tablespoons lemon juice

2 tablespoons sugar

Salt and pepper to taste

Salad:

1 (10-ounce) bag spinach

2½ cups sliced mushrooms

½ cup chopped walnuts

½ cup freshly grated Parmesan
cheese

Prosciutto Dressing:

Heat oil in small skillet over medium heat. Add prosciutto and garlic. Sauté 3 minutes, and then add wine, lemon juice and sugar. Simmer 5 minutes. Put in small bowl. Cool. Add salt and pepper to taste.

Salad:

Combine spinach, mushrooms, walnuts and cheese in a large bowl. Toss with dressing to taste. Serves 4 to 6.

Snow-on-the-Mountain Salad

¾ cup mayonnaise

3 tablespoons freshly grated Parmesan cheese

2 tablespoons fresh lemon juice

¼ teaspoon garlic salt

¼ teaspoon pepper

½ cauliflower head, separated into florets

2 heads romaine lettuce, washed, drained and torn into bite-size pieces

4 strips bacon, fried and crumbled

¼ cup minced onion tops or snipped fresh chives

Crumbled blue cheese as desired

Combine mayonnaise, Parmesan cheese, lemon juice, garlic salt and pepper. Toss with cauliflower and lettuce. Sprinkle bacon, onion tops and blue cheese on the top. Serves 6 to 8.

Long Hot Summer Tossed Salad

Must Be Chilled

1 head lettuce, washed, drained and torn into bite-size pieces

1 small head cauliflower, cut into florets

2 cups mayonnaise

1 medium onion, diced

1 pound bacon, cooked and crumbled

½ cup freshly grated Parmesan cheese

Arrange all ingredients in layers in order listed. Seal tightly. Refrigerate for 24 hours. Toss and serve. Serves 4 to 6.

Raspberry Chipotle Spinach Salad

Raspberry Chipotle Salad Dressing:

1   cup apple cider vinegar
    (real not apple flavored)
3   tablespoons Raspberry Chipotle
    sauce

¾   cup sugar
1   cup vegetable oil

Spinach Salad:

½   cup slivered almonds
3   tablespoons sugar
1   (8-ounce) package fresh spinach

1   cup sliced strawberries or 1 cup
    raspberries
½   cup finely sliced red onions

Raspberry Chipotle Salad Dressing:

Combine vinegar, sauce and sugar in mixing bowl or blender, gradually adding oil while whisking (or blending) until mixture is smooth. Use over spinach salad.

Spinach Salad:

Caramelize almonds in sugar over low heat until light brown; cool. Combine spinach, strawberries and onions. Toss with dressing and add almonds. Serves 4 to 6.

Hint: Raspberry Chipotle sauce is sold in bottles at grocery stores and gourmet shops.

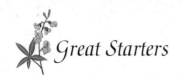

Strawberry Romaine Salad

Poppy Seed Dressing:

½ cup sugar

1 tablespoon poppy seed

1½ teaspoons minced onions

¼ teaspoon Worcestershire sauce

¼ teaspoon paprika

¼ cup cider vinegar

½ cup vegetable oil

Salad:

1 (2-pint) box strawberries

2 heads romaine lettuce

1 (3-ounce) package sliced almonds

Poppy Seed Dressing:

Put sugar, poppy seeds, onions, Worcestershire sauce and paprika in a blender. Turn on and add vinegar. While running, slowly add oil until mixed and thickened. Dressing can be stored in refrigerator for several days. If it separates, blend again.

Salad:

Clean and halve strawberries. Wash and tear romaine lettuce into bite-size pieces. Toss romaine lettuce, strawberries and almonds with dressing. Serves 12.

Variation: Replace the romaine lettuce with fresh spinach.

Poteet, the strawberry capital of the world, hosts the *"Strawberry Festival"* during the second week of April. Another festival is held in Palestine on the last weekend of April.

Crunchy Cabbage Salad

Must Be Chilled

Dressing:

3	teaspoons sugar	5	tablespoons vinegar
¾	cup oil		Flavor packet from noodles
½	teaspoon pepper		

Salad:

2½ cups cooked cubed chicken

3 tablespoons toasted sesame seed or ½ cup sunflower seed

1 small head cabbage, thinly sliced (about 6 cups)

5 tablespoons toasted slivered almonds

4 green onions, chopped

1 (3-ounce) package uncooked Ramen noodles

Dressing:

Mix all dressing ingredients and chill.

Salad:

Place chicken, sesame seeds, cabbage, almonds and onions in a large bowl. Chill. Break Ramen noodles into pieces, add to salad ingredients and toss with dressing at serving time. Serves 12.

Crispy Bacon Coleslaw

Must Be Chilled

¾	cup salad dressing	½	cup chopped peanuts
1	tablespoon sugar	4	slices bacon, cooked crisply, crumbled
4	cups shredded green cabbage		
1	cup shredded red cabbage		

Mix salad dressing and sugar in large bowl. Add cabbages, peanuts and bacon. Refrigerate until chilled. Serves 8.

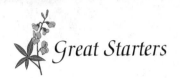

Lemon Coleslaw

Must Be Chilled

Dressing:

½ cup mayonnaise

½ cup sour cream

¼ cup fresh lemon juice
   (about 2 lemons)

2 tablespoons Dijon mustard

2 tablespoons olive oil

2 tablespoons sugar

1 tablespoon white wine vinegar

1 tablespoon prepared horseradish

Salt to taste

½ teaspoon celery seed

½ teaspoon pepper

Slaw:

8 cups shredded cabbage

½ red bell pepper, cut into
   matchstick strips

½ yellow bell pepper, cut into
   matchstick strips

½ green bell pepper, cut into
   matchstick strips

¼ red onion, diced

1 carrot, shredded

2 tablespoons fresh parsley,
   chopped

2 teaspoons grated lemon zest

Dressing:

Combine all ingredients in a bowl. Whisk to blend. Chill until cold.

Slaw:

In large bowl combine cabbage, bell peppers, onions, carrot, parsley and lemon zest. Toss with dressing to taste. Serves 6 to 8.

Hint: This is best served the day it is made.

Red Cabbage Salad with Poppy Seed Dressing

Must Be Chilled

Salad:

1   head red cabbage, finely shredded

3-4 avocados, peeled, pitted and thinly sliced

1½ pounds seedless grapes, cut in half

Dressing:

1½ cups powdered sugar

2   teaspoons dry mustard

2   teaspoons salt

⅔   cup vinegar

2   cups vegetable oil

3   tablespoons poppy seed

Salad:

Place shredded cabbage in a large bowl and cover with ice water. Refrigerate for 1 to 1½ hours. Drain thoroughly on paper towels or in salad spinner. Mix cabbage, avocados and grapes. Add dressing just before serving.

Dressing:

Combine sugar, mustard, salt and vinegar in blender. Slowly add oil and continue beating until thick. Add poppy seeds and beat a few more minutes. Serves 10 to 12.

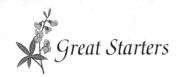

Hot German Potato Salad

Expect Recipe Requests

8	medium red potatoes, unpeeled	½	teaspoon dried rosemary, crumbled
4	teaspoons salt, divided	1	teaspoon dry mustard
3-4	bay leaves	½	teaspoon black pepper
8-12	slices bacon	4	teaspoons chopped onions
⅔	cup white wine vinegar	3	tablespoons flour
⅔	cup water	½	cup chopped parsley
¼-½	cup sugar		

Cover potatoes with cold water and bring to a boil. Add 2 teaspoons salt and bay leaves. Cook until just tender. Drain and cool. Remove the bay leaves. Slice the potatoes and reserve. Fry bacon and reserve 2 tablespoons bacon drippings. Cool and crumble bacon. Blend vinegar, water, sugar, rosemary, mustard and the remaining 2 teaspoons salt and the pepper. Sauté onions in bacon drippings. Add vinegar mixture and simmer for 15 minutes, stirring occasionally. Gradually add flour. Pour gravy over sliced potatoes and stir until potatoes are well coated. Add bacon and stir again. Sprinkle the top with parsley. Serves 6 to 8.

Spring time in North Texas is the perfect time for a stroll through the Dallas Arboretum and Botanical Garden in Dallas. It contains 66 acres and has more than 2,000 varieties of azaleas in the Johnson Color Garden. Visit any time of the year to see varying displays of flowers and foliage.

New Potato and Pea Salad

Must Be Chilled

Dressing:

¼ cup low-fat plain yogurt

¼ cup low-fat mayonnaise

1 teaspoon dried dill weed

1 tablespoon snipped chives

Leaf lettuce

Freshly ground pepper

Salad:

1 pound tiny new potatoes, quartered

2 cups snow peas or sugar snap peas

Dressing:

Stir together yogurt, mayonnaise, dill and chives. Cover and chill. To serve, mound potatoes and peas mixture, place on lettuce leaves and top with dressing. Sprinkle with pepper. Serves 5.

Salad:

Cook potatoes, covered in boiling water for 8 minutes. Add peas, cover and cook 2 to 4 minutes longer. Drain and cool.

Game Time Potato Salad

1 cup mayonnaise

¼ cup Dijon mustard

2 tablespoons fresh lime juice

1 medium tomato, chopped

2 tablespoons cilantro, chopped

½ jalapeño, finely chopped

2 green onions, chopped, tops included

½ medium red onion, thinly sliced

½ teaspoon cayenne pepper

1 garlic clove, minced

Salt and pepper to taste

16 new potatoes, (about 2 pounds) cooked, drained and sliced ½-inch thick

Fold together all ingredients, except the potatoes, and mix well. Season to taste and pour over warm potatoes. Serves 6.

Guacamole Salad

3	avocados	1	tablespoon lemon juice
¼	cup sour cream (you might need more)	½	teaspoon salt
2	tomatoes, chopped	6	slices bacon, cooked and crumbled
2	tablespoons sliced green onions		

Halve avocados and carefully scoop out pulp, reserving shells. Dice avocados and add sour cream. (Add more if avocados are not very ripe.) Add tomatoes, green onions, lemon juice and salt. Carefully spoon mixture back into shells and top with crumbled bacon. Serves 6.

Variation: Discard shells and serve as a dip.

Cool Bean Salad

Must Be Made Ahead

2 (14½-ounce) cans green beans, drained	¼ teaspoon garlic powder or 1 garlic clove, pressed
18 pitted ripe olives, halved	2 rounded tablespoons grated Parmesan cheese
1 (8-ounce) can water chestnuts	Italian or Greek feta dressing
1 (8-ounce) can sliced mushrooms	Fresh cilantro or parsley, optional
½ onion, thinly sliced and chopped	
¼ teaspoon pepper	

Mix green beans, olives, water chestnuts, mushrooms, onions, pepper, garlic and cheese. Toss and add Italian dressing or Greek feta dressing. Chill 24 hours. Garnish with cilantro or parsley if desired. Serves 8 to 12.

Variation: Sliced jicama or radishes can be substituted for water chestnuts.

Spicy Black Bean Salad

Salad:

1   (15-ounce) can black beans, drained and rinsed

1   large tomato, chopped

¼   cup seeded, chopped pickled jalapeños

½   bunch cilantro, chopped

Dressing:

Juice of 1 lemon

¼   cup olive oil

1   teaspoon ground cumin

1   (11-ounce) can yellow corn, drained

2   garlic cloves, chopped finely

Salt and pepper to taste

Liquid from jalapeños, optional

Salad:

Toss all ingredients.

Dressing:

Combine all ingredients and toss with salad. Serve with a Mexican entrée or alone with Fritos Scoops or tortilla chips as a dip.

Hint: Make a day ahead of time and add the tomatoes at the last minute.

Carrot-Yogurt Salad

Must Be Chilled

1   pound carrots, peeled and coarsely grated

2   medium tart apples, grated

1-2 tablespoons lemon juice

1-2 tablespoons honey

Dash celery seed

Salt and pepper to taste

1   cup drained yogurt

¼   cup raisins

¼   cup chopped almonds, toasted

½   cup finely chopped celery

Combine all ingredients; mix well and refrigerate. Stir before serving. Serves 6.

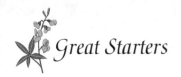

Broccoli-Bacon Salad

Must Be Made Ahead

Salad:

2 bunches fresh broccoli	½ cup walnuts, chopped
1 cup golden raisins	8 slices bacon, cooked crisp,
½ small red onion, sliced thinly	drained and crumbled

Dressing:

1 cup mayonnaise	2-4 tablespoons sugar
2 tablespoons milk	Whole walnut halves, optional
2 tablespoons vinegar	Crumbled bacon, optional

Salad:

Separate broccoli into florets. If using stems, peel and slice. Combine broccoli, raisins, onions, walnuts and bacon in a medium bowl. Serves 8.

Dressing:

Blend together all ingredients. Add to the salad and refrigerate overnight. When serving, sprinkle top with additional crumbled bacon and a few whole walnut halves.

Variation: Substitute 1 cup sunflower seeds for walnuts.

The *"Onion Festival"* is held in Noonday the second weekend in June. The East Texas #1015 sweet onion is the world's only tearless onion.

Danish Tomatoes

¾	cup extra virgin olive oil	6	medium tomatoes, peeled, sliced almost through (keep each tomato together but fanned out)
¼	cup balsamic vinegar		
1	garlic clove, minced		
½	teaspoon salt	4	tablespoons crumbled blue cheese or feta cheese
¼	teaspoon pepper	2	tablespoons chopped parsley

In small bowl, beat together the oil, vinegar, garlic, salt and pepper. Pour over the sliced tomatoes in a shallow serving dish. Sprinkle with blue cheese and chopped parsley. Let stand 30 minutes at room temperature to blend in flavors. Serves 6 to 8.

Hint: To peel tomatoes, dip in boiling water for 20 seconds, then plunge in cold water to stop cooking. Peel should slip off.

Jícama Slaw

2	medium or large jícamas	2	tablespoons vinegar
Ice water		2	tablespoons sugar
2	teaspoons lemon juice	1	teaspoon salt
¾	cup whipping cream		

Peel jícamas and julienne. Add the jícamas to a medium bowl of ice water; add lemon juice and stir well. In a small container, mix together whipping cream, vinegar, sugar and salt. Drain jícamas and pat very dry with a paper towel. Pour cream dressing mixture over jícamas and toss. Serve on greens of your choice.

Jícama is called the Mexican potato. It makes an excellent substitute for water chestnuts. It is also good sprinkled with lime juice and chili powder as a simple salad.

Oriental Salad

Must Be Made Ahead

Salad:

1 (4½-ounce) jar sliced mushrooms, drained	1 (8-ounce) can sliced water chestnuts, drained
1 (17-ounce) can green peas, drained	1 (4-ounce) jar diced pimientos, drained
1 (14-ounce) can bean sprouts, drained	1 large green bell pepper, sliced thinly
1 (12-ounce) can white shoepeg corn, drained	1 large onion, sliced thinly
	1 cup sliced celery

Dressing:

1 cup sugar	1 tablespoon soy sauce
1 cup vegetable oil	1 teaspoon dry mustard
½ cup vinegar	½ teaspoon salt
½ cup water	½ teaspoon paprika
2 tablespoons red wine vinegar	¼ teaspoon pepper

Salad:

Combine vegetables in a large bowl and toss lightly.

Dressing:

Mix all ingredients together and pour over vegetables. Cover and chill overnight.
Serves 10 to 12.

Marinated Vegetables with Provolone Salad

Must Be Chilled

⅔ cup olive oil
⅓ cup white wine vinegar
1 teaspoon minced garlic
1 teaspoon dried oregano, crumbled

⅛ teaspoon salt
6 ounces provolone cheese, cut into ¼-inch slices
2 cups small mushrooms
1 cup asparagus tips, blanched

Blend together oil, vinegar, garlic, oregano and salt. Cut cheese slices in 6 wedges. Arrange cheese, mushrooms and asparagus in glass baking dish. Pour dressing over. Chill covered 4 hours in refrigerator or overnight. Serves 4.

Red River Rotini Pasta Salad

Must Be Chilled

1 (12-ounce) package tri-color rotini pasta
2 medium yellow squash, cut in half then sliced
2 medium zucchini, cut in half then sliced
2 medium tomatoes, finely chopped

1-2 cups broccoli florets
1 (3.8-ounce) can sliced ripe olives, drained
½-1 (8-ounce) package cubed cheese
1 (8-ounce) bottle Kraft Zesty Italian dressing

Cook rotini according to package directions. Drain. Mix with yellow and zucchini squash, tomatoes, broccoli, olives and cheese. Add dressing. Chill, stirring occasionally.

Angel Hair Pasta Salad

Must Be Made Ahead

1 (16-ounce) package angel hair
   pasta, cooked and drained
4 tablespoons vegetable oil
3 tablespoons fresh lemon juice
1 teaspoon seasoned salt
1 teaspoon Accent, optional
1½ cups chopped celery
1 cup chopped onions
   (about 1 medium)

1 medium green bell pepper,
   chopped
1 (4-ounce) jar chopped
   pimientos, drained
1 (2½-ounce) can sliced ripe
   olives, drained
1½ cups mayonnaise
½ cup freshly grated Parmesan
   cheese

Combine pasta, oil, lemon juice, seasoned salt and Accent and refrigerate over-night. Add celery, onions, bell peppers, pimientos and olives. Mix cheese with mayonnaise and add to pasta. Mix well and chill. Makes 20 (½ cup) servings.

Variation: Add 1 to 2 pounds cooked shrimp or 2 cups chopped smoked chicken.

An RWC Favorite. We served this in the
Tea Room with smoked chicken.

Make Ahead Salad

1 (6.9-ounce) package chicken
   flavored rice and vermicelli mix
1 bunch green onions, chopped
1 (2-ounce) can chopped ripe
   olives, drained

2 (6-ounce) jars marinated
   artichoke hearts, marinade
   reserved from 1½ jars
¾ cup mayonnaise
1 green bell pepper, chopped
½ teaspoon curry powder

Prepare rice according to package directions. Cool. Mix together all the remain-ing ingredients and refrigerate for 2 days before serving.

Ensalada Macaroni

Must Be Chilled

4	quarts boiling water	3-4	green onions, chopped
2	tablespoons salt	1	(2.5-ounce) can sliced ripe olives, drained
4	cups dry macaroni		
1	tablespoon chili powder	2	celery ribs, chopped
1	(15-ounce) can black beans, drained and rinsed	¾	cup light Italian dressing
		¾	cup medium or mild picante sauce
1	(11-ounce) can Mexican style corn, drained	1	teaspoon seasoned salt

Bring water to boil in a large kettle. Add salt. When the water stops foaming, add the macaroni, stirring occasionally and cook 6 to 8 minutes or until tender. Drain the macaroni; rinse the kettle with cold water. Immediately put the macaroni into the kettle and add the chili powder. Stir until thoroughly mixed. Add beans, corn, green onions, olives and celery and stir. Mix the Italian dressing with the picante sauce and seasoned salt. Toss with salad. Chill. Serves 10 to 12.

Hint: Most Southwestern cooks prefer Gebhardt chili powder or another brand without additional spices for a purer chili taste. Chili powder should be heated, toasted in a skillet or cooked with hot ingredients to prevent a slightly bitter taste.

Easy to take to a picnic or a buffet!

111

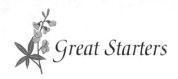

Mexican Cornbread Salad

Must Be Chilled

Cornbread:

1	tablespoon vegetable oil		1	teaspoon baking soda
3	cups buttermilk		1	teaspoon baking powder
2	eggs		1	teaspoon salt
2	cups yellow cornmeal		½	cup chopped jalapeños

Salad:

1   (1-ounce) package ranch dressing mix

1   (8-ounce) container sour cream

1   cup mayonnaise

1   recipe cornbread

2   (16-ounce) cans pinto beans, drained, divided

3   cups grated Cheddar cheese, divided

3   large tomatoes, chopped, divided

½   cup chopped green bell peppers, divided

½   cup chopped green onions, divided

1   (4½-ounce) can chopped green chiles, divided

1½ cups crisp, crumbled bacon pieces, divided

1   (15-ounce) can whole kernel corn, drained, divided

Cornbread:

Coat bottom and sides of a 10-inch cast iron skillet with oil and heat in oven. In a medium bowl, combine buttermilk and eggs. Add cornmeal, baking soda, baking powder, salt and jalapeños. Mix well. Pour batter in hot skillet. Bake in a preheated 450 degree oven for 20 minutes or until lightly browned. Cool and crumble.

Salad:

Combine ranch dressing mix, sour cream and mayonnaise in a small bowl. Place ½ of crumbled cornbread in the bottom of a large serving bowl. Top with 1 can of pinto beans. Follow with ½ of the cheese, tomatoes, bell peppers, green onions, green chiles, bacon and corn. Cover with ½ of the ranch dressing mixture. Repeat, ending with the dressing mixture. Cover and chill for 2 hours or more before serving. Makes 10 to 12 servings.

Tabbouleh

A Traditional Lebanese Salad

½ cup dry bulgur wheat
1 cup water
2 medium firm tomatoes, diced
2 cups finely chopped flat leaf
   parsley
3 sprigs finely chopped mint leaves

1 small white onion, finely chopped
½ teaspoon freshly ground pepper
4 tablespoons fresh lemon juice
4 tablespoons olive oil
Salt and pepper to taste

Soak bulgur in water for 10 minutes. Mix tomatoes, parsley, mint leaves, onions, pepper, and bulgur. Add lemon juice and oil and toss. Add salt and pepper.

Hint: Flavors develop better if this salad if chilled for several hours.

Artichoke-Chicken-Rice Salad

Must Be Chilled

2 (6-ounce) jars marinated
   artichoke hearts, drained and
   marinade reserved
1 (6.9-ounce) package reduced
   sodium flavored rice and
   vermicelli mix
2½ cups chopped cooked chicken
1 (6-ounce) can sliced water
   chestnuts, drained and
   chopped

1 (3-ounce) jar pimiento stuffed
   olives, drained and sliced
1 cup chopped green onions
1 cup fat-free mayonnaise
1½ tablespoons curry powder
1 teaspoon pepper
Lettuce leaves

Coarsely chop artichokes. Prepare rice and vermicelli mix according to package directions; stir in reserved marinade and cool. Mix artichoke hearts, rice mixture, chicken, water chestnuts, olives and onions. Combine mayonnaise, curry power, and pepper; stir into chicken mixture. Cover and chill 1 to 2 hours. Serve on lettuce leaves. Serves 8.

Chicken Pasta Salad

Must Be Chilled

1½ cups bowtie pasta
2 ears fresh corn
1 cup shredded cooked chicken
1 large tomato, seeded and chopped
¼ cup olive oil
3 tablespoons vinegar

3 tablespoons pesto sauce
1 tablespoon water or chicken broth
¼ teaspoon salt
⅛ teaspoon pepper
2 tablespoons finely grated Parmesan cheese
Fresh basil

Cook pasta according to package directions. Drain pasta, rinse in cold water and drain again. Cut the kernels off the cobs. (You should have about 1 cup.) Cook corn, covered in boiling water for 10 minutes or until corn is tender. Drain. Let cool slightly. Combine pasta, corn, chicken and tomato. In a quart jar combine the olive oil, vinegar, pesto, water or chicken broth, salt and pepper. Cover and shake well. Pour over pasta mixture; toss gently to coat. Cover and chill 2 to 24 hours. To serve sprinkle with Parmesan cheese and snipped basil. Serves 4.

Chicken Waldorf Salad

Must Be Chilled

1½ cups diced cooked chicken
⅔ cup whole small seedless white, red or green grapes
⅔ cup chopped celery
1 red apple with peel, chopped
½ cup chopped walnuts

¼ teaspoon celery salt
½ teaspoon salt, optional
⅛ teaspoon white pepper
⅔ cup mayonnaise
2 tablespoons lemon juice
Curry powder to taste

Combine all ingredients. Chill before serving. Serves 4.

An RWC Favorite served in the Tea Room.

Curried Chicken Salad with Cashews

Must Be Chilled

½ cup mayonnaise

½ cup sour cream

3 tablespoons coarsely chopped mango chutney

2 teaspoons curry powder

Salt and pepper to taste

3 cups diced cooked chicken breast

3 green onions including tops, finely chopped

2 celery ribs, thinly sliced

½ cup coarsely chopped cashews

Combine mayonnaise, sour cream, chutney, curry powder, salt and pepper in a large bowl. Add chicken, green onions, celery and cashews. Refrigerate for several hours or overnight. Serves 4 to 6.

Hint: One pound bone-in chicken cooked equals about 3 cups chopped meat or ½ pound.

Old-Fashioned Chicken Salad

Must Be Chilled

2 cups diced cooked chicken

1 cup diced celery

1 cup green grape halves

¾ cup toasted slivered almonds, divided

1¼ cups mayonnaise

1 tablespoon lemon juice

½ teaspoon salt

Fresh ground pepper to taste

Lettuce

Parsley

Toss chicken with celery, grapes, and ½ cup almonds. Combine mayonnaise, lemon juice, salt and pepper. Fold into chicken mixture. Cover and refrigerate. Serve on lettuce leaves, garnished with remaining ¼ cup almonds and parsley. Serves 4.

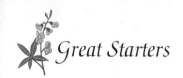

Taste of the Southwest Chicken Salad

Southwest Dressing:

½   cup lime juice

1   tablespoon Dijon mustard

1   tablespoon ground cumin

1   teaspoon minced garlic

1   teaspoon pepper

½   teaspoon salt

¼   cup vegetable oil

¾   cup olive oil

Salad:

6-8 skinless chicken breast halves, grilled

1   (16-ounce) can black beans, drained and rinsed

1   small red onion, chopped

1   red bell pepper, diced

1   green bell pepper, diced

⅓   cup chopped green onions

1   (16-ounce) bag frozen corn, thawed

⅓   cup chopped cilantro

Sliced avocados for garnish

Salsa for garnish

Sour cream for garnish

Chopped cilantro for garnish

Southwest Dressing:

Mix together all dressing ingredients in a 2-quart jar and let stand for 1 to 2 hours.

Salad:

Cut chicken into very thin strips about the size of skinny fries. In a large bowl, mix chicken with remaining salad ingredients. Toss with dressing and serve garnished with sliced avocados, salsa, sour cream and chopped cilantro. Serves 6 to 8.

Thai Chicken Salad

Must Be Chilled

Peanut-Ginger Dressing:

½	cup rice wine vinegar	1	tablespoon honey
2	garlic cloves	1	tablespoon molasses
⅓	cup creamy peanut butter	1	tablespoon Tabasco sauce
¼	cup lime juice	2	teaspoons peeled and grated ginger root
¼	cup fresh cilantro, chopped		
2	tablespoons apple cider vinegar	2	teaspoons soy sauce

Salad:

4	chicken breast halves, skinned and boned	2	medium carrots, coarsely shredded
6	tablespoons Peanut-Ginger Dressing, divided	2	medium cucumbers, thinly sliced
		1	large red bell pepper, cut in strips
3	ounces vermicelli	¼	cup fresh cilantro, chopped
4	cups romaine lettuce, torn in bite-size pieces		Chopped peanuts, optional
2	cups Chinese cabbage, thinly sliced		Sliced cucumber, optional

Peanut-Ginger Dressing:

Combine all ingredients in container of an electric blender; process until smooth. Makes 1½ cups.

Salad:

Grill chicken without grill lid over medium coals 15 to 20 minutes, turning once. Cut into thin strips. Combine chicken and 3 tablespoons Peanut-Ginger Dressing, tossing to coat, cover and refrigerate 8 hours. Cook vermicelli according to package directions, drain. Combine vermicelli and 3 tablespoons Peanut-Ginger Dressing tossing to coat. Cover and refrigerate 8 hours. At serving time combine romaine lettuce, Chinese cabbage, carrots, cucumber, bell peppers and cilantro, tossing well. Arrange on serving platter. Top with vermicelli and chicken; sprinkle salad with peanuts, if desired. Arrange cucumber slices around vermicelli, if desired. Serve salad with remaining Peanut-Ginger Dressing. Serves 6.

Hot Chicken Salad

4 cups cooked diced chicken (I use white meat)	1½ cups Miracle Whip (not mayonnaise)
2 cups diced celery	½ cup chicken broth
3 tablespoons lemon juice	1 cup grated Cheddar cheese
2 tablespoons grated onions	1½ cups crushed potato chips
½-1 cup sliced almonds	

Combine chicken, celery, lemon juice, onions, almonds, Miracle Whip, chicken broth and cheese. Put in 13x9x2-inch casserole. Top with crushed chips. Bake in a preheated 425 degree oven 10 to 15 minutes (just enough to heat). This can be made the night before; next day add chips and bake. Serves 12.

Country French Tuna Salad

Salad:

1 small head leaf lettuce, torn in bite-size pieces	½ cup finely chopped parsley
4 large ripe tomatoes, sliced	4 hard-cooked eggs, quartered
2 (6-ounce) cans of tuna in olive oil, drained, oil reserved	Chopped cucumber, optional
	Chopped fresh basil, optional
½ cup red onions, chopped	

Dressing:

½ cup oil reserved from the canned tuna	½ cup red wine vinegar
	Salt and pepper to taste

Salad:

Arrange lettuce on plates and put tomato slices on top. Crumble tuna over tomatoes and sprinkle with onions and parsley. Arrange eggs around the edges.

Dressing:

Whisk oil and vinegar in a small bowl and pour over salad. Add salt and pepper to taste. Garnish with cucumber and fresh basil. Serves 4.

Antipasto Salad

Salad:

1   head lettuce, torn into pieces

1   cup pitted ripe olives, drained

6   medium mushrooms, diced

½   cup freshly grated Parmesan cheese

½   cup provolone cheese, cut into ½-inch cubes

3   Roma tomatoes, sliced

½   cup garbanzo beans, drained and rinsed

1½ cups artichoke hearts, drained and halved

¼   pound pepperoni, sliced very thinly

Hearty Italian Dressing:

6   tablespoons olive oil

1   garlic clove, minced

¼   teaspoon salt

½   teaspoon black pepper, freshly ground

1½ teaspoons parsley, finely minced

½   tablespoon freshly grated Parmesan cheese

2   tablespoons chili sauce

½   teaspoon sugar

1   teaspoon Italian herb seasoning

1½ teaspoons Worcestershire sauce

1½ tablespoons red wine vinegar

Salad:

In a large salad bowl, combine all ingredients. Serves 6.

Hearty Italian Dressing:

In blender, mix all ingredients until well combined. Pour dressing over salad until lightly coated. This dressing is excellent on any pasta salad or fresh vegetable combination.

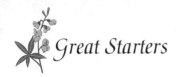
Shrimp and Tortellini Salad

Must Be Chilled

Salad:

1   (9-ounce) package fresh
    tortellini with 3 cheese filling

1   (9-ounce) package fresh spinach
    tortellini with cheese filling

2   pounds frozen salad shrimp,
    thawed and deveined

2   (15-ounce) cans artichoke
    hearts, drained and coarsely
    chopped

1   cup chopped green onion tops

2   cups julienned red, yellow and
    orange bell peppers

1   cup thinly sliced celery ribs,
    optional

Pesto Dressing:

1   cup fresh basil pesto

½   cup balsamic vinegar

½   cup packed brown sugar

½   teaspoon salt

Salad:

Cook tortellini according to package directions. The 2 tortellini packages may
be cooked together. Cool. Toss all the salad ingredients in a very large container
or bowl. Drizzle dressing evenly over ingredients and toss again lightly. Cover
container; refrigerate 1 hour. Transfer to a serving bowl or platter. Serves 8.

Pesto Dressing:

Mix all ingredients in a shaker or blend on low speed for one minute. Chill well
after blending.

Shrimp with Avocado and Hearts of Palm Salad

Must Be Chilled

Salad:

1   (7½-ounce) can hearts of palm, drained

2   large tomatoes

1   avocado, peeled and pitted

1   medium head red leaf lettuce, torn in bite-size pieces

1½ pounds cooked large shrimp, peeled and deveined, chilled

Sour Cream Dressing:

½   cup sour cream

½   cup mayonnaise

2   tablespoons fresh lemon juice

1   green onion, chopped

½   tablespoon seeded, finely chopped jalapeños

¼   teaspoon chili powder

¼   teaspoon dry mustard

Salad:

Cut hearts of palm, tomato and avocado into 1-inch pieces. Combine in a medium bowl. Mix with just enough dressing to coat lightly. Chill. Place lettuce on individual salad plates. Mound ¼ of vegetables in the center, surround with ¼ of shrimp. Serve with dressing on the side. Serves 4.

Sour Cream Dressing:

Combine all ingredients in small bowl. Chill.

Seaside Macaroni Salad

Salad:

1½ cups macaroni
6   cups boiling water
3   teaspoons salt, divided
1   teaspoon vegetable oil
2   cups shredded iceberg lettuce
3   hard-cooked eggs, sliced
Pepper to taste

½   (1-pound) package frozen cooked shrimp, thawed and cut in small pieces
1   (10-ounce) package frozen tiny peas, thawed
1   cup shredded Monterey Jack cheese
2   tablespoons chopped parsley or chopped chives, optional

Dijon-Mayonnaise Dressing:

1   cup mayonnaise
½   cup sour cream
2   teaspoons Dijon mustard

¼   cup sliced green onions
½   teaspoon freshly ground pepper

Salad:

Cook macaroni in boiling water with 2 teaspoons salt and oil. Drain and set aside to cool. Make dressing. Put the lettuce in the bottom of a clear 2-quart glass bowl. Stand the slices of egg around the sides of the bowl. Add the remaining 1 teaspoon of salt and the pepper. Then add the shrimp, peas and cheese. Spread dressing carefully over the top and sprinkle with parsley or chopped chives. May toss at the table or serve as a layered salad. Serves 6.

Dijon-Mayonnaise Dressing:

Mix all ingredients in a small bowl.

Tuna Salad with Avocado Dressing

Salad:

2	cups instant rice, cooked
2	(6-ounce) cans tuna, rinsed in hot water
1	(8½-ounce) can tiny green peas, drained
½	cup chopped onions

1	cup chopped celery
1	teaspoon salt
½	teaspoon pepper
1	dash Tabasco sauce
½	cup Hellmann's mayonnaise

Avocado Dressing:

2	medium avocados, peeled, pitted and chopped
½	cup Hellmann's mayonnaise
½	cup sour cream
3	drops Tabasco sauce

½	teaspoon Worcestershire sauce
½	teaspoon finely chopped onions
1	teaspoon lemon juice
Salt to taste	

Salad:
Toss all ingredients together and chill. Serves 6.

Avocado Dressing:
Blend all ingredients in blender until smooth. Serve on top of salad.

Sugar-Free French Dressing

Must Be Chilled

1	cup canola oil
1	(10½-ounce) can tomato soup
2	tablespoons granulated artificial sweetener
⅔	cup vinegar

1½	teaspoons salt
¼	teaspoon pepper
1	teaspoon dry mustard
1	teaspoon fresh minced onions
2	tablespoons Worcestershire sauce

Mix together all ingredients in a large covered container and shake well. Cover and chill. Makes 3 cups.

Low-Calorie Dijon-Honey Dressing
Must Be Chilled

½ cup light mayonnaise	1 tablespoon skim milk
2 tablespoons Dijon mustard	¼-½ cup cider vinegar
2 tablespoons honey	Pinch of ground red pepper

In a small bowl, whisk together all ingredients. Cover and chill.

Ranch Pepper Dressing
Must Be Chilled

½ cup fat-free mayonnaise	½ teaspoon cracked black pepper
¼ cup light sour cream	½ teaspoon onion powder
¼ cup low-fat buttermilk	1 garlic clove, minced
1 tablespoon finely chopped fresh parsley	

In a small bowl, whisk together all the ingredients. Cover and refrigerate for at least 3 hours to blend the flavors.

Avocado Dressing

1 avocado, peeled, pitted and coarsely chopped	½ cup fresh lime juice
1 small jalapeño, seeded	2 tablespoons sugar
¼ cup finely chopped red onions	2 cups canola oil
	Salt and pepper to taste

Puree the avocado, jalapeños, onions, lime juice and sugar in a blender until smooth. With the motor running, slowly add the oil until it emulsifies. Store in a glass container in the refrigerator. Bring to room temperature 1 hour before serving.

Village Dressing

Must Be Made Ahead

1	quart safflower oil	2	teaspoons Accent
4	garlic cloves, minced	1	tablespoon whole peppercorns
5	tablespoons fresh lemon juice	1	tablespoon salt
¼-½	pound Roquefort cheese, plus additional for garnish	½	teaspoon dry mustard
			Croutons, optional

Combine all ingredients in a blender until well blended. Follow directions exactly and make no substitutions. Age 3 weeks before using. Sprinkle Roquefort cheese and croutons over top of salad, if desired.

Hint: Best served with romaine lettuce.

Nutty Cashew Dressing

Must Be Chilled

1½	cups canola oil	3	teaspoons light soy sauce
¾	cup cashews	⅓	cup white vinegar
¾	cup water	3	tablespoons lemon juice
½	cup honey	6	garlic cloves, minced
4½	teaspoons dill weed		

Combine oil and cashews in a blender for 10 to 15 seconds. Add water, honey, dill weed, soy sauce, vinegar, lemon juice and garlic and blend another 10 seconds, just to mix. Cover and chill. Makes 4 cups.

Creamy Italian Dressing
Must Be Chilled

Homemade Mayonnaise:

2 large egg yolks

1 teaspoon Dijon mustard

1 teaspoon fresh lemon juice

Salt and pepper to taste

1 cup canola oil

Creamy Italian Dressing:

¼ cup heavy cream

2 tablespoons white wine vinegar

1 garlic clove, minced

2 tablespoons chopped fresh oregano

Salt and freshly ground pepper to taste

Homemade Mayonnaise:

In a medium bowl, beat together the egg yolks, mustard, lemon juice, salt and pepper with a whisk. Whisk in the oil, a few drops at a time, until the mixture thickens and begins to look like mayonnaise. Then beat in the remaining oil in a thin stream. Add a little more lemon juice if mixture is too thick.

Creamy Italian Dressing:

In a small bowl, beat together the heavy cream, vinegar, garlic, oregano, salt, pepper and homemade mayonnaise from the preceding recipe. Cover and chill at least 1 hour. Serve at room temperature. Makes 1½ cups.

Uncooked egg yolks should not be eaten by
the young, the elderly or people with impaired immune systems.

Dijon Vinaigrette

½ cup red wine vinegar	¼ teaspoon freshly ground pepper
¼ cup Dijon mustard	2 tablespoons sugar, optional
2 tablespoons fresh lime juice	¾ cup olive oil
¼ teaspoon salt	

In a blender, combine vinegar, mustard, lime juice, salt, pepper and sugar. Process until smooth, stopping to scrape down sides. With blender running, add oil in a slow, steady stream until smooth. Makes 1½ cups.

Hearty Italian Vinaigrette

Must Be Chilled

6 tablespoons olive oil	2 tablespoons chili sauce
1 garlic clove, minced	½ teaspoon sugar
¼ teaspoon salt	1 teaspoon Italian herb seasoning
1½ teaspoons minced fresh parsley	1½ teaspoons Worcestershire sauce
½ teaspoon freshly ground pepper	2½ tablespoons red wine vinegar
1 tablespoon freshly grated Parmesan cheese	

Combine all ingredients in a blender until smooth. Cover and chill.

***

**This vinaigrette is excellent on salad greens,
pasta salad or any vegetable combination.**

Entrées I

Stretching 80 miles along the Texas Gulf Coast is the Padre Island National Seashore. It is one of largest undeveloped ocean beaches in our country. The beautiful splash of color in the railroad vines is displayed against its sandy white shoreline and windswept dunes.

Photography by Richard Reynolds

Texas
Gulf Coast

A Texas Blossoms Menu for a

Texas Barbecue

Rio Frio Brisket
Confetti Slaw
Palo Pinto Beans
Potatoes Con Queso
Pan de Elote
San Saba Pecan Pie
Summer Lemonade Cookies
Texas Rangers

Tangy Beef Tenderloin

Must Be Made Ahead

1 cup ketchup	2 (0.7-ounce) envelopes Italian salad dressing mix
2 teaspoons prepared mustard	
½ teaspoon Worcestershire sauce	1 (4 to 6-pound) whole beef tenderloin
1½ cups water	

Combine ketchup, mustard, Worcestershire sauce, water and salad dressing mix. Mix well. Pierce tenderloin in many places with skewer and place in a large heavy duty self-sealing plastic bag. Pour sauce over meat and seal tightly. Place bag in a shallow pan or dish and refrigerate 8 hours, turning occasionally. Drain and reserve sauce. Place tenderloin on a rack in pan and insert meat thermometer. Bake in a preheated 425 degree oven for 30 to 45 minutes or until a meat thermometer registers 140 degrees for rare, 150 degrees for medium rare or 160 degrees for medium. Bring sauce to boil. Baste tenderloin occasionally with sauce. Bring the remaining sauce to a boil and simmer at least 5 minutes. Serve with the beef. Slice beef to desired thickness and number of servings needed. Serves 10 to 12.

Variation: Try this with an eye-of-round roast.

Classic Beef Tenderloin

Must Be Made Ahead

8 tablespoons butter
1 tablespoon garlic salt
1 tablespoon pepper
1 tablespoon Lawry's seasoned
   salt

1 tablespoon fresh chopped
   parsley
1 (4 to 5-pound) beef tenderloin

Melt butter in small pan and add garlic, pepper, salt and parsley. Tie tenderloin with string at 1-inch intervals. (If one end of tenderloin is slender tuck under to avoid over cooking.) Place tenderloin on heavy foil and broil 10 minutes on each side using ½ of sauce on each side. Wrap and refrigerate until next day. Bring to room temperature and bake in a 350 degree oven for 15 minutes or until done to taste depending on size of tenderloin. Use a meat thermometer for accuracy. Slice and serve. Serves 8.

A hostess' dream recipe.

Man Pleasers

Must Be Made Ahead

¼ cup soy sauce, plus
   1½ tablespoons, divided
3 tablespoons sliced fresh ginger
4 garlic cloves, sliced
1½ teaspoons sugar
3 green onion tops, sliced

½ teaspoon crushed red pepper
1½ pounds boneless beef sirloin, cut
   in ¾-inch cubes
2 tablespoons vegetable oil
1 tablespoon sesame seed, toasted

Combine the ¼ cup soy sauce, ginger, garlic, sugar, onions and red pepper. Marinate the beef at least 4 to 6 hours or overnight; drain thoroughly. Heat oil. Add the meat cubes and brown, stirring for about 2 minutes. Put meat on a small plate or bowl and sprinkle with 1½ tablespoons soy sauce and toasted sesame seeds. Serve with rice or noodles. Serves 4 to 6.

Variation: Serve individual cubes as an appetizer. Makes about 40.

Peppered Eye-of-Round

1	garlic head	2	cups sour cream
1	eye-of-round roast	4	tablespoons prepared horseradish
	Cracked pepper to taste	1	baguette

Peel garlic cloves and cut into slivers lengthwise. Prick roast with point of sharp knife about every inch all over the meat and place garlic slivers into the slits. Press cracked pepper on meat with your hands. Place roast on a double thickness of heavy aluminum foil with the sides folded up to catch any juice. Cook on charcoal grill (we used pecan wood chips for extra flavor) with indirect heat until meat thermometer reads 140 degrees for rare. This takes approximately 45 minutes, but watch carefully. Remove from heat and let stand 10 to 15 minutes. Slice paper-thin. Mix horseradish with sour cream, adjusting the amount of horseradish to taste. Slice baguette into ¼-inch slices and toast lightly. Serve several thin slices of meat on a slice of baguette with horseradish cream.

Variation: Serve as an appetizer.

Sirloin Steak with Garlic Peppercorn Sauce

2	tablespoons butter	2	pounds sirloin steak
¼	cup minced green onions	1	tablespoon cracked black peppercorns
2	tablespoons minced garlic		
½	cup dry white wine	1	teaspoon cracked white peppercorns
2	tablespoons Dijon mustard		
1	cup whipping cream	1	tablespoon olive oil
⅔	cup beef broth	¼	cup chopped fresh parsley

In medium saucepan melt butter, add onions and garlic. Sauté until the onions are transparent. Add wine and cook until reduced by ½, about 4 minutes. Whisk in mustard, cream and broth. Boil until reduced to 1½ cups, about 7 minutes. Coat both sides of steak with peppercorns. Heat oil in heavy large skillet. On medium-high heat cook steak to desired doneness. Transfer to platter. Add sauce to pan drippings, bring to boil, scraping up browned bits. Cook 1 minute longer. Add parsley and spoon over steak. Serves 6 to 8.

Ranch-Style Fajitas with Guacamole

Must Be Made Ahead

Fajitas:

2 pounds whole beef skirt, trimmed of fat and membrane

2 tablespoons Bolner's Fiesta fajita seasoning

¼ cup orange juice

¼ cup lime juice

2 tablespoons vegetable oil

2 green bell peppers, thinly sliced

1 large yellow onion, thinly sliced

12 flour tortillas, warmed

½ pint sour cream

Shredded lettuce

Guacamole:

2 avocados

1 tomato, diced

1 tablespoon finely chopped onion

¼ teaspoon garlic powder

⅛ teaspoon Worcestershire sauce

1 teaspoon lemon juice

Dash Tabasco sauce

Salt to taste

Fajitas:

In a self-sealing plastic bag, marinate meat in fajita seasoning, orange juice and lime juice for at least 3 hours. Heat oil in a medium saucepan and sauté green pepper and onion until tender. Grill meat until cooked. Slice. Place slices on flour tortillas with sour cream, shredded lettuce and guacamole and roll. Serves 4 to 6.

Guacamole:

Peel and pit avocados and mash in a small bowl. Add tomatoes, onions, garlic powder, Worcestershire sauce, lemon juice, Tabasco sauce and salt and mix gently.

T Bar S Ranch Roast Beef

Must Be Made Ahead

1	(6 to 8-pound) beef rump roast	¼	cup Worcestershire sauce
1	cup vegetable oil	¼	cup prepared mustard
¾	cup soy sauce	30	garlic cloves cut in half
½	cup lemon juice	1	tablespoon freshly ground pepper

Pierce roast at 1-inch intervals with a meat fork and place in a large heavy duty self-sealing plastic bag. Combine vegetable oil, soy sauce, lemon juice, Worcestershire sauce, mustard, garlic and pepper. Pour over the roast and chill 48 hours, turning roast occasionally. Remove meat from marinade and place roast on a lightly greased rack in an oven pan. Bake in a preheated 325 degree oven for 1 hour and 50 minutes or until a meat thermometer registers 145 degrees. Let stand 5 minutes before slicing. Serves 10 to 12.

Variation: Simmer marinade 8 to 10 minutes. Grill roast over indirect heat until pink. Baste 2 or 3 times with marinade the last 10 minutes of cooking time. Boil remaining marinade a few minutes and serve as gravy.

The *"Cantaloupe Festival"* is held in Pecos the second weekend in August. The soil, climate and water produce this world-famous variety of sweet and juicy cantaloupe.

German Sauerbraten
with Gingersnap Gravy

Sauerbraten:

1 (3½ to 4 pounds) beef rump roast	½ teaspoon crushed red pepper
Salt and pepper to taste	1 large onion, coarsely chopped
2 bay leaves	2 cups water
12 whole cloves	2 cups red wine vinegar
1 teaspoon whole black peppercorns	2 cups red wine
1 stick cinnamon, broken into 3 pieces	3 tablespoons butter
	3 tablespoons vegetable oil

Gingersnap Gravy:

4 tablespoons sugar	1½ cups finely ground gingersnaps
3 cups strained cooking liquid, from cooked sauerbraten	½ cup sour cream
	Salt and pepper to taste

Sauerbraten:

Place roast in a large crock. Sprinkle with salt and pepper and surround with the bay leaves, cloves, peppercorns, cinnamon, pepper flakes and onion. Combine water, vinegar and wine in a large saucepan. Bring to a brisk boil. Pour immediately over the roast, cover and let cool down about 1 to 2 hours. Refrigerate and marinate, turning daily for 3 to 5 days. Place roast on paper towels to dry, strain and reserve the marinade. Discard all the vegetables and seasonings. Melt butter in Dutch oven and add oil. Brown roast well on all sides and add reserved marinade. Cover and simmer slowly, turning occasionally, for about 3 hours or until tender. Remove meat from the cooking liquid, reserving the liquid to make gingersnap gravy. Wrap roast in heavy foil for 30 minutes before slicing. If you prefer, liquid may just be thickened with cornstarch.

Gingersnap Gravy:

Heat sugar in a Dutch oven or large skillet. Stir constantly until thoroughly melted and browned. Gradually add cooking liquid and then ground gingersnaps, stirring constantly with wire whisk until well blended and thickened. Add sour cream and salt and pepper to taste. If gravy is too thick, add a little water to cooking liquid. Serve meat and gravy with potato dumplings, mashed potatoes or egg noodles.

Variation: A venison roast can be substituted for the beef rump roast.

Rio Frio Brisket

Brisket:

1   (8 to 12-pound) beef brisket

Seasoning Rub: (For each pound of meat:)

½   teaspoon ground cumin

½   teaspoon garlic powder

½   teaspoon salt

½   teaspoon chili powder

½   teaspoon cornstarch

¼   teaspoon pepper

Texas Sauce:

Juice of 1 lemon

2   cups ketchup

2   tablespoons Worcestershire sauce

1   teaspoon prepared mustard

2   tablespoons brown sugar

2   tablespoons vinegar

2   tablespoons orange marmalade

2   tablespoons butter

Horseradish Sauce:

2   tablespoons prepared horseradish

¼   cup mayonnaise

¼   cup sour cream

Juice of ½ lemon

½   teaspoon sugar

Brisket:

Multiply the ingredients in the Seasoning Rub by the number of pounds of meat. Combine spices and rub ⅔ on the fat side of the brisket and ⅓ on the lean side. Grill brisket until it is dark and crusty on both sides, about 40 minutes, turning occasionally. Remove brisket from grill and place on a rack in a roasting pan. Cover and bake in a preheated 200 degree oven for 1 hour per pound. Serve with choice of sauce. Serves 10 to 16.

Texas Sauce:

Combine all ingredients except butter in saucepan. Bring to a boil and simmer 5 minutes. Stir in butter. Makes 3 cups.

Horseradish Sauce:

Mix all ingredients and chill. Makes ½ cup.

This was served at a bachelor party on the
banks of the Rio Frio. It can be cooked in stages.

Three Day Brisket

Must Be Made Ahead

Brisket:

1	(6-pound) brisket	1	teaspoon garlic salt
1	teaspoon onion salt		

Sauce:

1½	tablespoons brown sugar	2	tablespoons Worcestershire sauce
½	cup ketchup	1½	teaspoons dry mustard
¼	cup water		Dash pepper
1	teaspoon celery seed	1	teaspoon liquid smoke
3	tablespoons butter	½	teaspoon salt

Day 1:

Wrap brisket in heavy-duty foil and refrigerate overnight.

Day 2:

Unwrap and sprinkle with onion salt and garlic salt. Rewrap in foil. Bake in a preheated 300 degree oven for 5 hours. Cool and refrigerate overnight.

Day 3:

Slice thinly and cover with sauce, wrap in foil and bake in a preheated 325 degree oven about 1 hour.

Sauce:

Mix all ingredients and heat. Pour over brisket. Meat can be frozen covered with sauce.

Hint: Short, fat briskets with a thick covering of fat have the best flavor. Never use a trimmed brisket.

Entrées I

Lone Star Short Ribs
Must Be Made Ahead

Lone Star Rub:

5-6 pounds beef short ribs	¼ cup sugar
¾ cup paprika	2 tablespoons garlic powder
¼ cup ground pepper	2 tablespoons onion powder
¼ cup Gebhardt chili powder	1 tablespoon cayenne pepper
¼ cup salt	

Beer Mop Sauce:

12 ounces beer	2 garlic cloves, minced
½ cup cider vinegar	2 tablespoons Lone Star Rub
¼ cup corn oil	1 tablespoon Worcestershire sauce
½ medium onion, chopped	

Glaze and Barbecue Sauce:

1½ cups ketchup	2 garlic cloves, minced
1 cup beer	2 teaspoons cumin seeds, toasted and ground
¾ cup cider vinegar	1½ teaspoons anise seeds, toasted and ground
3 tablespoons minced cilantro	
3 tablespoons dark brown sugar	1½ teaspoons salt
3 tablespoons Worcestershire sauce	1 teaspoon Tabasco sauce

Lone Star Rub:

Mix together all dry rub ingredients. Massage each short rib with the dry rub. Place the ribs in a plastic bag and refrigerate overnight. The next day place the ribs, fat side up, in a smoker for 5 hours and cook to a temperature of 200 to 220 degrees.

Beer Mop Sauce:

Before placing the ribs in the smoker, mix the mop sauce. Baste ribs with the mop sauce every 30 to 60 minutes.

Glaze and Barbecue Sauce:

Prepare the glaze about 1½ hours before the meat is done. Mix the glaze ingredients in a medium saucepan and simmer for 30 minutes, stirring frequently.

Lone Star Short Ribs continued

Mop the glaze on the top and sides of the ribs twice during the last 30 to 60 minutes of cooking time. (Never apply glaze before the last hour or it will burn.) Return the remaining glaze to the stove, and simmer until it's reduced by ⅓, about 15 to 20 minutes. After removing the ribs from the smoker, allow them to sit for 10 minutes. Trim the fat and serve them with the reduced glaze on the side.

"Mop" get its name because the glaze is applied to
large amounts with a clean string mop. A small dishwashing
mop works well for the home cook.

Always Requested Chicken Fried Steak

2	pounds round steak, sliced ½-inch thick and tenderized	1	teaspoon freshly ground pepper
2	cups flour	1½	cups buttermilk
1	egg	1	tablespoon Tabasco sauce, optional
2	teaspoons baking powder	2	garlic cloves, minced
1	teaspoon baking soda		Vegetable shortening, preferably Crisco
¾	teaspoon salt		

Cut steak into four equal portions. Pound each portion until about ¼-inch thick. Place the flour in a shallow bowl. In a medium bowl, beat the egg. Mix together the baking powder, baking soda, salt and pepper. Add to egg. Blend in the buttermilk. Add Tabasco sauce and garlic. Dredge each steak first in the flour and then in batter. Pat more flour into each piece until surface is dry. Melt shortening in a deep skillet or Dutch oven until the shortening is at least 4-inches deep. Bring the temperature of the shortening to 325 degrees. Fry the steaks, pushing them down or turning them over as they bob to the surface, for 7 to 8 minutes, or until they are golden. Drain the steaks. Serve with cream gravy.

Once you make this...they'll ask for it again and again.

Spicy Short Ribs

Ribs:

3	pounds boneless beef short ribs	1	tablespoon vegetable oil
½	teaspoon salt	1	cup water (more if needed)
¼	teaspoon pepper		

Zesty Barbecue Sauce:

2	medium onions, chopped	½	cup lemon juice
1	garlic clove, chopped finely	¼	cup Worcestershire sauce
1	tablespoon vegetable oil	⅓	cup packed brown sugar
2	tablespoons chili powder	2	tablespoons prepared mustard
2	cups ketchup	1-2	teaspoons ground cumin
1	cup cider vinegar	2	tablespoons butter

Ribs:

Season short ribs with salt and pepper and brown them in the oil in a Dutch oven. Add the 1 cup water and simmer, covered, on low heat for 2 hours. Remove the ribs and reserve the pan juices to add to the barbecue sauce. Put ribs in broiler pan. Broil ribs 6 inches from heat, basting with sauce until the ribs are well glazed and brown, about 4 minutes each side. Serve with Zesty Barbecue sauce. Serves 6.

Zesty Barbecue Sauce:

In a saucepan sauté onions and garlic in oil until tender. Add chili powder and cook 1 minute. Add pan juices from the ribs, ketchup, vinegar, lemon juice, Worcestershire sauce, sugar, mustard, cumin and butter. Simmer uncovered 30 minutes, stirring often.

San Antonio Beef Rosé

3-3½ pounds round steak
½ cup flour
1½ teaspoons salt
¼ teaspoon pepper
½ cup vegetable oil
2 cups rosé wine
1½ cups water, divided

3 tablespoons onion soup mix
1 (6-ounce) can tomato paste
2 tablespoons brown sugar
1 cup (about 4-ounces) shredded sharp Cheddar cheese
8 ounces fresh mushrooms, halved
2 tablespoons snipped parsley

Cut steak into strips 3 to 4-inches long. Combine flour, salt and pepper and sprinkle over meat to lightly dredge. Brown dredged strips ⅓ at a time in oil in large frying pan. Combine wine, 1 cup water and onion soup mix and add to all of the meat. Cover tightly and cook slowly 45 minutes. Add tomato paste, ½ cup water and brown sugar to meat. Continue cooking 20 minutes, or until meat is tender, stirring occasionally. Add cheese and mushrooms and continue cooking slowly 10 minutes. Sprinkle with parsley and serve over rice or noodles. Serves 8 to 10.

Beef Hispania

Flour
1 pound cubed stew meat
2 tablespoons butter
1 (10¾-ounce) can cream of mushroom soup, undiluted
1 (4-ounce) can mushroom stems and pieces, and liquid

1 jalapeño pepper, seeded and finely chopped
¼ cup sherry
Small package of corn chips or Chinese noodles

Flour meat and brown in butter in pan; over medium heat. Add soup, mushrooms and liquid, jalapeños and sherry. Blend well. Reduce heat to low; cover and simmer for about 2 hours. Serve over noodles or corn chips. (I like Fritos.) Serves 4.

No-Peek Mystery Stew

2	pounds lean stew meat or beef tips	1	(10¾-ounce) cream of mushroom soup, undiluted
1	(2-ounce) package onion soup mix	½	cup red wine
1	cup ginger ale	1	tablespoon browning sauce
		6	medium fresh mushrooms, sliced

Mix all ingredients in heavy Dutch oven and cover with heavy duty aluminum foil before putting on a tight fitting lid. Bake for 3 hours in a preheated 300 degree oven. Don't lift lid while cooking. Serve over rice or noodles. Serves 6.

Variation: Omit ginger ale, red wine and browning sauce. Add 1 cup regular 7Up.

Hill Country Goulash

1	pound beef, cubed	2-3	tablespoons Worcestershire sauce
1	tablespoon olive oil	¾	teaspoon cider vinegar
2	medium onions, diced	6	tablespoons ketchup
¼	teaspoon dry mustard	1	(12-ounce) can beer, divided
½	teaspoon paprika	3	tablespoons flour
2	tablespoons brown sugar	1	(12-ounce) package noodles
1¼	teaspoons salt		

Brown meat in oil in large skillet. Add onions. Combine mustard, paprika, sugar, salt, Worcestershire sauce, vinegar and ketchup and add to meat. Stir and add 1 cup of beer. Stir, cover and cook on low heat 2½ hours or until meat is tender. Blend ½ cup beer with flour and add to meat and stir until thickened. Serve over cooked noodles. Serves 4.

Hint: Non-alcoholic beer is good too.

I usually double this recipe as it freezes well.

North Texas Meat Loaf

1½ pounds ground chuck
¼ cup minced onions
1⅓ cups fine soft bread crumbs
2 teaspoons salt
1 egg
4 teaspoons prepared horseradish

¾ teaspoon dry mustard
3 tablespoons minced green bell peppers
3 tablespoons ketchup
½ cup milk

Mix all ingredients and form into a loaf. Place the meat in an 8x4x3-inch loaf pan and bake in a preheated 400 degree oven for 1 hour. Serves 6.

Best Ever Buttermilk Fried Chicken

1 pound thinly sliced chicken breast
1 cup buttermilk, divided
¼ cup yellow cornmeal
¼ cup plus 2 teaspoons flour, divided

½ teaspoon salt
1 teaspoon coarsely ground pepper
¼ cup vegetable oil, divided
¾ cup chicken broth

Place chicken in a shallow dish and pour in ½ cup buttermilk, turning chicken to coat. In another dish combine cornmeal, ¼ cup flour, salt and pepper. Dredge chicken in cornmeal mixture, patting on the coating. In a large pan heat 2 tablespoons oil over medium high heat. Add ½ of the chicken and cook, turning once, until chicken is white throughout, about 6 minutes. Repeat with the remaining chicken and the remaining oil. Remove chicken and keep warm. Stir in the remaining 2 teaspoons of flour and cook, stirring 1 minute. Whisk broth and the remaining ½ cup buttermilk into pan drippings, scraping up browned bits in pan. Simmer, stirring, 2 minutes. Season with additional salt and pepper to taste. Serve gravy over chicken. Serves 4.

One Fast Chicken

1	(5 to 6-pound) chicken	Salt and pepper
1	lemon, halved	½-1 teaspoon dried summer savory,
4	whole garlic cloves	crumbled, optional
4	tablespoons unsalted butter	1 cup chicken broth or wine

Place oven rack on second from bottom level. Remove giblets from chicken for another use. Stuff chicken with lemon, garlic and butter. Season with salt, pepper and summer savory. Put chicken in a roasting pan in a preheated 475 degree oven and roast breast side up for 50 to 60 minutes. Tilt chicken over pan as you lift it out when done so juices run into pan. Pour off excess fat. Put juices in a saucepan and heat with broth or wine. Let liquid reduce by half. Serve sauce over chicken or in sauceboat. Serves 4.

East Texas Pecan Chicken

1	cup pecans	1 cup buttermilk
1	cup flour	6 skinless boneless chicken breast halves
1	tablespoon paprika	⅓ cup butter, melted
½	teaspoon salt	Fresh parsley, thyme or sage, optional
¼	teaspoon pepper	
1	egg, lightly beaten	

Toast pecans in a preheated 300 degree oven for 10 to 20 minutes. Watch carefully. Grind pecans to very fine texture. Combine pecans, flour, paprika, salt and pepper in a pie plate. Set aside. Combine egg and buttermilk. Dip chicken breasts into buttermilk mixture and dredge in flour mixture. Pour the melted butter into a 13x9x2-inch baking dish. Add chicken, turning once to coat with butter. Bake in a preheated 375 degree oven for 30 minutes. Chicken should be golden brown. Garnish with parsley, thyme or sage. Serves 6.

Chicken-Cheese Chilies Rellenos

2	chicken breast halves, poached	2	tablespoons finely diced onions
Salt and pepper		2	poblano peppers, seeded
2	ounces Monterey Jack cheese, shredded		

When the chicken is cool enough to handle, take the meat off the bone and chop it coarsely. Season lightly with salt and pepper to taste. Mix in the cheese and onions. Cut the tops off the poblano chilies and clean out the seeds and membranes. Stuff the chicken mixture into the chilies. Grill stuffed chilies lightly over charcoal grill until the skin splits and chars slightly and filling is hot. Serve with fresh salsa. Serves 2.

Bed Roll Chicken

Must Be Chilled

4	boneless skinless chicken breast halves	Dash salt	
4	tablespoons cream cheese, softened	1	egg
		1	tablespoon water
1½ teaspoons green peppercorns		Italian seasoned breadcrumbs	
Dash tarragon		¼	cup olive oil

Pound chicken breasts to uniform thickness with a mallet. Combine cream cheese, peppercorns, tarragon and salt. Spread mixture evenly on chicken breasts. Roll chicken starting with narrowest end; cheese will act as glue. Whisk egg in shallow bowl. Add water. Dip chicken breasts in egg mixture, then roll in breadcrumbs to cover. Chill for at least 30 minutes. Drizzle bottom of baking pan with olive oil to cover. Place rolled breasts in baking pan and pour the remaining oil over chicken. Bake, uncovered, in a preheated 350 degree oven for 25 minutes. Do not turn. Serves 2 to 4.

Hint: Recipe can be easily multiplied for larger groups.

Rockingham Chicken

Chicken:

1 (8-ounce) package Pepperidge
   Farm dressing

4 whole chicken breasts

¼ cup flour

½ teaspoon salt

¼ teaspoon paprika

Dash pepper

8 tablespoons melted butter or
   margarine, divided

Sauce:

½ pound fresh mushrooms, sliced

¼ cup minced onions

2 tablespoons butter

2 tablespoons flour

½ cup heavy cream

½ cup sour cream

½ teaspoon salt

¼ teaspoon pepper

Chicken:

Mix Pepperidge Farm dressing according to package directions. Split chicken breasts almost in half. Stuff with dressing mix and secure with toothpicks. Combine flour, salt, paprika and pepper in bag. Dip chicken in 4 tablespoons melted butter, then into flour mixture, and shake. Place in pan and drizzle remaining butter on top. Bake in preheated 325 degree oven for 45 minutes; turn chicken breasts over and continue baking for 45 minutes.

Sauce:

Sauté mushrooms and onions in 2 tablespoons butter. Cover and cook 10 minutes. Stir in flour; add cream, sour cream, salt and pepper. Heat slowly, stirring constantly to near boiling point. Remove chicken breasts to serving dish, pour sauce over and serve. Serves 4.

This is a great company dish!

Apricot Russian Chicken

1	cup apricot preserves	½	(2-ounce) package onion soup mix
1	(8-ounce) bottle Russian dressing	6	chicken breast halves

Mix apricot preserves, dressing and 1 envelope soup mix. Place chicken in greased baking dish and pour apricot mixture over chicken. Bake uncovered in a preheated 350 degree oven for 1 hour. Serves 6

Artichoke Chicken

8	boneless chicken breast halves	1	garlic clove, chopped
1	teaspoon garlic salt	1	(14-ounce) can artichoke hearts
½	teaspoon pepper	2	tablespoons flour
1	teaspoon paprika	⅔	cup Knorr liquid chicken bouillon
6	tablespoons butter, divided	4	tablespoons dry sherry
1	pound fresh mushrooms, sliced		

Season chicken with garlic salt, pepper and paprika. In skillet, melt 4 tablespoons butter and brown seasoned chicken. Place chicken in buttered baking dish. In skillet, melt the remaining 2 tablespoons butter and sauté mushrooms and garlic for 2 to 3 minutes. Add flour, bouillon and sherry and cook about 5 minutes. Arrange artichokes around chicken breasts and then pour mushroom mixture over chicken and artichokes. Bake uncovered in preheated 350 degree oven for 35 to 45 minutes. Baste during cooking. Serves 8.

Variation: Cut chicken in small pieces and serve as a brunch casserole.

Chicken Breasts Dijon

4	skinless boneless chicken breast halves	¼	cup whipping cream
⅛	teaspoon pepper	¼	cup Chablis or other dry white wine
1	tablespoon, plus 2 teaspoons Dijon mustard, divided	1	teaspoon green peppercorns in vinegar
2	tablespoons olive oil		

Place chicken between two sheets of heavy duty plastic wrap; using a meat mallet or rolling pin flatten to ¼-inch thickness. Sprinkle with pepper and spread one side of the chicken breasts with 1 tablespoon mustard. Cook chicken in oil in a large skillet over medium heat, 10 minutes, turning frequently. Remove from skillet and keep warm. Combine whipping cream, wine, the remaining 2 teaspoons mustard and peppercorns in skillet. Bring to a boil and cook until mixture thickens. Spoon over the chicken. Serves 4.

Hint: Milk may be substituted for cream to cut fat and calories without much change in flavor.

Chicken Wellington

1	(3-ounce) package cream cheese, softened	2	tablespoons milk
3	tablespoons margarine, melted, divided	1	tablespoon chopped chives or green onions
2	cups cubed cooked chicken	1	tablespoon chopped pimientos
¼	teaspoon salt	1	(8-ounce) can Crescent dinner rolls
Dash pepper		¾	cup crushed seasoned croutons

In medium bowl, blend cream cheese and 2 tablespoons margarine until smooth. Add chicken, salt, pepper, milk, chives and pimientos. Mix well. Separate Crescent dough into 4 squares. Spoon ½ cup meat mixture onto center of each square. Pull 4 corners of dough to top center of chicken mixture, twist slightly and seal edges. Brush tops with remaining margarine; dip into crouton crumbs. Bake on ungreased cookie sheet in preheated 350 degree oven for 20 to 25 minutes. Serves 4.

Poppy Seed Chicken

1 (3 to 4-pound) fryer or 4 to 5 chicken breast halves	2 (10¾-ounce) cans cream of chicken soup, undiluted
Celery salt	1 (8-ounce) container sour cream
Bay leaves	1 tablespoon poppy seed
Poultry seasoning	1 sleeve Ritz crackers
Salt and pepper to taste	8 tablespoons butter, melted

Simmer chicken in water with celery salt, bay leaves, poultry seasoning, salt and pepper to taste. Cool and cut in bite-size pieces. Mix chicken, soup, sour cream and poppy seeds in buttered casserole. Crush one sleeve of Ritz crackers and sprinkle over chicken mixture. Drizzle melted butter over crackers and bake in preheated 350 degree oven for 30 to 45 minutes or until bubbly. Serves 6.

Hint: Casserole can be made in advance, but add the Ritz cracker mixture just before baking.

Variation: Cooked, well-drained broccoli can be added to bottom of dish, if desired.

Variation: Use 6 chicken breast halves and increase poppy seeds to 3 tablespoons. Add 8-ounces grated Monterey Jack cheese. Mix 1½ tablespoons poppy seeds with the chicken and the remaining 1½ tablespoons poppy seeds with the mixture of 2 sleeves of Ritz crackers and 4 tablespoons butter.

The Ritz crackers are what really make this dish special.

Sweet and Sour Chicken

14	chicken thighs	2	cups pineapple juice
½	cup flour	1	teaspoon salt
1	teaspoon paprika	⅛	teaspoon pepper
2	tablespoons oil	4	teaspoons Worcestershire sauce
2	tablespoons butter	1	cup packed brown sugar
1	medium onion, chopped	½	cup lemon juice
1½	cups ketchup		

Wash and dry chicken. Put flour and paprika in a plastic bag and shake chicken pieces (one at a time) until coated. Heat oil and butter in a large frying pan until butter melts, and sauté chicken pieces on all sides over medium heat, until golden. As chicken pieces brown, transfer them to a 15x11x2-inch baking dish in a single layer. When all the chicken pieces have been transferred to the baking dish, add the onions to the drippings in the frying pan and sauté until soft. Add ketchup, pineapple juice, salt, pepper, Worcestershire sauce, brown sugar and lemon juice. Mix well. When heated through, pour contents of frying pan over chicken. Bake, uncovered, in preheated 325 degree oven for 2 hours. Serves 8 to 10.

Continental Chicken

25	boneless, skinless chicken breast halves	3	(10¾-ounce) cans cream of mushroom soup, undiluted
25	slices bacon	3	(2½-ounce) jars chipped beef
3	cups sour cream		

Pound chicken breasts until they are ¼-inch thick. Roll breasts, then wrap with a slice of bacon. Mix together sour cream and soup. In two 13x9x2-inch casserole dishes, layer dried beef, chicken breasts and sour cream mixture. Cover and bake in a preheated 350 degree oven for 1 hour. Uncover and bake an additional hour. Serves 25.

Variation: Add 3 tablespoons sherry and 3 (4½-ounce) jars sliced mushrooms, drained, to the sour cream mixture.

Country Captain

3   tablespoons flour

1-2 tablespoons curry powder

1½ pounds chicken breast strips or
    chicken tenders

4   tablespoons olive oil, divided

1   large onion, chopped

1   green bell pepper, diced

1   yellow bell pepper, diced

1   red bell pepper, diced

1   medium Granny Smith apple,
    peeled and diced

1   garlic clove, crushed

¾   teaspoon salt

1   tablespoon ground ginger

2   (14½-ounce) cans diced
    tomatoes, undrained

1   cup chicken broth

½   cup dark, seedless raisins

½   cup slivered almonds

Cooking spray

Combine flour and curry powder in a plastic bag. Add chicken pieces and shake to coat well. Heat 2 tablespoons olive oil over medium heat until hot. Brown chicken about 8 minutes, turning once. Transfer chicken to a platter and set aside. In same skillet, heat the remaining 2 tablespoons olive oil. Add onions, bell peppers and apples and cook about 10 minutes, stirring often. Stir in garlic and salt, cooking one more minute. Add ginger, tomatoes and broth and simmer about 8 minutes with chicken. Then stir in raisins. Put in 13x9x2-inch casserole that has been lightly sprayed with cooking spray. Sprinkle almonds on top. Bake in preheated 350 degree oven about 20 minutes.

No Fuss Chicken

1   (10¾-ounce) can cream of
    mushroom soup, undiluted

1   (6-ounce) roll garlic cheese, cubed

1   (6-ounce) roll jalapeño cheese,
    cubed

1   (4-ounce) can mushrooms and
    liquid

2-3 cups chopped cooked chicken

1   (9-ounce) can Chinese noodles

Put soup, garlic and jalapeño cheeses and mushrooms in top of double boiler and heat until cheese is melted. Add chicken and heat. Serve over Chinese noodles. Serves 4.

Slow Simmering Continental Chicken

6-8 boneless, skinless chicken breast halves

6-8 slices bacon

1 (2½-ounce) jar chipped beef

1 (10¾-ounce) can mushroom soup, undiluted

¼ cup sour cream

¼ cup flour

Pound chicken breasts until ¼-inch thick. Roll breasts and wrap with a slice of bacon. Arrange dried beef on the bottom of greased crock-pot. Lay rolled chicken on top of the dried beef. Mix the soup, sour cream and flour together; pour over chicken. Cover and cook on low for 8 to 10 hours or on high for 3 to 5 hours. Serves 6 to 8.

Use the LOW setting for all-day cooking.
One hour on HIGH equals 2 to 2½ hours on LOW.

Piñon Chicken

Must Be Made Ahead

Salt and pepper to taste

1 cup buttermilk

4 skinless, boneless chicken breast halves

¼ cup flour

1-2 tablespoons olive oil or butter

1 large garlic clove, minced

2 tablespoons piñon or pine nuts

2 tablespoons chopped fresh parsley

¼ cup finely diced smoked ham

¼ pound fresh mushrooms, sliced

¼ cup chicken broth

¼ cup dry white wine

In a large bowl or plastic bag add salt and pepper to buttermilk and add chicken. Turn to coat well. Refrigerate 3 to 4 hours or overnight. Remove chicken and toss with flour. Sauté in oil or butter until light brown. Add garlic, pine nuts, parsley, ham, mushrooms, more salt and pepper if desired, chicken broth and wine. Simmer over low heat about 10 minutes or until the chicken is done. Serves 4.

Chicken Strudel

1	(2½-pound) fryer, cut into pieces
2	medium onions, divided
2	tablespoons olive oil
1	(10-ounce) bag fresh spinach
½	pound Muenster cheese, shredded
2	tablespoons dry white wine
¼	teaspoon salt
½	teaspoon paprika, plus additional for garnish
¼	teaspoon pepper
1	egg
1	(16-ounce) package phyllo (10 leaves)
½	cup butter, melted
⅔	cup dried bread crumbs

Bring chicken to a boil in 3-inches of water with 1 onion. Simmer 35 minutes. When done remove chicken, discard the liquid and onion, and refrigerate for 30 minutes. Chop the other onion in fine pieces. In large non-stick skillet sauté onions in olive oil; then add spinach. Cover and cook 2 to 3 minutes. The spinach should just be wilted. Remove from heat. Stir in cheese, wine, salt, paprika, pepper and egg. Cut chicken into bite-size pieces and add to spinach mixture. Mix well. Lay one sheet phyllo on wax paper. Brush with butter and sprinkle with 1 tablespoon bread crumbs, continuing to make 4 more layers. On short side, spoon ½ of chicken mixture. Roll in 2-inch wide strips. Place seam side down on cookie sheet. Make second roll same as the first. Brush with butter. Using serrated knife cut half way through rolls in 4 places. Sprinkle with paprika. Bake in preheated 375 oven for 15 to 20 minutes until golden brown. Cool 5 minutes. Slice all the way through slits for entrée size servings, or slice in ½-inch intervals for appetizers. Serves 8 as an entrée or makes 24 to 30 appetizers.

A whole broiler-fryer is 50% edible meat. A 3 pound chicken yields approximately 3 cups of edible meat.

Rolled Turkey Breast

1	(7-ounce) jar roasted red peppers	¼	teaspoon salt
3½	tablespoons butter, divided	¼	teaspoon pepper
1	onion, chopped	1	cup dried breadcrumbs
1	garlic clove, minced	1	tablespoon chopped fresh parsley
¾	teaspoon dried basil, crumbled	1	(4-pound) boneless turkey breast

Drain peppers and pat dry. Reserve. Heat 3 tablespoons butter in a frying pan over medium heat. Add onions and cook until soft, about 2 minutes. Add garlic and basil and cook 1 minute. Remove from heat and stir in salt, pepper, breadcrumbs and parsley. Lay turkey, skin side down, on a work surface. Lightly pound meat to an even thickness. Spread breadcrumb mixture over turkey. Cover with red peppers. Roll up breast, starting with long side. Tie in several places with string. Put in roasting pan and rub with remaining ½ tablespoon butter. Put in a preheated 425 degree oven and reduce temperature to 350 degrees. Roast turkey until meat thermometer registers 180 degrees, about 2 hours. Remove turkey from pan. Let stand 10 minutes. Skim fat from pan juices. Add water and bring to a boil over medium high heat, scraping up browned bits from bottom of pan. Season to taste with salt and pepper. Slice turkey and serve with pan juices. Serves 12.

Day-Ahead Turkey

1	turkey	Lettuce

One day before serving, roast turkey as usual. Cut and bone as desired. Spray a 13x9x2-inch dish with cooking spray. Add turkey. Cover with lettuce. Cover with a dampened dish towel. Cover again with foil. Refrigerate overnight. One hour before serving, unwrap and remove dish towel. Leave the lettuce on and recover with foil. Start in cold oven and bake at 325 degrees for 20 to 40 minutes.

This is very moist and keeps the commotion
out of the kitchen on Thanksgiving Day.

Crown Roast of Pork

Great for Holidays or a Special Occasion

1   teaspoon salt
½   teaspoon pepper
1   teaspoon dried thyme, crumbled
1   teaspoon dried savory, crumbled
1   teaspoon dried marjoram, crumbled

1   teaspoon dried rosemary, crumbled
¼   teaspoon garlic powder
½   cup flour, or just enough to cover all of meat
1   (7 to 8-pound) crown pork roast
Cooking spray

Mix seasonings together with flour and rub over pork roast. Place bone side down on broiler rack sprayed with cooking spray. Place in a preheated 500 degree oven for 30 minutes to sear. Reduce heat to 300 degrees and bake 30 minutes per pound or until 160 degrees on a meat thermometer (about 3 to 3½ hours). Let rest 10 minutes before serving. Top rib bones with purchased little paper booties. Serves 8 to 10.

Roasted Pork with Bacon and Apricots

Cooking spray
1   medium red onion, sliced
Salt and pepper
2   pounds pork tenderloin
1   (1-pound) package bacon

1   (18-ounce) jar apricot preserves
1   tablespoon Worcestershire sauce
1   garlic clove, crushed
1   teaspoon ground ginger

Spray baking pan with cooking spray. Spread sliced onions on bottom of pan. Salt and pepper pork tenderloin, then wrap with bacon and put on top of onions. Mix preserves, Worcestershire sauce, garlic and ginger. Pour over pork and bake in a preheated 350 degree oven, uncovered, for 2½ hours or until pork is tender. Cover if it starts to get too brown. Serves 6.

Cranberry Pork Tenderloins

Tenderloins:

2 pork tenderloins

Salt, pepper and garlic powder to taste

Cranberry Sauce:

1 (16-ounce) can whole cranberry sauce

¼ cup chopped yellow onions

¾ cup orange juice

1 tablespoon brown sugar

¼ teaspoon ground cinnamon

¼ teaspoon ground ginger

Tenderloins:

Rub tenderloins with salt, pepper and garlic powder. Place on a rack in a roasting pan and roast in a preheated 350 degree oven for 30 minutes. Baste with the cranberry sauce and repeat basting every 15 minutes for the next 30 to 60 minutes until the desired doneness is reached. When the meat is done slice and serve topped with the reserved sauce.

Cranberry Sauce:

Mix all ingredients in a 2-quart saucepan and bring to a boil. Divide the sauce in ½. Reduce heat and keep ½ warm for basting. Reserve the other ½ to serve with the meat.

Hint: To prepare ahead, undercook the meat slightly; slice the meat and place in a serving casserole covered with the sauce. Refrigerate or freeze. Reheat before serving. You will probably want to make another recipe of the sauce if you do this.

Fruit-Stuffed Loin of Pork

1	(4-pound) pork loin roast prepared for stuffing	8	tablespoons butter, softened
1	cup pitted prunes	1	tablespoon dried thyme, crumbled
1	cup dried apricots	1	cup Madeira
1	garlic clove	1	tablespoon molasses
Salt and pepper to taste		1	bunch watercress, optional

Using the handle of a wooden spoon; push the dried fruits into the pocket in the roast, alternating prunes and apricots. Cut garlic into thin slivers. Make deep slits in the roast with the tip of a knife and push garlic into slits. Tie roast with twine and rub with salt and pepper. Set roast in shallow baking pan and smear the butter over the roast. Sprinkle with thyme. Stir Madeira and molasses together in small bowl and pour over roast. Set pan on middle rack of a pre-heated 350 degree oven and bake for 1½ hours, basting frequently. When roast is done, remove it from oven and let stand, loosely covered with foil for 15 to 20 minutes. Cut into thin slices, arrange slices on serving platter and spoon juices over the meat. Garnish platter with watercress, if desired and serve immediately. Serves 10 to 12.

Grilled Pork Tenderloin with Texas Rub

Must Be Chilled

3	tablespoons brown sugar	½	teaspoon dried oregano, crumbled
2	teaspoons garlic powder	½	teaspoon salt
2	teaspoons chili powder	2	pounds pork tenderloin
½	teaspoon pepper		

Combine sugar, garlic powder, chili powder, pepper, oregano and salt. Coat pork evenly with rub. Refrigerate 30 minutes or up to 3 hours for stronger flavor. Lightly grease grill rack. Preheat a gas or charcoal grill to medium heat or use indirect heat method. Grill 30 to 35 minutes or until pork registers 160 degrees with meat thermometer, turning occasionally. Remove from grill, cover with aluminum foil. Let stand 5 minutes before cutting into thin slices. Serves 6.

Herbed Pork Pinwheels

3 small red or yellow bell peppers, chopped	¾ teaspoon paprika
¾ cup finely chopped onions	3 tablespoons vegetable oil
¾ cup finely chopped celery	3 pork tenderloins (about ¾ pound each)
1½ teaspoons dried thyme, crumbled	1½ tablespoons fennel seed, crushed
¾ teaspoon garlic salt	1½ tablespoons lemon pepper seasoning
¾ teaspoon cayenne pepper	

Sauté peppers, onions, celery, thyme, garlic salt, pepper and paprika in oil until tender; set aside. Slice each pork tenderloin lengthwise down center, cutting to, but not through bottom. Place each between sheets of heavy-duty plastic wrap; pound to a 12x8-inch rectangle of even thickness using a meat mallet. Spoon ⅓ of pepper mixture onto tenderloin, spreading to within ½-inch of sides; roll tenderloin, jelly roll fashion, starting with 8-inch side. Tie with heavy string at 1½-inch intervals. Repeat procedure with remaining tenderloins and pepper mixture. Combine fennel seeds and lemon pepper; rub onto top and sides of tenderloins. Place seam side down, on a lightly greased rack in a shallow pan. Bake uncovered in a preheated 325 degree oven for 45 minutes or until done. Let stand 10 minutes, remove strings and slice. Serves 10.

My husband thought this was "unbelievably wonderful".

Hot and Sweet Pork

1 pound lean pork, cut into bite-size pieces	2 tablespoons vegetable oil
1 (1.25-ounce) package taco seasoning mix	1 (16-ounce) jar salsa
	1 (6-ounce) jar peach preserves

Coat pork with taco mix. Brown in a skillet with the oil. Add salsa and peach preserves. Simmer for 30 minutes. Serve over rice. Serves 3.

Crowd Pleasin' Chalupas

Pork:

2 (1-pound) packages dried pinto beans	1 teaspoon dried oregano, crumbled
1 (2-pound) boneless pork roast	1 tablespoon picante sauce
2 tablespoons chili powder	2 garlic cloves, minced
1 tablespoon ground cumin	Salt and pepper
	Corn chips

Toppings:

Diced onions	Chopped avocados
Diced tomatoes	Chopped lettuce
Grated cheese	Picante sauce

Pork:

Wash and clean beans carefully. Put beans, roast, chili powder, cumin, oregano, picante sauce and garlic in a large roaster pan and cover with water. Add salt and pepper. Bake 10 to 12 hours in a preheated 275 degree oven. Stir every hour. Remove roast and shred meat with 2 forks. Combine with bean mixture. Serve over corn chips. Serves 12 generously.

Toppings:

Set out bowls of onions, tomatoes, cheese, avocados, lettuce and picante sauce and let everyone add their own toppings.

**We serve this to groups who have been
working on special projects at our church.**

Indoor/Outdoor Barbecue Spareribs

Can Be Made Ahead

Ribs:

4-5 pounds pork spareribs

1 large onion, peeled, halved

¼ cup soy sauce

2 teaspoons dried oregano, crumbled

1 teaspoon salt

½ teaspoon pepper

Sauce:

1 large yellow onion, finely chopped

1 large garlic clove, finely chopped

1 tablespoon olive oil

1 (14½-ounce) can Italian tomatoes and liquid

1 cup chili sauce

2 tablespoons brown sugar

5 tablespoons honey

⅓ cup soy sauce

¼ cup dry sherry

1 teaspoon liquid smoke

Dash cayenne pepper

1 tablespoon chili powder

Spareribs:

Cut the spareribs into 3-inch sections. Put in a large kettle and cover with cold water. Add onion halves, soy sauce, oregano, salt and pepper. Bring to a boil and simmer until tender, about 1 hour. Remove the ribs from the water. When ribs are cool enough to handle, cut into individual pieces. Ribs can be refrigerated for up to 2 days at this point.

Sauce:

In a large skillet sauté onions and garlic in olive oil until translucent. Add tomatoes and liquid, breaking the tomatoes into small pieces with a spoon as you stir the sauce. Add chili sauce, brown sugar, honey, soy sauce, sherry, liquid smoke, cayenne and chili powder. Simmer 30 minutes. Remove from heat and let stand. Taste sauce. You may want to add more honey. Reserve about 1 cup sauce to serve with cooked ribs. To finish outside, place ribs on a wire grid and smoke over indirect heat for 10 minutes. Baste with sauce. Turn and baste every 5 minutes until ribs are done. Sauce burns easily. To finish in oven, place ribs in a broiler proof pan. Brush with sauce and heat in a preheated 300 degree oven. Turn and baste every 7 to 8 minutes until ribs are done. If desired, you can broil

the ribs for a minute or two. If the ribs have been refrigerated, start in a cold 275 degree oven and bake 15 minutes. Turn, baste and follow baking directions. Serves 4.

Hint: Leftover sauce keeps about a month, refrigerated. Use in meat loaf or as a cocktail sauce for shrimp or oysters.

Family Style Barbecued Pork Chops

2	tablespoons vegetable oil	¼	teaspoon pepper
6-8	loin pork chops	¼	cup, plus 2 tablespoons packed brown sugar
1	medium onion, diced		
3	garlic cloves, minced	¼	cup water
1	(6-ounce) can tomato paste	3	tablespoons Worcestershire sauce
½	cup cider vinegar		
¼	teaspoon salt	1	teaspoon dry mustard
		1	teaspoon chili powder

Heat oil in skillet and brown chops. Place in 11x7x2-inch baking dish. Sauté onions and garlic in skillet. Stir in tomato paste, cider vinegar, salt, pepper, brown sugar, water, Worcestershire sauce, mustard and chili powder. Simmer 5 minutes. Pour sauce over chops. Turn chops to coat. Cover. Bake in a preheated 350 degree oven for 45 to 60 minutes. Serves 6 to 8.

Lamb Shanks Provençal

Must Be Made Ahead

Lamb Shanks:

4	lamb shanks	Olive oil
1	carrot, chopped	Chicken stock
2	celery ribs, chopped	Salt to taste
1	onion, peeled and chopped	

Tomato Sauce:

1	tablespoon olive oil	4	tomatoes, chopped
½	cup diced onion	2	tablespoons fresh basil, julienned
2	garlic cloves, chopped		Salt to taste

Garlic Butter Sauce:

3	tablespoons butter	1	tablespoon chopped parsley
2	garlic cloves, chopped		

Lamb Shanks:

Place lamb shanks in roasting pan with carrots, celery and onions. Sprinkle lightly with olive oil and roast in a preheated 350 degree oven uncovered for 1 hour. Remove from oven and add enough chicken stock to cover the lamb shanks. Cover and roast 1 hour more. Salt to taste.

Tomato Sauce:

While the lamb is cooking put 1 tablespoon olive oil in a saucepan and sauté onions until wilted. Add chopped garlic and stir quickly. Add tomatoes, fresh basil and salt to taste. Bring to a boil, remove from heat and keep warm.

Garlic Butter Sauce:

When ready to serve, make garlic butter sauce by sautéing butter, garlic and parsley until butter starts to foam. Divide tomato sauce among the 4 plates; place lamb shank on each and pour garlic butter over the shanks. Serves 4.

Hint: The chicken stock in which the shanks were cooked may be strained and used as a wonderful rich bouillon.

An easy dish, prepared ahead of time that makes an elegant presentation.

Leg of Lamb Swedish Style

Lamb:

1 (5 to 5½ pound) leg of lamb
Garlic cloves, sliced, optional
1 tablespoon salt

1 teaspoon dry mustard
Onion, optional

Basting Mixture:

1 cup strong coffee
2 teaspoons sugar
2 teaspoons light cream, divided

¼ cup brandy
½ cup water

Sauce:

2 tablespoons flour
¼ cup light cream

2 tablespoons currant jelly

Lamb:

Wipe lamb with a damp cloth. If you wish, make small slits in the lamb with a sharp knife and insert slices of garlic. Rub lamb with salt and mustard. (If you don't use garlic, cover the lamb with slices of onion.) Place in an open roasting pan and roast in a preheated 350 degree oven for 75 minutes. Remove from oven. Serves 8 to 10.

Basting Mixture:

Combine all ingredients. Remove lamb from oven and baste all over. Roast an additional 75 to 90 minutes.

Sauce:

Remove lamb to a heated platter. Skim fat from roasting pan. Stir flour, cream and currant jelly into pan. Cook stirring constantly, until bubbly.

Lamb Stew

¾	pound Italian sausage	2	whole bay leaves
3	large onions, diced	½	bunch fresh parsley or
2	garlic cloves, diced		½ teaspoon dried, crumbled
2	pounds cubed leg of lamb	3	tomatoes, diced
1	large eggplant, peeled and cut in large cubes		Salt and pepper to taste
		2	cups red wine

Brown Italian sausage in a skillet. Remove sausage and drain. Reserve 2 table-spoons of sausage drippings. Sauté onions and garlic in sausage drippings. Add cubed lamb and brown. Place sausage, onions, garlic, lamb, eggplant, bay leaves, parsley, tomatoes, salt, pepper and wine in a large casserole. Bake in a preheated 300 degree oven for 2 hours. Remove bay leaves. Serves 6 to 8.

Veal with White Wine

1	large garlic clove, chopped	¼	cup white wine
¼	cup olive oil	¼	cup water
¼	cup flour	¼	teaspoon dried parsley, crumbled
½	teaspoon salt	⅛	teaspoon salt
⅛	teaspoon pepper	⅛	teaspoon pepper
1½	pounds veal, cut into 6 pieces		

Sauté garlic in olive oil until browned. Mix flour, salt and pepper. Coat veal with flour mixture and put in skillet. Add white wine, water, parsley, salt and pepper. Cover and simmer 20 minutes. Serves 4 to 6.

Veal Delicious

1 pound veal cutlets, cut in 1-inch pieces	¼ cup olive oil
½ cup flour	1⅓ cups crushed tomatoes
1 teaspoon salt, divided	¼ teaspoon dried parsley, crumbled
¼ teaspoon pepper, divided	¼ teaspoon dried oregano, crumbled
1 large garlic clove, sliced thinly	

Coat veal with flour mixed with ½ teaspoon salt and ⅛ teaspoon pepper. In heavy skillet sauté garlic in olive oil until browned. Add veal to garlic and brown both sides. Mix tomatoes, the remaining ½ teaspoon salt, parsley, oregano and the remaining ⅛ teaspoon pepper. Pour over veal and simmer for 25 minutes. Serves 3 to 4.

Hint: You can use canned tomatoes with roasted garlic in this recipe if you omit the garlic.

Boerne Wiener Schnitzel

2-3 pounds veal cutlets or thinly sliced bottom round beef	1 teaspoon dried basil, crumbled
8 slices bread, crumbled	2 eggs
1 teaspoon paprika	Salt and pepper to taste
	Vegetable shortening

Slice through the edge of the meat to keep it from curling. Mix bread crumbs with paprika and basil in a medium bowl. Set aside. Beat eggs in a shallow bowl. Add salt and pepper. Dip meat in egg mixture and then in crumb mixture, patting in the crumbs until all the meat is covered. Fry in about 1-inch of hot shortening until golden brown on both sides. Serve 4 to 6.

Pheasant Normandy

2 (2½-3 pound) pheasants	¼ cup fresh lemon juice
¼ cup butter	2 teaspoons salt
2 cups peeled, coarsely chopped tart apples	½ teaspoon pepper
	1 tablespoon cornstarch
½ cup Calvados	1 tablespoon cold water
2 cups heavy cream	

Tuck pheasant wings under the body and tie legs together. Sauté the birds in butter in a heavy skillet until lightly browned on all sides. Remove and keep warm. Sauté apple pieces briefly in the remaining butter. Remove and spread apples in the bottom of a 13x9x2-inch baking dish. Place the pheasants on top. Drain fat from the skillet. Add Calvados and scrape the bottom of skillet to deglaze it. Pour over the birds. Cover the baking dish with aluminum foil and bake in a preheated 375 degree oven for 45 minutes. Add the cream, lemon juice, salt and pepper and bake uncovered for another 30 minutes or until juices are clear, not pink and drumsticks move easily. (Pheasants are never as tender as chicken.) Put the pheasants on a serving dish and keep warm. Combine cornstarch with the water and stir the paste into liquid in the baking dish. Pour liquid into a medium saucepan and cook over medium heat, stirring constantly for a minute or two until the sauce thickens to a gravy like consistency. Pour sauce over the pheasants and serve. Serves 4.

Variation: Use chicken instead of pheasants. Cooking time is about the same.

Calvados is apple brandy from Normandy.

Leg of Venison with Potato Dumplings

Must Be Made Ahead

Potato Dumplings:

2 pounds potatoes, unpeeled, cooked the day before	Salt to taste
2 cups flour	Nutmeg to taste
2 eggs	¾ cup croutons

Venison:

½ cup vinegar	3 pounds leg of venison
1 cup water	4 tablespoons vegetable oil
4 whole cloves	1 tablespoon flour
1 bay leaf	1 tablespoon lemon juice
1 onion, quartered	½ cup sour cream
Salt and pepper to taste	½ cup red wine

Potato Dumplings:

Peel and mash potatoes in a large bowl. Add flour, eggs, salt and nutmeg. Knead to a firm dough. Shape dumplings, poke a hole in each and put in several croutons. Close over the holes. Drop into boiling water in a large pot and cook for 10 to 15 minutes. Try one test dumpling in the boiling water; if it falls apart, add more flour into the dough. Serves 4.

Venison:

Cook together the vinegar, water, cloves, bay leaf, onions, salt and pepper for 5 minutes in a small saucepan. Place the meat in a 13x9x2-inch baking dish. Pour mixture over the meat. Cover, refrigerate and marinate for 3 to 4 days, turning once a day. Pat the meat dry and brown in hot oil in a large heavy pot. Add 1 cup of marinade. Cover and simmer for 1½ hours over medium heat. Remove meat to a hot platter and keep warm. To liquid, add flour, lemon juice, sour cream and wine to make a smooth gravy.

Sweet and Sour Rabbit

½ cup flour	½ teaspoon salt
Salt and pepper to taste	1 cup pineapple pieces
1 (2½-pound) rabbit cut into serving pieces	1 medium green bell pepper, cut into thin half-slices
½ teaspoon pepper	1½ tablespoons cornstarch
2 tablespoons vegetable oil	¼ cup sugar
1 cup pineapple juice	½ cup water
¼ cup vinegar	

Combine flour, salt and pepper to taste and dredge rabbit in mixture. Heat oil in a large heavy pan and brown rabbit on all sides. Add pineapple juice, vinegar and salt. Cover pan and cook over low heat 40 minutes or until meat is tender. Add pineapple and green peppers and cook a few minutes longer until green pepper is tender. Mix cornstarch and sugar; stir in water. Stir this mixture gradually into liquid in the pan and cook slowly about 5 minutes. Serve warm.

Aegean Clam Spaghetti

Cooking spray	2 (6½-ounce) cans minced clams, broth reserved
1 teaspoon margarine	
1 large garlic clove, minced	2 tablespoons cornstarch
1 medium zucchini, sliced in ½-inch slices	2 teaspoons Greek seasoning
	1 (8-ounce) package spaghetti, cooked, drained
1 large tomato, diced	
¼ teaspoon dried oregano, crushed	½ cup freshly grated Parmesan cheese

Spray a large non-stick skillet with butter-flavored spray. Melt margarine and add garlic and zucchini and sauté about 2 minutes. Add tomato and oregano and cook 2 minutes longer. Add enough water to reserved clam broth to equal 1¾ cups and add to vegetable mixture. Stir in cornstarch, Greek seasoning and clams. Bring to boil and cook 1 minute. Toss with spaghetti and sprinkle with cheese. Serves 4.

Clam Linguine
with Bacon, Chiles and Garlic

2   jalapeños, halved and seeded

Salt and pepper to taste

¼   cup olive oil, divided

1   pound linguine

3   ounces bacon, diced
    (about ½ cup)

2   teaspoons minced garlic

¼   teaspoon crushed red pepper

2   pounds clams in the shell,
    scrubbed and rinsed
    (Littlenecks are fine.)

¼   cup dry white wine

4   tablespoons unsalted butter

¾   cup coarsely chopped fresh
    parsley, divided

1   tablespoon lemon juice

2   teaspoons grated lemon zest

¼   cup freshly grated Parmesan
    cheese

1   lemon, cut in 4 wedges

Brush jalapeño halves with olive oil and season with salt and pepper. Place on foil on baking sheet and roast in a preheated 400 degree oven for 10 minutes. When cool, dice finely. Cook linguine according to package directions. Meanwhile, in a large skillet heat the remaining olive oil and sauté the bacon until just browned. Add the jalapeños, garlic and red pepper and cook another minute. Turn the heat to high. Add the clams and wine and cover. Cook until the clams open, about 3 to 5 minutes. Remove and throw out any clams that have not opened! Add the butter, ¼ cup parsley, lemon juice and zest. Toss until the butter melts. Drain the pasta and toss with ingredients in the skillet. Add the rest of the parsley. Top each serving with cheese and serve with a lemon wedge.

Gulf Coast Crab Cakes

Must Be Chilled

½ cup finely chopped onions

½ cup finely chopped celery

6 tablespoons unsalted butter, divided

1 pound lump crabmeat

⅓ cup fine dry breadcrumbs

½ cup mayonnaise

½ teaspoon Old Bay seasoning

½ teaspoon Worcestershire sauce

Tabasco sauce to taste

2 tablespoons minced fresh flat-leafed parsley

Salt and pepper to taste

Lemon wedges, optional

In a skillet cook onions and celery in 4 tablespoons butter over moderately low heat, stirring until tender and then transfer to a bowl. Pick over crab carefully to remove all bits of shell and cartilage. Stir in crab and breadcrumbs. In a small bowl whisk together mayonnaise, Old Bay seasoning, Worcestershire sauce, Tabasco sauce, parsley, salt and pepper to taste and stir in crab mixture until combined well. Line a baking sheet with wax paper. Form crab mixture into 6 flattened rounds about 3-inches wide and ¾-inch thick and transfer to baking sheet. Cover crab cakes with plastic wrap and chill at least 1 hour and up to 4 hours. In a heavy skillet heat 1 tablespoon butter over moderate heat until foam subsides and cook half of crab cakes until golden brown, about 2 to 3 minutes on each side. Cook remaining crab cakes in the remaining tablespoon of butter. Serve with lemon wedges if desired. Serves 3 as a main course or 6 as appetizers.

Baytown Pan Fried Oysters

1   pint fresh or frozen oysters,
    drained
½   sleeve of saltine crackers, finely
    crushed

Regular or butter flavored vegetable
    shortening

Place oysters on crumbs and with a fork smash the oysters until they are flat and coated with crumbs. In a skillet melt shortening to a depth of ¼-inch. Fry oysters until brown, about 1 to 2 minutes on each side. If frying in batches, keep warm in a preheated 250 degree oven. Serve with potato salad, coleslaw and your choice of ketchup, cocktail sauce or horseradish sauce. Serves 2.

Halibut Provençal

2   (7-ounce) fresh halibut steaks
Cooking spray
½   cup diced tomatoes
½   cup fresh breadcrumbs
1   garlic clove, minced

2   large fresh basil leaves, minced
1   tablespoon olive oil
½   teaspoon salt
½   teaspoon pepper
½   cup fresh grated Parmesan cheese

Rinse halibut and drain on paper towels. Spray an 8x8x2-inch baking pan with cooking spray. Place halibut in baking dish and top with tomatoes. In a small pan, sauté breadcrumbs, garlic and basil in olive oil about 3 minutes. Add salt and pepper to taste. Sprinkle crumb mixture over tomatoes. Top with cheese. Bake in a preheated 425 degree oven for 10 to 12 minutes until fish flakes. Serves 2.

Caddo Lake Catfish
with Parsley-Pecan Sauce

Parsley-Pecan Sauce:

2   cups packed fresh parsley, using only leaves and tender stems

½   cup olive oil

½   cup broken pecan meats or pine nuts

1   large garlic clove, minced

½   cup grated Parmesan cheese

½   cup grated Romano cheese

2   tablespoons unsalted butter

Salt to taste

Catfish:

6   catfish fillets, 5-6 ounces each

2   cups flour

1   tablespoon cayenne pepper

1   tablespoon, plus 1 teaspoon salt

2   or more tablespoons vegetable oil

2   or more tablespoons unsalted butter

2   cups Parsley-Pecan Sauce

Parsley-Pecan Sauce:

Place all ingredients in food processor and scrape down the sides until mixture is a smooth paste. This may be made ahead and frozen or used at once.

Catfish:

Dredge fillets in a mixture of flour, cayenne and salt. Heat oil and butter. Sauté one side of fillet for 4 minutes on low heat. Turn and spread sauce on cooked side. Cover pan with lid and cook slowly until fish flakes, approximately five minutes. Serves 6.

Vera Cruz Flounder

8	ounces flounder fillets, dredged in flour	½	small onion, sliced
3	tablespoons butter	1	teaspoon ground coriander
2	tablespoons garlic butter	4	tomato wedges
1	poblano pepper, sliced	1	teaspoon dried parsley, crumbled

In a skillet, sauté flounder in butter until golden brown. In another skillet, melt garlic butter. Add pepper and onion slices and cook until soft. Add coriander, tomato and parsley stirring until heated. Pour over flounder fillets and serve.

Sole au Gratin

2	pounds sole fillets	¼	cup grated Parmesan cheese, divided
4	tablespoons butter		
½	pound fresh mushrooms, sliced	2	(14-ounce) cans artichoke hearts, drained
3	tablespoons flour		
2	cups milk or half-and-half	1	cup grated Swiss cheese
Salt and pepper to taste		Paprika	

Bake sole in a preheated 350 degree oven on a cookie sheet for 20 minutes or until fish flakes. Drain on a paper towel. Melt butter; add mushrooms and sauté 5 minutes. Remove mushrooms and add flour, cooking until bubbly. Add milk and cook until thick, stirring constantly. Season with salt and pepper. Add mushrooms. Spread bottom of a buttered 2-quart casserole with ½ the grated Parmesan cheese. Add sole, artichokes and Swiss cheese in layers. Cover with mushroom mixture. Sprinkle with the remaining Parmesan cheese mixed with a little paprika. Bake in a preheated 350 degree oven for 30 minutes until hot and bubbling. Serves 6.

Rainbow Trout Piccata

2	tablespoons butter, divided	4	tablespoons chopped parsley
1	tablespoon olive oil	2	tablespoons capers
4	(4-ounce) trout fillets	2	teaspoons grated lemon zest
½	cup lemon juice		

Melt 1 tablespoon butter and olive oil in skillet; add trout, flesh side down, and cook until golden, about 2 minutes. Turn fish and cook 2 minutes longer. Remove fish from skillet. Keep fish hot. In same skillet over low heat, melt the remaining tablespoon of butter and add lemon juice, parsley, capers and lemon zest, stirring constantly while deglazing pan. Pour sauce over hot cooked trout. Serves 2 to 4.

Sautéed Salmon
with Sour Cream Sauce

Salmon:

2	salmon steaks or fillets	2	tablespoons fresh lemon thyme
2	tablespoons olive oil	2	tablespoons fresh tarragon
¾	cup white wine	2	tablespoons fresh dill
2	tablespoons fresh onion chives		

Sour Cream Sauce:

½	cup sour cream	2	tablespoons lemon juice
1	tablespoon fresh dill		

Salmon:

In a large skillet, sauté salmon in oil until lightly browned on each side. Add wine, chives, lemon thyme, tarragon and dill. Cook about 7 to 10 minutes on each side. Serve with sour cream dressing. Serves 2.

Sour Cream Sauce:

Combine sour cream, dill and lemon juice in a small bowl.

Garlic Broiled Shrimp

Must Be Made Ahead

2	pounds medium shrimp	1	cup olive oil
4	tablespoons finely minced parsley		Salt to taste
4	garlic cloves, minced		Freshly ground pepper

Peel and wash shrimp and place in a 2-quart casserole. Mix the parsley, garlic and olive oil in a blender. Pour mixture over the shrimp and marinate overnight. When ready to cook shrimp, remove them from the marinade with a slotted spoon leaving some of the marinade on the shrimp. Place them in a shallow pan. Salt lightly and broil 3 minutes on each side, being careful not to overcook. Sprinkle with freshly ground black pepper. Serves 8.

Padre Island Shrimp Creole

⅓	cup vegetable shortening	¼	cup chopped green bell pepper
¼	cup flour	1½	teaspoons salt
1	cup hot water	2	whole bay leaves
1	pound raw shrimp, peeled and deveined	½	teaspoon dried thyme, crumbled
			Dash cayenne pepper
½	cup chopped green onions with tops	1	(8-ounce) can tomato sauce
4	garlic cloves, finely chopped	1	lemon slice
½	cup chopped fresh parsley	2	cups cooked rice

Melt shortening; blend in flour and brown very slowly until it is dark brown, stirring constantly. Add water gradually and cook until thick, stirring constantly. Add shrimp, onions, garlic, parsley, green peppers, salt, bay leaves, thyme, cayenne, tomato sauce and lemon slice. Cover and simmer 20 minutes. Remove bay leaves. Serve over rice.

Bachelor's Shrimp

2   pounds shrimp, peeled
8   tablespoons butter or margarine, melted
1   teaspoon pepper

½   teaspoon salt
¼   teaspoon cayenne pepper
½   teaspoon paprika

Place shrimp in a shallow pan in a single layer. Add pepper, salt, cayenne and paprika to the melted butter or margarine, mix well, and pour over the shrimp. Bake in a preheated 400 degree oven for 6 minutes; remove from oven and heat broiler. Place the pan 4 inches from the heat and broil for about 3 minutes or until hot and slightly browned. Serves 4.

Shrimp and Chicken in a Nest

8   tablespoons butter
1   tablespoon minced shallots
1½ pounds raw shrimp, cooked, cut into large pieces (about 2 cups)
¼   cup sherry
4   tablespoons flour
3   cups half-and-half

4   boneless, skinless cooked chicken breasts, cut into large pieces (about 4 cups)
2   cups artichoke hearts
Salt and pepper to taste
Patty shells
Shredded Gruyère cheese

Melt butter; add shallots and sauté 1 minute. Add shrimp and sauté 2 minutes, stirring with a fork. Add sherry, cover and cook until liquid is reduced. Add flour and cook until bubbly. Add half-and-half and cook until thickened. Mix in chicken and artichoke hearts and heat thoroughly. Add salt and pepper. Serve in patty shells lined with cheese. Serves 8.

Seafood Strudel

Must Be Made Ahead

Béchamel Sauce:

3 tablespoons butter
3 tablespoons flour
1½ cups milk

1 small onion studded with 3 or 4 whole cloves
½ small bay leaf

Filling:

3 cups cooked seafood (shrimp or crab or lobster chunks)
1½ cups Béchamel Sauce

6 green onions with tops, minced
6 tablespoons fresh minced parsley

Strudel:

½ box phyllo dough
8 tablespoons butter, melted

Béchamel Sauce:

Melt the butter over low heat, add the flour and stir for 3 to 5 minutes. Slowly add in milk and then the onion and bay leaf. Cook and stir until thickened and smooth. Remove the onion and the bay leaf. Serve unused sauce on the side.

Filling:

Mix seafood, béchamel, onions and parsley together and chill.

Strudel:

To assemble put phyllo dough on large sheet of aluminum foil. Fold dough in half like a book. With pastry brush, paint every other leaf with melted butter. Open in the middle so that all sheets lay flat, one on top of the other. Put filling evenly in a pile along lower long end of the dough. Using foil to help, roll up like a jelly roll. Place seam-side down on a cookie sheet, cover well with foil and refrigerate for 24 hours. When ready to bake, make diagonal slits through part of the strudel at half-inch intervals with a serrated knife. Brush with melted butter and bake uncovered in a preheated 400 degree oven for approximately 30 minutes or until brown and heated through. Serve immediately. Serves 4.

Entrées II (One Dish Meals)

Texans descend on the Hill Country in large numbers annually to see their favorite wildflower, the bluebonnet. It arrives in early spring, spreading over the rolling hills, rocky terrain and highway shoulders in a wonderful display of deep blue for the love of all to see. Many artists immortalize these wonderful landscapes.

Photograph provided by the Wildseed Farms

Texas Hill
Country

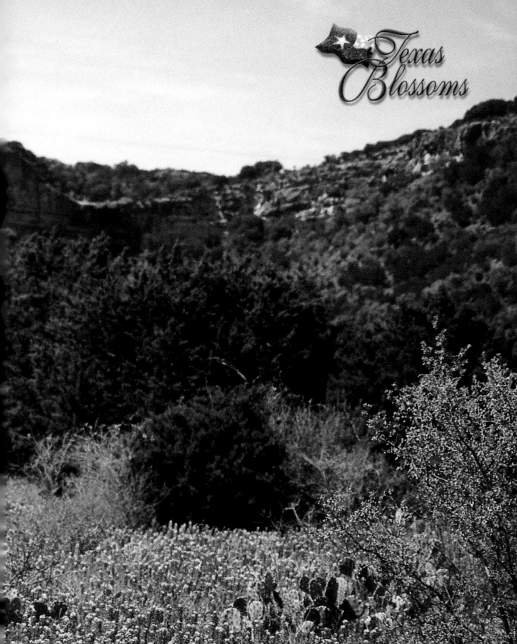

A Texas Blossoms Menu for a

Super Bowl Party

Gazpacho Dip

Frozen Margarita Punch

Super Bowl Chili

State Fair Jalapeño Cornbread

The Best Chocolate Cake in Texas

Orange Pralines

Mazetti

1 (12 to 16-ounce) bag medium or wide noodles	1 (10-ounce) can tomatoes and green chiles, drained
1½ pounds ground beef	1 (4-ounce) can mushroom pieces and stems
1 onion, chopped	5-6 dashes Tabasco sauce, optional
1 green bell pepper, chopped	1 pound Monterey Jack cheese, grated
1 (10¾-ounce) can cream of mushroom soup, undiluted	
1 (10¾-ounce) can tomato soup, undiluted	

Cook noodles according to package directions. Brown beef and drain well. Sauté onions and peppers until tender. Mix meat, onions, bell peppers, soups, tomatoes and green chiles, mushrooms and Tabasco sauce with the noodles and spoon into a 3-quart casserole. Top with the cheese and bake in a preheated 350 degree oven for 30 minutes. Serves 12.

Hint: I usually put this into 2 (9x9x2-inch) baking dishes and freeze one of them uncooked. To cook frozen casserole, thaw in the refrigerator overnight and follow the baking instructions. You might have to increase the baking time 10 to 15 minutes.

Sour Cream Enchilada Casserole

1 cup water	1 tablespoon chili powder
2 tablespoons, plus ¼ cup picante sauce, divided	1 teaspoon garlic powder
	¾ cup ripe olives, sliced
12 corn tortillas, divided	8 tablespoons butter or margarine
2 pounds ground beef	2 tablespoons flour
1 onion, chopped	1½ cups milk
1 teaspoon salt	1 (16-ounce) container sour cream
⅛ teaspoon pepper	2 cups (about 8-ounces) shredded Cheddar cheese
2 teaspoons ground cumin	

Combine water and 2 tablespoons picante sauce in large shallow dish. Place tortillas in picante sauce mixture; let stand 5 minutes. Drain. Cook ground beef and onions in a heavy skillet until brown; drain. Stir in salt, pepper, cumin, chili powder, garlic powder, olives and remaining ¼ cup picante sauce; simmer meat mixture 5 minutes. Melt butter in heavy saucepan over low heat; add flour, stirring until smooth. Cook 1 minute, stirring constantly. Gradually stir in milk; cook over medium heat, stirring constantly, until thickened and bubbly. Remove from heat and add sour cream; stir until well blended. Place ½ of tortillas in 13x9x2-inch baking dish. Pour ½ of sour cream sauce over tortillas; spoon ½ of meat mixture evenly over sauce. Sprinkle ½ of cheese over meat mixture. Repeat layers with remaining ingredients. Bake in a preheated 375 degree oven for 25 minutes. Serves 8 to 10.

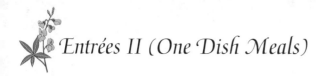

South of the Border Casserole

12 corn or flour tortillas, divided

1½ pounds ground beef

1   medium onion, chopped

1   tablespoon chili powder

Salt and pepper to taste

1   (15-ounce) can Ranch Style
    beans and liquid

1   pound Velveeta or Hot Mexican
    Velveeta cheese, sliced

1   (10¾-ounce) can cream of
    chicken soup, undiluted

1   (10-ounce) can tomatoes and
    green chiles

Line the bottom of a greased 13x9x2-inch baking dish with 6 tortillas torn to fit. Brown the ground beef with the onions, chili powder, salt and pepper. Drain the meat and spread over the tortillas. Next layer the beans and the sliced cheese. Cover with the remaining tortillas. Combine soup with tomatoes and chiles and pour over the casserole. Cover with foil and bake in a preheated 350 degree oven approximately 1 hour. Serves 8 to 10.

Rising Star Texas Casserole

1¼ pounds extra lean ground beef

2   teaspoons salt

2   teaspoons sugar

2   (14½-ounce) cans tomatoes and
    liquid

1   (8-ounce) can tomato sauce

2   garlic cloves, minced

Pepper to taste

1   (8-ounce) package noodles,
    cooked and drained

1   cup sour cream

1   (3-ounce) package cream
    cheese, softened

6   green onions and tops, chopped

1   cup grated sharp Cheddar cheese

Cook and drain beef. Add salt, sugar, tomatoes and liquid, tomato sauce, garlic and pepper in skillet and cook over low heat for 5 to 10 minutes. Combine noodles with sour cream, cream cheese and onions. In a greased 3-quart casserole, arrange meat and noodle mixture in alternate layers. Top with grated cheese. Bake in a preheated 350 degree oven for at least 30 minutes. Serves 8 to 10.

Kids Love It Casserole

1½ pounds ground beef	1 (28-ounce) jar traditional Prego pasta sauce
1 medium onion, chopped	
1 garlic clove, minced	Salt and pepper to taste
1 tablespoon, plus ¼ cup vegetable oil, divided	7 ounces macaroni or rotini
	8 ounces sharp Cheddar cheese, shredded, divided
1 (10-ounce) package frozen chopped spinach	
	½ cup breadcrumbs
Water as needed	2 eggs, well beaten

Brown beef, onions and garlic in 1 tablespoon oil. Cook spinach according to package directions. Drain, reserving liquid. Add enough water to the spinach liquid to make 1 cup liquid. Combine liquid with pasta sauce, salt and pepper. Stir into meat mixture and simmer 10 minutes. Cook macaroni according to package directions. Combine spinach with pasta, ¾ of the cheese, breadcrumbs, eggs and the remaining ¼ cup of oil. Spread in 13x9x2-inch baking dish. Top with meat sauce. Bake in a preheated 350 degree oven for 30 minutes. Sprinkle the remaining cheese on top for the last few minutes. Let stand 10 minutes before serving. If you like you may cover with foil for 25 minutes, uncover and sprinkle more cheese on top for the last 5 minutes. Serves 8 to 10.

Bluebonnet Tours are available in early April in the Texas Hill Country cities of Burnet, Llano, Buchanan Dam, Lampasas, Marble Falls and Kingland.

Dump Stew

1 pound ground beef	1 (14½-ounce) can sliced carrots and liquid
1 (10¾-ounce) can tomato soup, undiluted	1 (14½-ounce) can cut green beans and liquid
1 (14½-ounce) can stewed tomatoes and liquid	1 (15¼-ounce) can whole kernel corn and liquid
1 (14½-ounce) can sliced new potatoes and liquid	1 (14½-ounce) can sliced zucchini and liquid

Divide ground beef into four patties; brown and cook in a large stew pot. Pour off any grease and break patties into bite-size pieces. Add remaining ingredients and heat thoroughly. Stew may also be served over rice or noodles. Serves 8 to 10. Leftovers freeze very well.

Variation: Add cooked chicken instead of ground beef.

Bronco Riders Chili

Must Be Made Ahead

1 pound lean coarsely ground beef	½ teaspoon dried oregano, crumbled
1 teaspoon oil	¼-½ teaspoon cayenne pepper
2 cups water	1 teaspoon sugar
1 small bay leaf	½ tablespoon paprika
3 tablespoons chili powder	1 tablespoon flour
2 teaspoons salt	2 tablespoons cornmeal
1 garlic clove, minced	
¾ teaspoon ground cumin	

Sear beef in hot oil until the meat is gray, but is not browned. Add water, bay leaf, chili powder, salt, garlic, cumin, oregano, cayenne, sugar and paprika. Simmer, covered at least 30 minutes. Refrigerate overnight. Remove fat from the top and reheat. Make a paste of the flour, cornmeal and a little water. Add to reheated chili and stir until smooth. Cook at least 7 minutes. Remove bay leaf. Serves 2 as an entrée.

Beef

Mrs. Lyndon B. Johnson's Pedernales River Chili

4 pounds chili-ground beef chuck or round steak	1 teaspoon ground cumin
1 large onion, chopped	Salt to taste
2 garlic cloves, minced	2-6 dashes Tabasco sauce
1 teaspoon dried oregano	2 cups hot water
2 tablespoons chili powder	1½ cups canned whole tomatoes with juice

Place the meat, onion and garlic in a large, heavy frying pan or Dutch oven. Cook over medium heat until the meat is lightly browned. Add the oregano, chili powder, cumin, salt and Tabasco sauce. Pour in the water and tomatoes and bring to a boil. Reduce the heat to a simmer and cook for 1 hour. Skim off the fat during cooking.

Texican Stew

May Be Made Ahead

1 pound lean ground beef	½ (17-ounce) can whole kernel corn, drained
1 teaspoon seasoned salt	1 (15-ounce) can pinto beans, drained and rinsed
1 garlic clove, finely minced	½ teaspoon ground cumin
1 medium yellow onion, finely chopped	1 cup water
1 (14½-ounce) can diced tomatoes and liquid	2 teaspoons instant beef bouillon, optional
½ cup medium picante sauce	Chopped fresh cilantro, optional

In a non-stick skillet brown beef, seasoned salt, garlic and onions. Add tomatoes and liquid, picante sauce, corn, pinto beans, cumin and water. Cover and simmer 20 minutes. If you want soup, add 2 additional cups water and the optional bouillon. Just as good or better the next day. Serves 4.

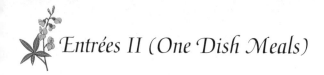

Brazos Valley Chili

1	tablespoon vegetable oil	2½ cups water	
1	medium onion, chopped	1	tablespoon chili powder
2	garlic cloves, minced	1	teaspoon rubbed sage
1	pound ground beef, crumbled	1	teaspoon dried oregano, crumbled
1	(14½-ounce) can peeled tomatoes and liquid		
1	(8-ounce) can tomato sauce	1	teaspoon ground cumin
2	(15-ounce) cans kidney beans, drained	1	teaspoon dill seed
		1	teaspoon pepper
1	jalapeño, chopped	Dash salt	
		Chopped onions for garnish	

Heat oil in a large skillet or Dutch oven. Add onions and garlic and cook until onions are soft. Add beef and cook until brown. Drain off excess drippings. Stir in tomatoes and liquid, tomato sauce, kidney beans, jalapeños, water, chili powder, sage, oregano, cumin, dill, pepper and salt and bring to a boil, stirring constantly. Lower heat and let simmer for at least an hour. Top with a heap of raw chopped onions. Serves 4 to 6.

The *"Pepper Festival"* is held on the last weekend of October in Palestine. To celebrate the very hot jalapeño pepper, travel to Laredo in the middle of February for the *"Jalapeño Festival."*

Super Bowl Chili
Best Made Ahead

2 pounds lean ground beef
1 large onion, chopped
2 garlic cloves, pressed
1 (28-ounce) can whole tomatoes, drained and liquid reserved
3 (8-ounce) cans tomato sauce
2 (15-ounce) cans pinto beans and liquid

1 (4½-ounce) can chopped green chiles and liquid
1½ teaspoons salt
2 tablespoons chili powder
½ teaspoon cayenne pepper
1 teaspoon dried oregano, crumbled

Brown beef, onions and garlic in 6-quart stock pot or Dutch oven; drain. Add tomatoes, tomato sauce, pinto beans, green chiles, salt, chili powder, cayenne and oregano. Add enough water to the liquid from the tomatoes to fill ½ the tomato can and add to the chili. Simmer approximately 2 hours. Serves 15 to 16.

Variation: For spicier chili add 1 (10-ounce) can tomatoes and green chiles in place of 1 (8-ounce) can tomato sauce.

Wildflower Tours are held in March and April in the Texas Brazos-Republic Trail cities of Brenham, Chappell Hill and Round Top. Texas is home to 5,000 species of wildflowers.

A Texas Blossoms Menu for a

Fiesta

Black Bean Salsa
South of the Border Casserole
Fiesta Time Tossed Salad
Sopaipillas
Mexican Wedding Cake
Sangría Blanco

Chicken Almond Casserole

4   cups chopped cooked chicken
2   cups finely chopped celery
¼   cup finely chopped onions
2   hard-cooked eggs, chopped
½   cup slivered almonds, toasted
2   (10¾-ounce) cans cream of
     chicken soup, undiluted

½-1 cup mayonnaise
½   cup chicken broth
¼   cup lemon juice
½   teaspoon salt
¼   teaspoon pepper
1   cup crushed round buttery
     crackers or 1½ cups crushed
     potato chips

Combine chicken, celery, onions, eggs, almonds, soup, mayonnaise, chicken broth, lemon juice, salt and pepper. Spoon into a 13x9x2-inch lightly greased baking dish. Sprinkle with cracker crumbs or potato chips. Bake in a preheated 350 degree oven for 40 minutes. Serves 8 to 10.

Hint: When you're in a hurry buy a roasted chicken at the deli or buy the refrigerated roasted chicken.

Chicken Tetrazzini

May Be Made Ahead

8 boneless, skinless chicken breast halves

1 pound spaghetti

1 tablespoon salt

4 celery ribs, chopped

1 pound mushrooms, sliced

1 large green bell pepper, chopped

1 large red bell pepper, chopped

1 large onion, chopped

3 tablespoons butter

1 (10¾-ounce) can cream of chicken soup, undiluted

1 (14½-ounce) can chicken broth

1 (4-ounce) jar pimientos

1 (14½-ounce) can stewed tomatoes

1 (10-ounce) can tomatoes and green chiles

1 tablespoon garlic powder

Salt and pepper to taste

1 pound Velveeta cheese, diced

2 cups grated sharp Cheddar cheese

Simmer chicken in water in a large pot until tender. Chop into chunks. Cook spaghetti in boiling water with salt for approximately 11 minutes. Drain. Sauté celery, mushrooms, bell peppers and onions in butter and set aside. Add soup, chicken broth, pimientos, stewed tomatoes and tomatoes and green chiles to spaghetti. Then add chicken chunks, sautéed vegetables, and garlic powder. Fold in Velveeta cheese, salt and pepper. Spoon into a 13x9x2-inch casserole and top with grated sharp Cheddar cheese. Bake in a preheated 350 degree oven for 25 to 30 minutes. May be made ahead and refrigerated. Bring to room temperature before baking or start in a cold oven. Increase cooking time 10 or 15 minutes if the casserole is cold and you are using a cold oven. Serves 10 to 12.

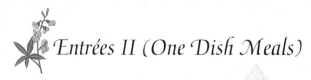

Chicken Florentine
May Be Made Ahead

4 tablespoons butter	1 (2-ounce) jar diced pimientos
¼ cup flour	1 large onion, chopped
1 cup milk	1 celery rib, chopped
1 cup chicken broth	2 teaspoons seasoned salt
5 ounces small egg noodles, cooked and drained	1 teaspoon Accent, optional
	½ teaspoon cayenne pepper
2 cups sour cream	1 teaspoon paprika
⅓ cup lemon juice	1 teaspoon salt
1 (10-ounce) package frozen chopped spinach, cooked and drained	2 teaspoons pepper
	2 fryers, cooked, boned and chopped
1 (8-ounce) can chopped mushrooms, drained	1½ cups grated Cheddar cheese
1 (8-ounce) can water chestnuts, drained	

Melt butter in stockpot and blend with flour. Add milk and chicken broth. Cook over low heat, stirring continuously, until thickened. Mix in noodles, sour cream, lemon juice, spinach, mushrooms, water chestnuts, pimientos, onions, celery, seasoned salt, Accent, cayenne pepper, paprika, salt and pepper. In greased 4-quart baking dish, alternate layers of noodle mixture and chicken. Top with cheese and bake in a preheated 350 degree oven for 30 minutes or until bubbly. May be prepared ahead. May be frozen uncooked, but don't add the grated Cheddar cheese until baking time. Thaw frozen casserole overnight in the refrigerator and bring to room temperature before baking. Serves 12.

Southwestern Chicken

2	cups chopped onions	2	canned jalapeño peppers, seeded and finely chopped
2	tablespoons butter	1	tablespoon liquid from the jalapeños
1	(10-ounce) package frozen chopped spinach, cooked and well drained	½	teaspoon salt
2	cups sour cream	1	(12-ounce) package corn chips
2	(10¾-ounce) cans cream of chicken soup, undiluted	4-6	cups diced cooked chicken breast
4	green onion tops, sliced	2	cups grated Monterey Jack cheese

Sauté onions in butter and add spinach, sour cream, soup, green onions, jalapeños, liquid and salt. Reserve. In a 13x9x2-inch baking dish layer ½ the corn chips, ½ the chicken, ½ the spinach mixture and ½ the cheese. Repeat. Bake in a preheated 350 degree oven for 30 to 40 minutes or until bubbly. You can assemble the casserole the night before. Bring to room temperature before baking or start in a cold oven increasing cooking time 15 or 20 minutes. Serves 8 to 12.

Oriental Style Chicken

1	cup chopped celery	1	(10¾-ounce) can cream of chicken soup, undiluted
1	cup chopped onions		
1	tablespoon butter or margarine	1	cup instant rice
4	cups cubed cooked chicken	¼	cup soy sauce
1	(10¾-ounce) can cream of mushroom soup, undiluted	1	(16-ounce) can Chinese vegetables, drained
		1	(3-ounce) can Chinese noodles

Sauté celery and onions in butter until tender. Add chicken, soups, rice, soy sauce and vegetables. Pour into greased 2-quart casserole dish. Bake in a preheated 350 degree oven for 45 minutes. Sprinkle noodles over top. Bake 5 minutes longer. Serves 6 to 8.

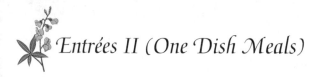

Santa Fe Chicken

1	(6-ounce) package cornbread stuffing mix with seasoning packet	½	cup chopped red bell pepper, optional
2	(3-ounce) cans white chicken, drained	½	cup fresh parsley, chopped
1	(4½-ounce) can Underwood chicken spread	1	(11-ounce) can whole kernel corn, drained
1	(7-ounce) can chopped green chiles	1	(10¾-ounce) can cream of mushroom soup, undiluted
		1	cup sour cream
		1	cup (about 4-ounces) grated Monterey Jack cheese

Combine stuffing with chicken, chicken spread, green chiles, red bell peppers and parsley in a large bowl; toss until combined. Add corn, soup and sour cream and stir well. Spread in a lightly greased 2-quart shallow baking dish. Cover and bake in a preheated 350 degree oven for 35 minutes or until thoroughly heated. Uncover, sprinkle with cheese, and bake an additional 5 minutes or until cheese is melted and bubbly. Serves 4 to 6.

See fall foliage every weekend in October at the "Autumn Trails Festival" in the East Texas Piney Woods city of Winnsboro located 22 miles west of Pittsburg on Texas Highway 11.

Chicken Asparagus Olé

6	boneless chicken breast halves	8	ounces sharp Cheddar cheese, grated
3	teaspoons instant chicken bouillon	¼	teaspoon Tabasco sauce
1	medium onion, finely chopped	2	teaspoons soy sauce
8	tablespoons butter	1	teaspoon salt
1	(8-ounce) can sliced mushrooms	½	teaspoon pepper
1	(10¾-ounce) can cream of mushroom soup, undiluted	1	teaspoon Accent, optional
1	(10¾-ounce) can cream of chicken soup, undiluted	1	(2-ounce) jar diced pimientos, drained
1	(5⅓-ounce) can evaporated milk	2	(15-ounce) cans whole asparagus, drained
		½	cup sliced almonds

Cover chicken with water, add bouillon and simmer until the chicken is done, about 30 minutes. Cut into bite-size pieces. In large pan sauté onions in butter until tender but not brown. Add mushrooms, soups, milk, cheese, Tabasco sauce, soy sauce, salt, pepper, Accent and pimientos. Simmer sauce until cheese melts. Place a layer of chicken in the bottom of a greased 13x9x2-inch baking dish. Cover with half of the asparagus and half the sauce. Repeat layers ending with sauce. Top with almonds. Bake, covered in a preheated 350 degree oven for 30 to 45 minutes. Uncover and bake approximately 15 to 20 minutes or until bubbly. Serves 10 to 12. Freezes well.

Extra-Rich Wild Rice and Chicken Casserole

1 (6-ounce) can sliced mushrooms	1½ cups chicken broth
1 (6.4-ounce) box long grain and wild rice	1½ cups cream or milk
½ cup chopped onions	3 cups diced cooked chicken
8 tablespoons butter	½ cup diced pimientos
½ cup flour	¼ teaspoon pepper
	½ cup slivered, blanched almonds

Drain mushrooms and reserve liquid. Prepare rice according to package directions. Sauté onions in butter until transparent. Stir in flour; add chicken broth and reserved mushroom liquid. Add cream; cook until thick, stirring constantly. Combine with mushrooms, chicken, pimientos and pepper and mix well. Pour into a 13x9x2-inch baking dish. Sprinkle almonds on top. Bake in a preheated 350 degree oven for 25 minutes. Serves 8 to 12.

Turkey Pot Pie

2 cups diced cooked turkey	½ cup water
1 tablespoon flour	1 (10¾-ounce) can cream of mushroom soup
1 cup chopped onions	
1 cup sliced celery	2 cups sliced cooked carrots
½ teaspoon dried thyme, crumbled	1 cup cooked green beans, drained
⅛ teaspoon pepper	
1 tablespoon margarine	1 (6-ounce) can refrigerated biscuits

Toss turkey and flour in a plastic bag. Set aside. Cook onions, celery, thyme and pepper in margarine until tender. Mix water with soup; add onion mixture, carrots, green beans and turkey. Pour into a 2-quart casserole. Split biscuits in half and place on top. Bake in a preheated 350 degree oven for 30 minutes. Serves 5.

Pot Luck Chicken

Must Be Made Ahead

1 (6.4-ounce) package long grain and wild rice	¾ cup mayonnaise
1 medium onion, chopped	4 cups chopped cooked chicken
1 tablespoon butter	½ teaspoon curry powder
1 cup chopped celery	Salt to taste
1 (6-ounce) can sliced water chestnuts, drained	1 tablespoon sugar
2 (10¾-ounce) cans cream of chicken soup, undiluted	1 cup grated Cheddar cheese
	1 cup grated Monterey Jack cheese
	½ cup toasted slivered almonds

Cook rice according to package directions. Sauté onions in butter until barely tender. Mix together rice, onions, celery, water chestnuts, soup, mayonnaise, chicken, curry powder, salt and sugar. Pour into a 13x9x2-inch baking dish and chill overnight. Return to room temperature and bake in a preheated 350 degree oven for 30 minutes covered and 30 minutes uncovered. The last 10 minutes of cooking top the casserole with grated cheeses and almonds. Serves 8.

The oldest botanical gardens in Texas are located in the North Texas city of Fort Worth. The Fort Worth Botanical Gardens and Japanese Garden contain the fragrances of over 2,000 different plants. A fragrance garden has been created for the blind, but it can be enjoyed by everyone. Seasonal plants bloom throughout the year with the most color and excitement occurring in the spring.

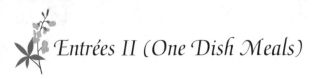

Arroz con Pollo

Best Made Ahead

2 teaspoons salt	¼ pound smoked ham, diced
¼ teaspoon black pepper	1½ cups canned tomatoes
1 teaspoon ground cumin	4 ripe plum tomatoes, peeled and cubed
1 teaspoon dried oregano, crumbled	½ teaspoon saffron
1 (3-4 pound) chicken, cut in serving pieces	3 cups chicken broth
2 teaspoons olive oil, divided	1 cup converted rice
½ cup finely chopped onions	12 stuffed green olives, sliced
1-2 teaspoons finely chopped garlic	1 (9-ounce) package frozen peas
1 large bell pepper cut in 1-inch chunks	¼ cup grated Parmesan cheese
	Chopped parsley

Mix salt, pepper, cumin, and oregano and rub this mixture on the chicken. Brown chicken in 1 teaspoon olive oil in a non stick skillet and put in a 3 or 4-quart casserole or Dutch oven. Pour off chicken fat and add the remaining 1 teaspoon olive oil to the skillet. Add onions, garlic, bell peppers and ham and cook until the vegetables are wilted. Add tomatoes, saffron and broth. Bring to a boil and scrape up browned bits. Add rice and olives and pour over chicken. Stir and cover tightly. Bake 25 to 30 minutes in a preheated 375 degree oven. Stir in peas, cheese and parsley. Bake 5 minutes more. Cool. Refrigerate several hours or overnight. Bring to room temperature and reheat at 350 degrees until bubbly, about 20 minutes. Serves 6.

Brunswick Stew

Best Made Ahead

1	(6-pound) stewing hen or 2 (3-pound) broiler-fryers	4	cups frozen corn
3	quarts water	3	teaspoons salt
2	large onions, cubed	1	teaspoon pepper
2	cups fresh or frozen okra, sliced	1	teaspoon sugar
2	(14½-ounce) cans stewed tomatoes	1	tablespoon Worcestershire sauce
		1	tablespoon paprika
2	cups fresh or frozen lima beans	1	tablespoon lemon juice
6	medium potatoes, peeled and cubed		Dash Tabasco sauce

Simmer chicken in water until tender, about 1 hour. Remove chicken from broth. Skin, bone and cut into bite-size pieces (you should have about 6 cups of cooked chicken). Add onions, okra, tomatoes, lima beans, potatoes and corn to broth. Simmer until lima beans and potatoes are tender. Stir occasionally to prevent sticking. Add chicken, salt, pepper, sugar, Worcestershire sauce, paprika, lemon juice and Tabasco sauce. Taste and adjust seasonings. Serves 10.

The Indians introduced maize (corn in English) to the Spanish and English. The *"Corn Festival"* is celebrated in Holland on the third Saturday in June.

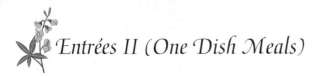

Creamy Ham and Potato Bake

Casserole:

1   (2-pound) package southern style frozen hash brown potatoes, thawed

2   cups sour cream

½   teaspoon pepper

6   ounces Cheddar cheese, grated

1   (10¾-ounce) can cream of chicken soup, undiluted

8   tablespoons butter, melted

2   cups cubed ham

⅓   cup chopped green onions

Topping:

4   tablespoons butter, melted

2   cups crushed corn flakes

Casserole:

Combine all casserole ingredients. Spoon mixture into a greased 13x9x2-inch casserole dish.

Topping:

Combine topping ingredients and sprinkle over top of casserole. Bake in a preheated 350 degree oven for 1 hour. Serves 10.

Touring the "Dogwood Trails" is a popular event among Texans from around the state. One of the best times and places to see the delicate white blossoms scattered throughout the forests is late March and early April in the East Texas town of Palestine.

A Texas Blossoms Menu for a

Bridal Luncheon

Sparkling Strawberry Mimosas
Chicken Waldorf Salad
Mango Mousse
Strawberry Romaine Salad
Streusel Topped Strawberry Muffins
Bavarian Angel Dessert

The Clubhouse

Nestled under stately pecans and red oaks in a picturesque enclave of northeast Richardson is the home of the Richardson Woman's Club, a blend of past and present. An aura of bygone days surrounds the old farmhouse where small meetings and luncheons are held. The "new" is Founder's Hall which accommodates larger gatherings. The structures are connected by porches, decks, terraces, and walkways. Painted in a soft yellow, spanning the hilly terrain, the buildings create a sense of tranquility. A winding drive passes an historic old stone well and meanders down to the beautiful old house. On a gentle slope behind the house is a romantic Victorian-style gazebo that is favored by brides as a wedding site.

Food Styling by Lee Stanyer

Photography by David Bullock

Photography Assistance by Carley Blackman

Floral Designs by Ute Schnetzinger, AIFD, Gunter's Greenhouse and Florist

China and Crystal Provided by Polly DuPont

Texas
Blossoms

Richardson Woman's Club

The *Texas Blossoms* reflects the true meaning of the Richardson Woman's Club. Volunteering time for community projects, sharing good food and promoting friendship are of great importance to the women of this organization. Organized in 1955, members of RWC, as the club is called, soon became well-known for their annual Holiday Tour of Homes. The event continues to grow and draws over 3,000 people. Featured are the Tea Room, the Bake Shop, the Holiday Bazaar and Country Store with arts and crafts and the beautifully decorated homes for the upcoming Holiday Season. Many arrive early, standing in line to be first to enjoy a delicious lunch in the Tea Room. Favorites of those recipes are included in this book as well as favorites from our annual spring Bridge Festival. After lunch in the Tea Room, many visit the Bake Shop to fill their baskets with an assortment of homemade pies, cakes, cookies and candies to be enjoyed during the Holiday Season and to shop at the Holiday Bazaar before driving to the inspiring homes.

The East Texas town of Tyler, in Smith County, is well known nationally for it's flourishing rose industry. Many of the nation's commercially grown rose bushes are packed and shipped from this area. This huge industry began more than 100 years ago and has established Tyler as the Rose Capital of the Nation. It is home to the largest municipal rose garden. The Municipal Rose Garden has more than 30,000 rose bushes in 500 varieties filling fourteen acres. The blooming season peaks in mid May and continues through November. This thriving business gives rise to the Texas Rose Festival held every October.

Texas Style Pasta Casserole

1 pound hot or sweet Italian sausage, casings removed	¼ teaspoon cayenne pepper
1 pound ground beef	2 (15½-ounce) cans black beans, drained and rinsed
1 large onion, chopped	Salt and pepper
4 garlic cloves, chopped	1 pound mostaccioli pasta, freshly cooked
1 teaspoon dried oregano, crumbled	½ cup grated Parmesan cheese
½ teaspoon dried thyme, crumbled	¼ cup chopped fresh cilantro
1 (20-ounce) can diced tomatoes and liquid	12 ounces Monterey Jack cheese or mozzarella cheese, grated
2 tablespoons ketchup	

Sauté crumbled sausage and ground beef with onions, garlic, oregano and thyme in a heavy, large saucepan until sausage and beef are brown, about 5 minutes. Add tomatoes and liquid, ketchup and cayenne and simmer 5 minutes longer. Add black beans and heat through. Season with salt and pepper. Add mostaccioli, Parmesan cheese and cilantro and toss to combine. Transfer to a 13x9x2-inch baking dish and sprinkle with grated cheese. Bake in a preheated 400 degree oven until cheese melts, about 30 minutes. Serves 8 to 12.

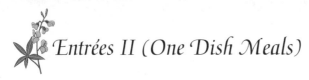

Pepperoni Pasta Alfredo

8 ounces bowtie pasta	¼ cup white wine
1 (1.6-ounce) package Knorr Alfredo sauce mix	1 teaspoon Worcestershire sauce
1½ cups milk	⅓ cup chopped red bell peppers
1 tablespoon butter	⅓ cup chopped yellow bell peppers
4 ounces grated mozzarella cheese	⅓ cup chopped green bell peppers
Salt and pepper to taste	1-2 garlic cloves, minced
1 tablespoon dried basil, crumbled	3-4 ounces frozen Chinese pea pods, sliced diagonally
½ teaspoon dried oregano, crumbled	40 slices pepperoni (about ⅓ of an 8-ounce package), cut into quarters
½ teaspoon dried thyme, crumbled	
1 teaspoon dried parsley, crumbled	½ pound mushrooms, sliced
¼ large onion, chopped	4 ounces frozen peas
1-2 celery ribs, chopped	Garlic salt, optional
3 tablespoons olive oil	⅓ cup shredded Parmesan cheese

Cook pasta, just to al dente stage, drain. Prepare sauce mix with milk and butter according to package directions and simmer. Add mozzarella cheese gradually with salt and pepper. Add basil, oregano, thyme, and parsley. Stir until smooth. Remove from heat. Sauté onions and celery in olive oil until soft. Add wine and Worcestershire sauce. Add bell peppers, garlic and pea pods, cooking slightly after each addition, so that all will remain somewhat crunchy. Cool slightly. Add the sauce mixture, pepperoni, mushrooms, and peas. Add garlic salt and adjust seasoning to taste. Pour into a 13x9x2-inch baking dish and sprinkle with Parmesan cheese. Bake covered in a preheated 350 degree oven for 30 minutes or until hot in middle and the edges are bubbly. May be refrigerated or frozen before baking. Remove from refrigerator and let sit out for 30 minutes before baking. If frozen, thaw thoroughly and bring to room temperature before baking as instructed. Serves 4 to 6.

Lazy Day Salmon Casserole

1¼ cups sour cream
1 garlic clove, crushed
2 (3-ounce) packages cream cheese, softened
1 teaspoon Worcestershire sauce
½ teaspoon salt
⅛ teaspoon pepper

1 (16-ounce) can red salmon, drained
½ cup chopped green bell peppers
¼ cup grated onions
2 tablespoons pimientos
1 (6-ounce) package medium egg noodles, cooked and drained
Parmesan cheese, grated

Blend sour cream, garlic, cream cheese, Worcestershire sauce, salt and pepper. Fold in salmon, bell peppers, onions and pimientos. Combine with noodles. Pour into 1½-quart greased casserole. Sprinkle with grated Parmesan cheese. Bake uncovered in a preheated 350 degree oven for 30 minutes. Serves 6.

Shrimp and Wild Rice Casserole

1 (12-ounce) package raw frozen shrimp, thawed and drained
1½ cups sliced fresh mushrooms
2 celery ribs, chopped
1 small onion, chopped
1 tablespoon olive oil
2 cups cooked wild rice (about ½ cup uncooked)

1 (10¾-ounce) can cream of shrimp soup, undiluted
2 teaspoons Worcestershire sauce
1 (2-ounce) jar chopped pimientos, drained, divided
Parsley for garnish

Peel shrimp and remove tails if necessary. In small skillet sauté mushrooms, celery and onions in olive oil until tender and lightly browned. Combine shrimp, wild rice, soup, Worcestershire sauce and half the pimientos. Pour mixture into 8x8x2-inch casserole dish. Bake in a preheated 350 degree oven for 30 to 35 minutes or until bubbly. Garnish with the remaining pimientos and parsley. Serves 6.

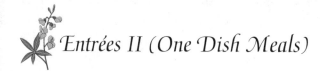

Texas Star Shrimp and Chicken Casserole

Must Be Made Ahead

2	(16-ounce) packages frozen broccoli florets, thawed and well drained	1	(16-ounce) package frozen ready-to-eat cooked shrimp, thawed and tails removed
1	(10¾-ounce) can cream of chicken soup, undiluted	4	cups cooked chopped chicken
1	(10¾-ounce) can cream of celery soup, undiluted	1	cup (about 4-ounces) shredded Cheddar cheese
1	cup mayonnaise	½	cup soft breadcrumbs
3	tablespoons lemon juice	1	tablespoon butter or margarine, melted
¼	teaspoon white pepper	¼	teaspoon paprika

Spread broccoli evenly in a greased 13x9x2-inch baking dish. Stir together soups, mayonnaise, lemon juice and white pepper. Spread about ⅓ of the mixture evenly over broccoli; top with shrimp and chicken. Spread remaining soup mixture evenly over the shrimp and chicken. Cover and chill overnight. Remove from refrigerator and let stand for 30 minutes. Bake covered, in a preheated 350 degree oven for 30 minutes. Uncover, and sprinkle with cheese. Combine breadcrumbs and butter; sprinkle over cheese. Bake 15 minutes more or until hot and bubbly. Sprinkle with paprika. Serves 10 to 12.

Located in the Texas Gulf Coast region just above Beaumont lies the "Big Thicket". One will marvel at the great diversity of this special place. Hardwood pines stand next to cypress forests, soft meadows share space with blackwater swamps, and sandhills coexist with untouched pines. The "Big Thicket" is home to more than a 1,000 flowering plants.

Tuna Stuffed Muffs

Best Made Ahead

1 very large onion, finely chopped	1 teaspoon dill weed
1 very large carrot, finely chopped	1 tablespoon grated Parmesan cheese
3 tablespoons olive oil	
1 (28-ounce) can Italian style tomatoes and liquid	1 cup low-fat small curd cottage cheese
1 (8-ounce) can tomato sauce	1 (3-ounce) package Neufchâtel cheese, at room temperature
½ cup sliced black olives, divided	2 eggs, beaten
1 (13-ounce) can tuna, drained	16 uncooked manicotti (little muffs) pasta shells
⅓ cup finely chopped green bell peppers	
1 tablespoon instant minced onions	2 cups shredded mozzarella cheese

Sauté onions and carrots slowly in the oil in a heavy skillet. When tender, add tomatoes and break up into small pieces. Add tomato sauce and half the olives. Allow to simmer over very low heat while preparing filling. Mix remaining olives, tuna, green peppers, onions, dill, Parmesan cheese, cottage cheese, Neufchâtel cheese and eggs together thoroughly with a fork. Fill shells, using a fork or what ever is easy. (I have used a long handled baby spoon, a butter knife, an iced tea spoon, a baby fork, a seafood fork and probably something else long forgotten.) Cover the bottom of a 13x9x2-inch pan with the sauce making sure you have enough left to finish the top of the casserole. Arrange 10 manicotti down the center then 3 on either side. Cover with the remaining sauce, seal casserole tightly with foil and refrigerate. Pasta will be most tender if you let it set a few hours. Bake, covered, in a 375 degree oven for 1 hour. Remove foil, sprinkle on mozzarella cheese and bake, uncovered, another 10 minutes. Serves 6 to 8.

This recipe takes time to make, dirties lots of dishes
and pans, but you will find the rave reviews make it all worth while.

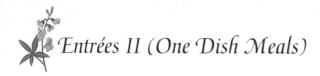

New-Fangled Lasagna
Must Be Made Ahead

1 (10-ounce) package frozen chopped spinach, thawed and drained

1 (12-ounce) carton low-fat cottage cheese

1 egg, beaten

Cooking spray

2 teaspoons olive oil

¾ cup minced onions

1 cup sliced mushrooms

2 garlic cloves, minced

2 (14½-ounce) cans no-salt-added tomatoes, drained and chopped

¼ cup minced fresh parsley

¼ cup Burgundy or other dry red wine

¼ cup tomato paste

2 teaspoons dried basil, crumbled

1½ teaspoons dried oregano, crumbled

1 teaspoon dark brown sugar

½ teaspoon pepper

¼ teaspoon salt

6 lasagna noodles, uncooked, divided

5 cups thinly sliced zucchini, divided (about 1¼-pounds)

1¼ cups (about 5-ounces) part-skim mozzarella cheese, finely shredded, divided

2 tablespoons freshly grated Parmesan cheese

Press spinach between paper towels. Combine spinach, cottage cheese and egg in a medium bowl; stir well and set aside. Coat a large, non-aluminum saucepan with cooking spray; add oil and place over medium heat until hot. Add onions and sauté 3 minutes or until tender. Add mushrooms and garlic; sauté 2 minutes or until mushrooms are tender. Add tomatoes, parsley, wine, tomato paste, basil, oregano, brown sugar, pepper and salt; stir well. Reduce heat and simmer, uncovered, 20 minutes. Remove tomato mixture from heat and set aside. Coat a 12x8x2-inch baking dish with cooking spray. Spoon one-third of tomato mixture into dish. Arrange 3 noodles lengthwise in a single layer over tomato mixture; top with 1¼ cups spinach mixture. Layer 2½ cups zucchini over spinach, and sprinkle with ½ cup mozzarella cheese. Repeat layers and top with remaining tomato mixture. Cover and refrigerate 8 hours. Bake, uncovered, in a preheated 350 degree oven for 1 hour 30 minutes. Uncover and sprinkle with the remaining ¼ cup mozzarella cheese and Parmesan cheese. Let stand 5 minutes before serving. Serves 6.

Hint: Pasta sauce can be substituted for the tomatoes, tomato sauce, basil, oregano, brown sugar, salt and pepper.

Green Chiles Rice Casserole

Can Be Made Ahead

1   cup chopped onions

4   tablespoons margarine or olive
    oil

4   cups rice, cooked
    (about 1 cup raw)

2   cups sour cream

1   cup cream style cottage cheese

1   bay leaf, crumbled

1   teaspoon salt

Pepper to taste

3   (4½-ounce) cans chopped green
    chiles

2   cups grated sharp Cheddar
    cheese

Parsley, optional

Cook onions in margarine until soft. Mix with cooked rice, sour cream, cottage cheese, bay leaf, salt and pepper. Grease a 13x9x2-inch baking dish and put in layers of ½ of the rice mixture, ½ of the green chiles and ½ of the cheese. Repeat. Bake in preheated 375 degree oven about 25 minutes, uncovered. Add chopped parsley for garnish. Serves 6 to 8.

This can be made the day before and heated the
day it is served. Every time I make it, people ask
for the recipe. It is simple and very good.

Entrées III (Brunch and Breakfast)

Lady Bird Johnson Wildflower Center

A "must see" is the Lady Bird Johnson Wildflower Center in Austin. Mrs. Johnson's passion to beautify America with roadside flowers started when her husband was President of the United States. Her commitment continues today in The Wildflower Center, the nation's only non-profit organization devoted to the preservation of native North American wildflowers and other plants. The Wildflower Center houses the largest collection of information about wildflowers. Many states besides Texas have spectacular roadside views, especially in the spring.

Photograph provided by
Lady Bird Johnson Wildflower Center

Texas
Blossoms

Texas Hill
Country

Texas
Blossoms

Entrées III (Brunch and Breakfast)

A Texas Blossoms Menu for a

Brunch
Italian Country Garden Strata
Apple-Cranberry Bake
Double Good Lemon Bread
Angel Biscuits

Texas Sunrise Breakfast
Must Be Made Ahead

Butter, softened
16 slices white bread, crusts removed, divided
2½ cups cooked, cubed ham or cooked sausage, divided
1   (8-ounce) package grated sharp Cheddar cheese, divided

7   large eggs, beaten
3½ cups milk
½   teaspoon dry mustard
½   teaspoon salt
2   cups cornflakes, crumbled
½   cup melted butter or margarine

Butter the bread lightly and place 8 slices on the bottom of a 13x9x2-inch baking dish. Sprinkle with ½ of the ham or sausage and ½ of the cheese. Add the remaining bread slices. Sprinkle with the remaining ham or sausage and cheese. Beat eggs, milk, dry mustard and salt together in a medium bowl. Pour over the cheese and ham mixture. Cover and refrigerate overnight. Remove from refrigerator 1 hour before baking. Sprinkle with crumbled cornflakes and drizzle with melted butter or margarine. Bake uncovered in a preheated at 350 degree oven for 60 minutes. Serves 12.

Good Start Cheese Strata
Must Be Made Ahead

12 slices white bread, crusts trimmed

12 ounces sliced American cheese

1 (10-ounce) package frozen chopped broccoli, cooked and drained

2 cups finely diced cooked ham

6 eggs, slightly beaten

3½ cups milk

2 tablespoons dried minced onions

½ teaspoon salt

¼ teaspoon dry mustard

Shredded Cheddar cheese for topping, optional

Cut 12 "doughnuts and holes" from bread and set aside. Fit the remaining bread scraps in the bottom of a 13x9x2-inch casserole. Place the American cheese slices in a layer over the bread. Add a layer of broccoli and then a layer of ham. Arrange bread doughnuts and holes on top. Combine eggs, milk, onions, salt and mustard in a medium bowl. Pour into the casserole. Cover and refrigerate at least 6 hours or overnight. Remove from refrigerator and let stand for 30 minutes. Bake uncovered in a preheated 325 degree oven for 45 to 50 minutes. Remove from the oven and sprinkle with Cheddar cheese and return to oven for 5 minutes. Let stand about 10 minutes to firm up. Cut into squares. Serves 12.

Hint: "Doughnuts" are easier to cut out of frozen bread.

Country Breakfast
Must Be Made Ahead

Eggs:

1 cup diced Canadian bacon or ham

¼ cup chopped green onions

3 tablespoons butter or margarine

12 eggs, beaten

1 (3-ounce) can mushroom pieces

Cheese Sauce:

2 tablespoons butter

2 tablespoons flour

½ teaspoon salt

⅛ teaspoon pepper

2 cups milk

1 cup grated Cheddar cheese

Topping:

4 tablespoons melted butter or margarine

⅛ teaspoon paprika

2½ cups soft breadcrumbs

Eggs:

Sauté Canadian bacon and onions in butter until tender, but do not brown. Add eggs and mushrooms and scramble until set; remove from heat.

Cheese Sauce:

In a medium saucepan melt butter; blend in flour, salt and pepper. Add milk gradually and then add the cheese. Cook and stir until bubbly and smooth. Fold the cooked eggs and mushrooms into the cheese sauce and pour into a 12x7x2-inch baking dish.

Topping:

Combine topping ingredients and sprinkle over the top. Cover and refrigerate overnight. Remove from the refrigerator and let stand at least 30 minutes. Bake uncovered in a preheated 350 degree oven for 30 minutes. Serves 8 to 10.

Brunch Enchiladas

Must Be Made Ahead

Enchiladas:

12 ounces ground ham
2 cups grated Cheddar cheese
½ cup sliced green onions, including tops
1 (4½-ounce) can chopped green chiles, drained

1 fresh jalapeño, finely chopped, optional
8 flour tortillas
Cornmeal

Egg Topping:

6 eggs, slightly beaten
2 cups half-and-half
1 tablespoon flour

¼ teaspoon garlic powder
Tabasco sauce to taste
Grated Cheddar cheese for topping

Enchiladas:

Mix together the ham, cheese, onions, green chiles and jalapeños in a medium bowl. Put ⅓ cup mixture in each tortilla and roll. Place in a greased and cornmeal dusted 13x9x2-inch baking dish.

Egg Topping:

Combine the eggs, half-and-half, flour, garlic powder and Tabasco sauce. Pour over enchiladas. Cover and chill overnight. Remove from refrigerator about 30 minutes before baking. Sprinkle additional cheese on top. Bake covered in a preheated 350 degree oven for 30 minutes and then uncovered for 25 to 30 minutes. Serves 8.

Egg and Artichoke Casserole

1	bunch green onions, finely chopped	1	(14-ounce) can artichoke hearts
1	large garlic clove, finely chopped	12	eggs
6	tablespoons butter	12	ounces shredded Cheddar cheese
			5-6 saltine crackers, crumbled

Brown onions and garlic in butter in a small skillet. Spread in a 13x9x2-inch baking dish. Drain and rinse artichoke hearts. Cut each piece into fourths and spoon over onion mixture. Beat eggs, add cheese and blend well. Pour over vegetable mixture. Bake in a preheated 350 degree oven for 35 to 40 minutes. Remove from oven and sprinkle with crackers. May be refrigerated or frozen. Reheat before serving. Cut into small squares and serve. May be served at room temperature. Serves 12.

Variation: May be served as an appetizer.

Guiltless Spinach-Cheddar Squares

1½	cups egg substitute	¼	cup dry breadcrumbs
¾	cup skim milk	¾	cup shredded fat-free Cheddar cheese, divided
1	tablespoon dried minced onions		
1	tablespoon grated Parmesan cheese	1	(10-ounce) package frozen chopped spinach, thawed and well drained
¼	teaspoon garlic powder		
⅛	teaspoon ground black pepper	¼	cup diced pimientos

In a medium bowl, combine egg substitute, milk, minced onions, Parmesan cheese, garlic powder and black pepper. Set aside. Sprinkle breadcrumbs evenly onto the bottom of a lightly greased 8x8x2-inch baking dish. Top with ½ cup Cheddar cheese and spinach. Pour egg mixture evenly over spinach; top with remaining Cheddar cheese and pimientos. Bake in a preheated 350 degree oven for 35 to 40 minutes or until set. Let stand 10 minutes. Serve hot. Serves 8.

Variation: To serve as an appetizer, cut into 2-inch squares. Serves 16.

Italian Country Garden Strata

Must Be Made Ahead

¾ cup diced onions
½ cup diced green onions
8 ounces fresh mushrooms, sliced
2 tablespoons olive oil
1 red bell pepper, cut into thin strips
1 green bell pepper, cut into thin strips
5 cups 1-inch cubes Italian bread (about half a loaf), divided

1½ cups (about 6-ounces) shredded Cheddar cheese, divided
½ cup Parmesan cheese, divided
6 large eggs
1¾ cups milk
1 tablespoon Dijon mustard
½ teaspoon salt
½ teaspoon pepper
¼ teaspoon Tabasco sauce

Sauté onions, green onions and mushrooms in a large skillet in hot oil until tender. Stir in bell peppers. Cook for 10 minutes, stirring often until liquid evaporates. Spread 2½ cups bread cubes in a lightly greased 13x9x2-inch baking dish. Top with half of vegetable mixture. Sprinkle with ¾ cup Cheddar cheese and ¼ cup Parmesan cheese. Repeat layers. Whisk together the eggs, milk, mustard, salt, pepper and Tabasco sauce in a medium bowl. Pour over strata. Cover and chill overnight. Remove from refrigerator and let stand at least 30 minutes. Bake uncovered in a preheated 350 degree oven for 45 minutes or until set. Serves 12 to 15.

Top Hat Cheese Soufflé

⅓ cup butter
⅓ cup flour
1 teaspoon salt
Dash cayenne pepper

1½ cups milk
2 cups grated sharp Cheddar cheese
6 eggs, separated

Melt butter in a medium saucepan and blend in flour, salt and cayenne. Gradually add milk. Cook and stir until slightly thickened. Add cheese and stir until melted. Remove from heat. Gradually add slightly beaten egg yolks. Cool. Beat egg whites stiffly. Fold sauce into egg whites. Pour into a 2-quart dish. With the tip of a spoon make a slight indentation or track around top of soufflé 1-inch from edge to form a top hat. Bake in a preheated 300 degree oven for 1 hour and 15 minutes. Serve immediately. Serves 6.

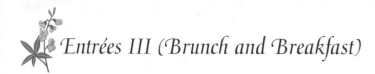

Rancher's Frittata

3	tablespoons butter or margarine	¼	teaspoon pepper
2	cups frozen hash brown potatoes with onions and peppers	1	cup (about 4-ounces) shredded Monterey Jack cheese
6	large eggs	6	slices bacon, cooked and crumbled
2	tablespoons milk		
¼	teaspoon salt		Diced fresh tomatoes for garnish

Melt butter in a 10-inch nonstick skillet over medium heat. Add frozen potatoes, and cook 10 minutes or until browned. Whisk together the eggs, milk, salt and pepper in a small bowl. Pour over potatoes. As mixture starts to cook, gently lift edges with a spatula. Tilt skillet so the uncooked portion flows underneath. If center remains uncooked, carefully turn frittata over, and cook 5 minutes or until center is done. Place frittata on a serving platter. Sprinkle with cheese. Cover with aluminum foil and let stand for 5 minutes. Uncover and sprinkle with crumbled bacon. Garnish with tomatoes and serve immediately. Makes 6 servings.

Lost Maples French Toast

	Cooking spray	½	cup maple syrup
4	slices honey wheat bread, cubed	1	teaspoon vanilla extract
4	ounces cream cheese, cubed	1	teaspoon ground cinnamon
4	eggs		Apples or pears for garnish, optional
1	cup milk		Pecans for garnish, optional

Spray an 8x8x2-inch baking dish with cooking spray. Spread bread cubes evenly in dish and top with cream cheese cubes. Mix together the eggs, milk, syrup, vanilla and cinnamon in a small bowl. Pour over the bread cubes and bake in a preheated 350 degree oven for 45 minutes. Garnish with fruit or pecans. Serves 4.

Mañana's Seafood Casserole

Must Be Made Ahead

8   slices white bread, crusts
     removed, cubed
2   cups crabmeat or cooked shelled
     shrimp or mixture of each
1   large onion, chopped
1   cup chopped celery
1   green bell pepper, chopped
1   teaspoon salt

1   teaspoon pepper
1   (10¾-ounce) can cream of
     mushroom soup, undiluted
½   cup mayonnaise
4   eggs, beaten
3   cups milk
1½ cups grated Cheddar cheese

Place cubed bread in a 13x9x2-inch baking dish. Top with the crabmeat and shrimp.
In a large bowl combine the onions, celery, green peppers, salt, pepper, mushroom soup, mayonnaise, eggs, milk and cheese. Pour over seafood. Cover and
chill overnight. Remove from refrigerator and let stand for at least 30 minutes.
Bake in a preheated 325 degree oven for 1 hour and 15 minutes. Serves 8 to 12.

Fredericksburg Peach French Toast

3   fresh peaches
1   (3-ounce) package cream
     cheese, softened
2   tablespoons chopped pecans
12 slices bread

2   large eggs
½   cup milk
½   teaspoon ground cinnamon
¼   teaspoon vanilla extract
Butter

Chop 1 peach and slice the other 2. Stir pecans and chopped peach into cream
cheese in a small bowl. Spoon 1½ tablespoons of cream cheese mixture onto
6 bread slices; spread evenly. Top with remaining slices of bread. Beat together
the eggs, milk, cinnamon and vanilla in a small bowl. Dip each sandwich into
mixture; turning to coat. Melt 1 tablespoon butter over medium high heat in a
large skillet or griddle. Cook 2 sandwiches at a time for 3 minutes a side, adding
more butter as needed. Serve topped with remaining peach slices and your
favorite syrup. Serves 6.

Texas Ranch Cornbread Quiche

½   pound ground beef
½   onion, chopped
1   teaspoon salt, divided
Dash ground cinnamon
Dash white pepper
¾   cup yellow cornmeal
1   egg, beaten
¼   teaspoon baking soda
1   (15-ounce) can cream style corn

½   cup buttermilk
6   ounces grated Cheddar or colby cheese
1   (4½-ounce) can chopped green chiles, drained
5   slices bacon, chopped, fried and drained
½   green or red bell pepper, diced
Fresh cilantro leaves

In large skillet, brown meat. Add onions, ½ teaspoon salt, cinnamon and white pepper. Drain and set aside. In a medium bowl, mix cornmeal, eggs, baking soda, the remaining ½ teaspoon salt, corn, buttermilk and cheese. Grease an 8x8x2-inch pan and dust with cornmeal. Pour half of cornmeal batter into pan. Place meat mixture on top of batter. Sprinkle green chiles, bacon, bell peppers and cilantro on meat. Pour remaining batter on top. Bake in a preheated 350 degree oven for 40 to 50 minutes or until golden brown on top. Let cool for 10 minutes before serving. Serves 4 to 6.

Ham N' Swiss Pie

2   cups cooked ham
1   cup shredded Swiss cheese
½   cup chopped onions
4   eggs

2   cups milk
1   cup buttermilk biscuit baking mix
¼   teaspoon salt
⅛   teaspoon pepper

Grease a 9-inch pie plate. Sprinkle ham, cheese and onions in plate. Beat eggs, milk, baking mix, salt and pepper until smooth in a medium bowl. Pour into pie plate. Bake in a preheated 400 degree oven for 35 to 40 minutes or until golden brown and a knife inserted in center comes out clean. Cool for 5 minutes. Leftovers microwave well. Serves 6.

Variation: Two cups cooked, drained sausage can be substituted for ham.

Chicken-Pecan Quiche

Crust:

1 cup flour	1 cup shredded sharp Cheddar cheese
¾ cup chopped pecans	½ teaspoon salt
¼ teaspoon paprika	⅓ cup vegetable oil

Filling:

3 eggs, beaten	¼ cup minced onions
1 (8-ounce) container sour cream	¼ teaspoon dried dill weed
¼ cup mayonnaise	3 drops Tabasco sauce
½ cup chicken broth	½ cup shredded Cheddar cheese
2 cups chopped cooked chicken	¼ cup pecan halves

Crust:

Combine flour, pecans, paprika, cheese, salt and oil in a medium bowl. Set aside ¼ of mixture. Press remainder in bottom and up sides of a 9-inch quiche dish. Prick bottom with a fork. Bake in a preheated 350 degree oven for 10 minutes.

Filling:

Combine eggs, sour cream, mayonnaise and chicken broth. Stir in chicken, onions, dill weed, Tabasco sauce and cheese. Pour into prepared crust. Sprinkle reserved crust mixture over filling. Top with pecan halves. Bake in a preheated 325 degree oven for 45 minutes. Serves 6 to 8.

Pecan Pancakes

2 eggs, well beaten	1 teaspoon salt
2 cups milk	4 tablespoons vegetable oil
2 cups flour	½ cup chopped pecans
2 tablespoons baking powder	Cooking spray

Beat all ingredients in a medium bowl until well blended. Cook on a hot griddle sprayed with cooking spray. Serve with your favorite syrup.

Cheesy Crab Quiche

3	eggs, slightly beaten	3	tablespoons butter
1	cup sour cream	1¼	cups shredded Swiss cheese
½	teaspoon Worcestershire sauce	⅔	cup lump crabmeat
¾	teaspoon salt	1	baked (9-inch) pie crust
1	white onion, sliced paper thin		

Combine eggs, sour cream, Worcestershire sauce and salt in a small bowl. Sauté onions in butter in a medium skillet. Mix onions with cheese, crabmeat and egg mixture. Pour into baked pie crust. Bake in a preheated 325 degree oven for 50 to 60 minutes or until a knife inserted in center comes out clean.

Pumpkin-Spice Pancakes

2⅓	cups buttermilk baking mix	2	eggs
2	tablespoons sugar	1¼	cups milk
½	teaspoon ground cinnamon	⅓	cup canned pumpkin
¼	teaspoon ground nutmeg	¼	cup vegetable oil
¼	teaspoon ground ginger		

Beat all ingredients with a wire whisk or hand mixer until smooth. Pour by scant ¼ cup onto lightly greased hot griddle. Cook until edges are dry; turn and cook until golden. Serve with maple syrup or spiced apples.

Brunches are a wonderful time to entertain in a more relaxed atmosphere. They usually take place between 10:00 a.m. and 1:00 p.m. The secret to success is to plan ahead and to use recipes that can be prepared in advance. Consider serving anything from eggs and cheese to seafood.

Salmon Quiche

Crust:

1	cup whole wheat flour	½	teaspoon salt	
⅔	cup shredded sharp Cheddar cheese	¼	teaspoon paprika	
¼	cup chopped almonds	6	tablespoons corn oil	

Filling:

1	(16-ounce) can red salmon, drained and liquid reserved	½	cup shredded sharp Cheddar cheese
3	eggs, beaten	1	tablespoon grated onions
Water		¼	teaspoon dried dill weed
¼	cup mayonnaise	3	drops Tabasco sauce, optional
1	cup sour cream		

Crust:

Combine flour, cheese, almonds, salt, paprika and oil in a medium bowl. Roll out and place in a 9-inch pie plate. Trim and flute the edge. Bake in a preheated 400 degree oven for 10 minutes. Remove from oven and cool. Lower oven temperature to 325 degrees.

Filling:

In a large bowl flake salmon and mix with eggs. Add enough water to reserved salmon liquid to make ½ cup liquid. Mix with mayonnaise and add to salmon. Add sour cream, cheese, grated onions, dill and Tabasco sauce. Pour into baked pie crust. Bake for 45 minutes. Serves 8.

Deluxe Chicken-Pecan Crêpes

Crêpes:

1 cup flour	1 tablespoon vegetable oil
1½ cups milk	¼ teaspoon salt
2 eggs	

Cream Sauce:

8 tablespoons butter	1½ teaspoons salt
½ cup flour	¼ teaspoon white pepper
4 cups milk, scalded	

Filling:

3 cups chopped cooked chicken	2 egg yolks, beaten
1½ tablespoons chopped fresh parsley	4 cups prepared cream sauce, divided
½ cup chopped onions	1 teaspoon salt
1 cup light cream, divided	1½ cups chopped pecans, divided

Crêpes:

In a bowl combine the flour, milk, eggs, oil and salt. Whisk until blended. Heat a lightly greased 6-inch skillet. Remove from heat; spoon in about 2 tablespoons batter. Lift and tilt to spread batter evenly. Return to heat; brown on one side only or cook on a lightly greased inverted crêpe pan. To remove, invert crêpe to paper towel. Continue making crêpes until batter is used.

Cream Sauce:

In a large saucepan melt butter and gradually add flour. Cook over low heat, stirring constantly, until well blended. Gradually add milk, stirring constantly until mixture becomes thick and smooth. Add salt and pepper and simmer for 5 minutes. Set aside.

Filling:

Simmer chicken, parsley and onions in ¾ cup cream for 5 minutes in a large saucepan. Combine beaten egg yolks with ½ the cream sauce. Add to chicken mixture with salt and 1 cup chopped pecans. Cook over low heat until mixture is

 *Crêpes*

Deluxe Chicken-Pecan Crêpes continued

thickened. Spread generous tablespoon of filling down center of each crêpe; roll up, leaving ends open. Place crêpes seam-side down in a buttered 13x9x2-inch baking dish. Stir the remaining ¼ cup cream into the remaining sauce to thin. Pour over crêpes. Sprinkle with the remaining ½ cup pecans. Bake in a preheated 350 degree oven for 15 to 20 minutes. Serves 10.

Creamy Salmon Crêpes

Crêpes:

1 cup flour	1½ cups milk
Pinch salt	2 tablespoons brandy
3 eggs	3 tablespoons butter, melted

Filling:

1 (16-ounce) can red salmon	1 hard-cooked egg, finely chopped
6 pimiento stuffed olives, chopped	¼ cup light cream
1 tablespoon lemon juice	½ cup whipping cream
1 medium onion, finely chopped	1 cup grated Cheddar cheese

Crêpes:

Mix together the flour, salt, eggs, milk, and brandy in a medium bowl. Allow to stand for 30 minutes. Melt butter in crêpe pan. Pour melted butter into batter and make crêpes.

Filling:

Combine salmon, olives, lemon juice, onions, egg and light cream in a medium bowl. Place filling in crêpes and roll. Put in a greased 13x9x2-inch baking dish. Pour whipping cream over the crêpes and sprinkle with cheese. Bake in a preheated 350 degree oven for 20 minutes. If making ahead, fill crêpes and place in baking dish. Cover and refrigerate. Pour whipping cream over crêpes and sprinkle with cheese just before baking as directed.

Accompaniments

Wildflowers of Richardson

Texas wildflowers are not only an eagerly awaited scenic attraction in the city of Richardson in the spring – they are a tradition – a tradition in which families enjoy the colorful beauty of wildflowers in an environment of festive music and community friendship. The City of Richardson celebrates the tenth anniversary of its annual "Wildflower! Arts & Music Festival" in the spring of 2003. The vision of this festival emerged following a visit to a Texas wildflower seed farm in the late 1980's. Information on growing wildflowers and photographs of beautiful fields of multicolored wildflowers, sparked the imagination of the city's Parks & Recreation planners. It was a perfect match for Richardson's strongly supported city beautification and cultural growth. The wildflowers first came to the city in the fall of 1990, when over eight acres of seeds were planted. Beautiful patches of wildflowers scattered throughout Richardson along city streets and in its parks flourished the following spring for the enjoyment of all. The wildflower coverage has grown to over eighty-five acres. Wildflowers in this photograph include poppies, cornflowers and ox-eyed daisies.

Photography by John Guthrie

North
Texas

Texas
Blossoms

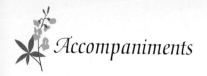

Artichokes and Green Beans Italiano

4 tablespoons butter	1 (2-ounce) jar diced pimientos with liquid
¾ teaspoon Italian herb seasoning, crumbled	1 (14-ounce) can artichoke hearts, drained and cut in quarters
¼ teaspoon garlic salt	½ cup chopped pecans
1 (9-ounce) package frozen French style green beans, thawed and drained	

Melt the butter in a 2-quart saucepan over medium heat. Stir in Italian herb seasoning, garlic salt, green beans and pimientos. Cover; cook, stirring occasionally until green beans are crispy tender, 5 to 7 minutes. Stir in artichokes and pecans. Cover; continue cooking 2 to 3 minutes until artichokes are heated. Serves 4 to 6.

Hint: Instead of Italian herb seasoning, you may substitute a mixture of ¼ teaspoon oregano, ¼ teaspoon marjoram, ¼ teaspoon basil and ½ teaspoon rubbed sage, crumbled together.

Baked Butter Beans

2 strips bacon	2 tablespoons brown sugar
¼ cup chopped onions	¼ teaspoon dry mustard
1 (16-ounce) can large butter beans, liquid drained and reserved	¼ teaspoon black pepper

Cook bacon until crisp; drain and crumble. Leave 1 tablespoon bacon drippings in the pan and cook onions until soft, about 5 minutes. Combine butter beans, ¼ cup liquid drained from beans, bacon, onions, brown sugar, dry mustard and black pepper. Pour into an 8x8x2-inch greased casserole and bake, uncovered, in a preheated 350 degree oven for 30 minutes. If beans become too dry, add more of reserved bean liquid. Serves 3 to 4.

Asparagus Spring Rollups

1	(8-ounce) package ⅓ less fat cream cheese	3	quarts water
2	tablespoons snipped fresh chives	1	tablespoon olive oil
2	tablespoons milk	1	tablespoon salt
1-2	tablespoons snipped fresh dill	8	dried lasagna noodles
1	garlic clove, minced	24	asparagus spears
1	tablespoon lemon juice	6	ounces thinly sliced smoked salmon
½	teaspoon freshly ground pepper	8	whole fresh chives

Combine cream cheese, snipped chives, milk, dill, garlic, lemon juice and pepper in a small bowl and set aside. In a large stock pot bring water and the olive oil to a boil; add salt and lasagna noodles and cook for 10 to 12 minutes or until pasta is nearly tender. Cut asparagus spears to 5-inch lengths. Add asparagus to pasta and cook for 3 minutes. Drain and rinse with cold water. Drain again and pat pasta dry with paper towels. Spread about 2 tablespoons of the cream cheese mixture evenly over each lasagna noodle. Divide salmon evenly among the noodles, placing a single layer of salmon on each noodle. Place 3 asparagus spears on one end of each noodle, letting the tips extend beyond the edge. Roll up each noodle. Tie each with a whole fresh chive. Stand rolls up to serve. Serves 8.

Kaleidoscope Black Beans and Rice

1	(15-ounce) can black beans, drained and rinsed	¾	cup water
1	(10-ounce) can diced tomatoes and green chiles and liquid	1	teaspoon salt
		1	cup uncooked instant white rice
1	cup frozen corn	1	green onion, sliced

In a skillet combine the beans, tomatoes and green chiles, corn, water and salt. Bring to a boil; stir in rice. Cover and remove from heat. Let stand for 5 minutes or until the liquid is absorbed. Sprinkle with onions. Serves 6.

Cowboy Beans

2	pounds ground beef	1	(10-ounce) can diced tomatoes and green chiles
1	onion, chopped	1	(10¾-ounce) can tomato soup, undiluted
1	bell pepper, chopped		
2	tablespoons olive oil	1	(4½-ounce) can chopped green chiles
2	(15-ounce) cans Ranch Style beans		
2	(15-ounce) cans pork and beans	1	pound mild Cheddar or Velveeta cheese, cubed or grated

Brown ground beef, onions and green peppers in oil. Add Ranch Style beans, pork and beans, tomatoes and green chiles, tomato soup and green chiles. Cover and simmer for 1 hour. To make in a slow cooker, brown beef and simmer 3 to 4 hours. Add cheese just before serving. Serves 6 to 8.

Holiday Broccoli

2	(10-ounce) packages frozen broccoli spears	2 tablespoons cornstarch
1½ cups water, divided		1 cup sour cream
½	(4.2-ounce) package chicken noodle soup with diced chicken white meat	¼ cup shredded Cheddar cheese

Cook broccoli according to package directions. Drain and arrange in a shallow 1½-quart baking dish. Boil 1¼ cups water in a saucepan, add 1 envelope soup mix and simmer 5 minutes. Blend cornstarch with ¼ cup water. Stir gradually into soup. Boil, stirring constantly for 2 minutes. Blend in sour cream and pour over broccoli. Sprinkle with cheese and broil under preheated broiler 3 to 4 inches from the heat until the cheese is melted. Serves 6 to 8.

I used to make this for Christmas
dinner, but it's so good I make more often now.

Broccoli and Corn Bake

1	(10-ounce) package frozen chopped broccoli, thawed	2	eggs, beaten
8	tablespoons butter, melted	1	slice toasted bread, crumbled (about ½ cup)
1	(14½-ounce) can cream style corn		Additional butter, optional

Mix broccoli, butter, corn and eggs. Place in a buttered 9x9x2-inch pan. Sprinkle top with breadcrumbs and dot with butter. Bake in a preheated 350 degree oven for 30 minutes. Serves 4 to 6.

Hint: Use a vegetable peeler to peel off tiny slices of butter when topping a casserole.

Cream of the Crock Broccoli

2	(10-ounce) packages frozen chopped broccoli, partly thawed	⅓	cup chopped onions
		½	teaspoon Worcestershire sauce
1	(10¾-ounce) can cream of celery soup, undiluted	¼	teaspoon pepper
1½	cups shredded sharp Cheddar cheese (about 6 ounces), divided	1	sleeve round buttery crackers (about 25), crushed
		2	tablespoons butter or margarine

In a large bowl, combine broccoli, soup, 1 cup cheese, onions, Worcestershire sauce and pepper. Pour into a greased slow cooker. Sprinkle crackers on top and dot with butter. Cover and cook on high for 1½ to 3 hours. Sprinkle with remaining cheese. Cook 10 minutes longer or until the cheese is melted. Serves 8 to 10.

Hint: Always use a slow cooker with the cover on, or it will be necessary to increase cooking time.

Curried Brussels Sprouts

2	(10-ounce) packages frozen Brussels sprouts	½	teaspoon sugar
2	tablespoons butter	½	cup chicken broth
1	garlic clove	1	tablespoon cornstarch
½	teaspoon curry powder	¼	cup water
		¼	cup toasted almonds

Cook Brussels sprouts according to package directions; drain. Melt butter in a saucepan and add garlic, curry powder and sugar. Bring to a boil over low heat. Remove garlic and stir in chicken broth. Dissolve cornstarch in water; add to liquid and bring to a boil. Pour over sprouts; garnish with almonds. Serves 4 to 6.

Red Cabbage Supreme

1	tablespoon butter	½	teaspoon salt
1	large yellow onion, finely chopped	1	tablespoon dark brown sugar
1	head red cabbage, cored and thinly sliced	1	cup water
1	Golden Delicious apple, thinly sliced	1	tablespoon red wine vinegar

Melt butter in a large skillet and sauté onions about 2 minutes. Add cabbage and apple and continue cooking for 5 minutes, stirring often. Add the salt, brown sugar, water and vinegar and cook covered over low heat for about 30 minutes or until as tender as desired. Stir once or twice and see if more water is needed. Serves 3 to 4.

This is much lower fat than most recipes and is just as delicious.

Saucy Baked Cabbage

2   cups crushed corn flakes
8   tablespoons margarine, melted
5-6 cups shredded cabbage
1   small onion, finely chopped
1   (10¾-ounce) can cream of
    celery soup, undiluted

1   cup milk
½   cup mayonnaise
1   cup shredded Cheddar cheese
Additional margarine, optional

Mix cornflakes and margarine. Put ½ mixture in bottom of a 13x9x2-inch baking dish. Put cabbage and onions over the cornflake mixture. Mix together soup, milk, mayonnaise and cheese. Pour over cabbage. Add remaining cornflake mixture and dot with additional margarine. Bake in a preheated 350 degree oven for 40 minutes or until tender. Serves 4 to 6.

Haywire Carrots

2   tablespoons butter
2   tablespoons flour
¾   teaspoon dry mustard
½   teaspoon salt
¼   teaspoon paprika
⅛   teaspoon pepper

2   cups milk
¼   cup grated Parmesan cheese
2   (14½ ounce) cans sliced carrots,
    drained
½   cup onions from 1 (2.8-ounce)
    can French fried onions

In a small saucepan melt the butter and blend in flour, mustard, salt, paprika and pepper. Add milk; cook and stir until thickened and bubbly. Stir in Parmesan cheese. Combine with carrots and pour into a 1½-quart casserole. Bake covered in a preheated 350 degree oven for 30 minutes. Uncover and sprinkle onions over the casserole. Return to oven and bake uncovered 3 to 5 minutes more. If desired double the seasonings. Leftovers can be combined with 1 (8-ounce) can of green peas and reheated. Serves 6 to 8.

Classy Carrots

1 (16-ounce) can small Belgian carrots, drained and liquid reserved

1 tablespoon instant orange breakfast drink

¼ teaspoon salt

1 tablespoon cornstarch

½ teaspoon ground nutmeg

2 tablespoons butter

1 tablespoon chopped fresh parsley

1-2 tablespoons sugar

2 tablespoons Cointreau or orange juice

Place carrot liquid, instant orange drink, salt, cornstarch and nutmeg in a medium saucepan and bring to boil over medium heat stirring constantly until mixture thickens. Add butter, parsley, sugar, Cointreau and carrots. Cook 3 or 4 minutes over low heat. Serve hot. Serves 4.

Baked Swiss Cauliflower

1 cup grated Swiss cheese

½ cup mayonnaise

½ cup sour cream

4 green onions, tops included, chopped

1 (0.65-ounce) package garlic cheese salad dressing mix

2 cauliflower heads, cut into florets, cooked and drained

½ cup bacon bits or 8 slices bacon cooked crisp, drained, crumbled

½ cup Italian style breadcrumbs

In the top of a double boiler melt the cheese and mayonnaise. Add sour cream, green onions and salad dressing mix. Place cauliflower in a baking dish and top with the sauce. Sprinkle the bacon and breadcrumbs on top and bake in a pre-heated 350 degree oven for 30 minutes. Serves 8.

Terlingua Corn Casserole

1 (15¼-ounce) can whole kernel corn with liquid	1 tablespoon butter or margarine
1 (14¾-ounce) can cream style corn	2 eggs, beaten
1-2 green onions, chopped	1 (8-ounce) package cornbread mix
½ medium green bell pepper, chopped	1 cup sour cream
	Cheddar cheese, grated

Put both corns in medium mixing bowl. Sauté onions and green peppers in butter. Add to corn. Add eggs and stir in cornbread mix. Pour into 8x8x2-inch greased baking dish. Spread sour cream on top and cover with grated cheese. Bake in a preheated 400 degree oven for 30 to 35 minutes. Serve immediately. Serves 8.

Variation: One-half (4½-ounce) can of green chiles could be substituted for green pepper.

Eggplant Southwestern

2 large or 3 small eggplants, peeled	1 (10¾-ounce) can cream of mushroom soup, undiluted
1 large onion, grated	4 tablespoons margarine
1 bell pepper, chopped	Salt and pepper to taste
3 eggs, beaten	2 cups grated cheese of your choice
1 tablespoon Worcestershire sauce	2 cups cracker crumbs
1 (10-ounce) can diced tomatoes and green chiles	Additional margarine, optional

Boil eggplants until tender; drain and mash. Add onions, bell peppers, eggs, Worcestershire sauce, tomatoes and green chiles, soup and margarine. Mix well. Mix cheese and cracker crumbs. Alternate layers of eggplant mixture with crumb mixture in a 13x9x2-inch casserole dish, ending with crumb mixture. Dot with additional margarine on top, if desired. Bake in a preheated 325 degree oven for approximately 50 minutes. Serves 10 to 12.

Eggplant Parmesan

1 (8-ounce) can tomato sauce	1 (1-pound) eggplant, peeled and sliced ¼-inch thick
¼ teaspoon dried basil, crumbled	
¼ teaspoon dried thyme, crumbled	1-2 ounces grated part-skim mozzarella cheese
Olive oil-flavored cooking spray	
	3-4 ounces freshly grated Parmesan cheese

Make the sauce by combining the tomato sauce, basil and thyme in a small pan. Bring to a boil; remove from heat and allow to stand. Preheat broiler. Spray broiler pan with cooking spray. Place eggplant in a single layer on the pan. Lightly spray the top of the eggplant with cooking spray. Broil 5 inches from the heat until light brown, about 3 to 5 minutes. Remove from oven; turn eggplant and broil 2 to 5 minutes longer. Change the oven temperature to 400 degrees. Put a thin layer of sauce in bottom of a 10x10x2-inch dish. Top with ½ of the eggplant slices. Add the mozzarella cheese. Top with the remainder of the eggplant slices. Spoon the rest of the sauce over the eggplant and sprinkle heavily with Parmesan cheese. Cover tightly with foil and bake 20 minutes. Uncover and bake until the cheese browns, about 3 minutes. Serves 4 to 6.

An eggplant with an indentation on the
bottom is less likely to be bitter.

Hot and Sassy Corn

Must Be Made Ahead

8 tablespoons butter	1 medium onion, chopped
1 (8-ounce) package cream cheese	3 (8-ounce) cans whole kernel corn
1-2 chopped jalapeños	

Melt butter and cream cheese over low heat. Add jalapeños, onions and corn. Pour into a 9x9x2-inch casserole. Refrigerate overnight. Bake in a preheated 350 degree oven for 30 minutes. Serves 4.

Tangy Green Beans
Must Be Made Ahead

Green Beans:

2 (14½-ounce) cans whole Blue
   Lake green beans

1 onion, sliced

1 tablespoon canola or vegetable oil

1 tablespoon sugar

Kosher salt, to taste

White pepper, to taste

Sauce:

1 cup sour cream

1 teaspoon lemon juice

½ teaspoon horseradish

2 teaspoons chopped onions

½ cup mayonnaise

¼ teaspoon prepared mustard

Green Beans:

Mix green beans, onions, oil, sugar, salt and pepper and refrigerate 8 hours or overnight. Drain.

Sauce:

Mix sour cream, lemon juice, horseradish, chopped onions, mayonnaise and mustard. Pour sauce over drained green bean mixture just before serving. Serves 6 to 8.

Variation: Sauce makes a good vegetable dip.

Lazy C Limas

1 (16-ounce) package frozen baby
   lima beans

4 tablespoons margarine

2 tablespoons red wine vinegar

1 teaspoon dried dill weed

¼ teaspoon pepper

½ teaspoon salt

½ (8-ounce) can sliced water
   chestnuts, drained

Cook limas according to package directions. Heat together margarine, vinegar, dill weed, pepper and salt. Drain beans; add water chestnuts, but do not cook. Pour hot sauce over beans, toss and serve. Beans are just as good or better when reheated the next day. Serves 4.

Highfalutin' Hominy

4   (15½-ounce) cans hominy, drained

2   (4½-ounce) cans chopped green chiles, drained

3   (8-ounce) containers sour cream

2   cups shredded Monterey Jack cheese

¼   cup, plus 2 tablespoons minced onions

1-2 jalapeños, seeded and finely chopped

¼   cup fine, dry breadcrumbs

¼   cup butter or margarine

Whole canned green chiles, sliced in half lengthwise

Pimiento strips

Combine hominy, green chiles, sour cream, cheese, onions and jalapeños. Place in a 13x9x2-inch glass baking dish. Spread mixture with breadcrumbs and dot with butter. Bake, uncovered in a preheated 325 degree oven for 30 minutes. Garnish with green chile halves and pimiento strips. Serves 12.

Lazy Man's Loaded Potato Casserole

6-7 medium potatoes

6   tablespoons butter, divided

8   ounces shredded Cheddar cheese

2   teaspoons salt

¼   teaspoon pepper

½   cup chopped green onions

2   cups sour cream

Boil unpeeled potatoes until tender. Dice. Melt 4 tablespoons butter in a sauce-pan. Remove from heat and add cheese, salt, pepper, onions and sour cream. Fold in diced potatoes. Pour into a greased 13x9x2-inch pan and top with the remaining 2 tablespoons butter cut in small pieces. Bake uncovered in a pre-heated 350 degree oven for 30 to 45 minutes. Serves 8.

Palo Pinto Beans

Best Made Ahead

1	ham hock	1	tablespoon cumin seed
5½	cups water	1	tablespoon chili powder
1	medium onion, finely diced, divided	1	(12-ounce) can lager beer
1¼	cups dry pinto beans, soaked overnight and drained	1	(14½-ounce) can chopped tomatoes or 1 cup fresh chopped tomatoes
1	tablespoon vegetable oil	2	tablespoons chopped cilantro
2	jalapeños, peeled, seeded and diced	2	teaspoons salt, or more, to taste

Simmer the ham hock in water for 1½ hours. Skim the fat or refrigerate until the fat can be lifted off. Combine the ham hock, ham stock, ½ the onions, and beans in a 6-quart stockpot. Bring to a boil; reduce heat; simmer for 2 hours or until beans are tender. Add more boiling water if necessary. Heat the oil in a large skillet until hot; add the remaining onions, jalapeños, cumin and chili powder. Sauté 3 minutes or until the onion browns. Add beer, tomatoes and cilantro; cook 2 minutes more. Add the mixture to the beans and season with salt to taste. Good made a day ahead. Serves 8.

Hint: Chicken stock may be substituted for ham hocks and ham stock.

Epazote is a Mexican herb, usually available in Hispanic markets. You can add ½ teaspoon crumbled dried Epazote or 1 or 2 fresh sprigs. It's supposed to reduce the gastric problems caused by beans.

The World's Championship *"Pinto Bean Cook-Off"* is held the first weekend in July in Kingsville. The Spanish named the bean "Pinto," meaning spotted.

Make Ahead Mashed Potatoes

Cook As You Wish

5 pounds potatoes (about 9 large), peeled and quartered	1 teaspoon salt
	¼ teaspoon pepper
2 (3-ounce) packages cream cheese	2 tablespoons butter or margarine
1 cup sour cream	Grated Cheddar cheese, optional
2 teaspoons onion salt	

Cook potatoes in boiling, salted water until tender. Drain well. Mash until smooth. Add cream cheese, sour cream, onion salt, salt, pepper and butter. Beat until smooth and fluffy. Place in refrigerator container. Cover and chill. To serve place the desired amount of potatoes in a greased casserole dish. Dot with butter and top with grated cheese as desired. Bake in a preheated 350 degree oven until heated, about 30 minutes. Recommended storage time is 2 weeks. Serves 8 to 10. (You can serve the potatoes or part of them when they are first made.)

Potatoes Con Queso

⅓ cup butter	1 (4½-ounce) can chopped green chiles, drained
3 tablespoons flour	
2 cups milk	2 tablespoons chopped pickled jalapeños
8 ounces shredded Monterey Jack cheese (about 2 cups), divided	½ teaspoon salt
1 (2-ounce) jar diced pimientos, drained	2 pounds baking potatoes, peeled and thinly sliced (about 3 cups)

Melt butter in a medium saucepan over low heat. Add flour, stirring until smooth and add the milk. Cook, stirring constantly, until slightly thickened and the mixture coats a spoon. Stir in 1½ cups cheese; remove from heat, and stir until cheese melts. Add pimientos, green chiles, jalapeños and salt, stirring well. Place ½ of potato slices in a lightly greased 2-quart rectangular baking dish; top with ½ of cheese mixture. Repeat layers. Bake, covered, in a preheated 350 degree oven for 20 minutes; uncover and bake 40 minutes more. Sprinkle with the remaining ½ cup cheese and bake 5 minutes more. Serves 6 to 8.

Tater Cakes

1½ pounds russet potatoes, peeled
½ cup sliced green onions (about 1 bunch)
2 eggs, beaten
½ cup milk

3 tablespoons flour
Salt and freshly ground black pepper to taste
2 tablespoons vegetable oil

Wash potatoes and cut in half. Grate the potatoes in a food processor. Put the potatoes in a bowl and cover with cold water. Combine onions with eggs, milk, flour, salt and pepper. Stir until blended. Drain potatoes in a colander and pat dry with a clean kitchen towel. Add potatoes to egg mixture. Heat oil in skillet and carefully drop in potato mixture, using a ¼ cup measure. Cook until golden brown on both sides. Potato cakes can be warmed in a 200 degree oven for 5 minutes before serving. In the rare event of leftovers, reheat and top with an egg for breakfast. Serves 4.

Spinach Fantastic

1 (6.2-ounce) package long grain and wild rice mix
2 (10-ounce) packages frozen chopped spinach, thawed
2 cups (about 8 ounces) shredded Monterey Jack cheese

4 tablespoons butter or margarine, melted
1 tablespoon chopped onions
¾ teaspoon dry mustard
½ teaspoon salt

Cook rice according to package directions. Squeeze spinach to remove excess moisture. Combine rice, spinach, cheese, butter, onions, mustard and salt and spoon into a lightly greased 2-quart shallow casserole. Bake uncovered in a pre-heated 350 degree oven for 35 to 40 minutes. You may make this casserole ahead and chill it covered up to 8 hours. Remove from refrigerator; let stand at room temperature 30 minutes; bake as directed. Serves 6.

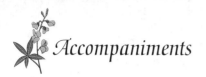

Jalapeño Cheese Spinach

Best Made Ahead

2	(10-ounce) packages frozen chopped spinach	¼	teaspoon black pepper
4	tablespoons butter	¾	teaspoon celery salt
2	tablespoons chopped onions	¾	teaspoon garlic salt
2	tablespoons flour		Salt to taste
½	cup evaporated milk	1	(6-ounce) roll jalapeño cheese, chopped
4	teaspoons Worcestershire sauce		Buttered breadcrumbs
	Cayenne pepper to taste		

Cook spinach according to package directions omitting the salt. Drain well and reserve liquid. Melt butter in saucepan over low heat. Add onions, cook until soft. Add flour, stirring until blended and smooth, but not brown. Add evaporated milk and ½ cup spinach liquid. Stir in Worcestershire sauce, cayenne, black pepper, celery salt, garlic salt, salt and cheese. Stir until cheese is melted. Combine with cooked spinach. Put into a greased 2-quart casserole and refrigerate overnight. If the casserole has been refrigerated, top with breadcrumbs and start in a cold oven set at 350 degrees and bake about 30 minutes or until hot and bubbly. To serve immediately, top with breadcrumbs and bake in a preheated 350 degree oven for 20 to 30 minutes. Serves 5 to 6.

Calico Calabacitas

Calabacitas Means Little Squash in Spanish

1½ pounds of fresh tomatoes
⅓ pound chorizo, optional
1 teaspoon butter
1 teaspoon olive oil
1 large onion, chopped
1-2 garlic cloves, minced
2 bell peppers, sliced
1 pound yellow squash, sliced thinly

1 pound zucchini, sliced thinly
1 (10-ounce) package frozen corn, thawed
2-3 tablespoons fresh cilantro
Salt and pepper to taste
1 (6-ounce) package sliced Muenster cheese, cut in strips

Peel, core, seed and chop tomatoes. Allow to drain. In a small skillet cook the chorizo 2 to 3 minutes. Drain on 2 layers of paper towels. In a large pot melt the butter and add the olive oil. Sauté the onions about 2 minutes; add the garlic, bell peppers and tomatoes and cook 2 minutes longer. Add yellow squash, zucchini, corn, cilantro, salt and pepper and cook over low heat until the vegetables are almost done, about 10 minutes. Add the chorizo. (At this point the vegetables may be put in a 13x9x2-inch casserole and may be frozen or refrigerated for several hours. Don't add the cheese until reheating.) To finish the dish, add the cheese, cover the pot and let steam about 2 minutes or until the cheese is melted, If the casserole dish is cold: reheat, starting in a cold oven set at 325 degrees for 25 to 30 minutes. Top with cheese and return to oven until the cheese melts. Serves 6.

Hint: Chorizo is a spicy Mexican sausage. It tends to be greasy, so precooking is recommended.

Sweet Potatoes and Cranberry Casserole

½ cup flour	1 (40-ounce) can sweet potatoes
1 teaspoon ground cinnamon	or yams, drained
½ cup packed brown sugar	1 cup raw cranberries
½ cup rolled oats	1½ cups miniature marshmallows
⅓ cup butter or margarine, softened	

Mix flour, cinnamon, brown sugar and oats with the butter. Toss 1 cup of flour mixture with the sweet potatoes and cranberries. Put in a greased 13x9x2-inch casserole and top with remaining flour mixture. Bake in a preheated 350 degree oven for 35 minutes. Top immediately with marshmallows. Serves 6 to 8.

Sweet Potato Chips

2 large sweet potatoes, unpeeled, thinly sliced	1 teaspoon salt
	1 teaspoon chili powder
1 tablespoon olive oil	

Toss all ingredients. Potatoes should be lightly oiled. Place on wire racks on cookie sheets and bake in a preheated 400 degree oven for 10 minutes. Check and continue to bake until browned. Drain on paper towels. Serves 3.

Variation: Slice potatoes as thinly as possible; place in ice water for about 10 minutes to remove starch. Drain well and pat dry with paper towel. Heat desired amount of oil in a heavy skillet or deep fryer to 375 degrees. Place slices in hot oil and fry until light golden color. Do not burn. Drain on paper towel. Sprinkle with salt or a mixture of cinnamon and sugar, if desired.

Gilmer is the home of the sweet potato festival known as the *"Yamboree."* It occurs in the second weekend of October and celebrates the survival of the sweet potato after weevils almost destroyed the whole crop.

Spinach-Stuffed Tomatoes

3 strips bacon	Dash vinegar
¼ cup chopped onions	Dash garlic salt
½ pound fresh spinach, torn into small pieces	4 medium tomatoes
½ cup sour cream	½ cup shredded mozzarella cheese

Cook bacon until crisp. Drain, reserving 2 tablespoons of the drippings. Crumble bacon and set aside. Cook onions in reserved drippings until tender. Add spinach and cook, covered 3 to 5 minutes or until tender. Remove from heat and add sour cream, bacon, vinegar and garlic salt. Cut tops from tomatoes and scoop out centers. Drain the tomato shells on paper towels. Lightly salt shells, fill with the spinach mixture and place in an 8x8x2-inch baking dish. Bake in a preheated 375 degree oven for 20 to 25 minutes. Top with cheese and return to oven until the cheese melts, about 2 or 3 minutes. Serves 4.

Top Hat Tomatoes

4 medium tomatoes	⅛ teaspoon dried oregano, crumbled
3 tablespoons chopped green onions	⅛ teaspoon cayenne pepper
2 tablespoons chopped green bell peppers	⅛ teaspoon pepper
1 tablespoon butter	Cooking spray
¼ cup Italian seasoned breadcrumbs	2 tablespoons grated Parmesan cheese
2 tablespoons chopped fresh parsley	

Cut tops from tomatoes and carefully scoop out pulp; set both aside. Cook green onions and green peppers with butter in skillet over medium heat, stirring constantly until tender. Remove from heat; stir in tomato pulp, breadcrumbs, parsley, oregano, cayenne and pepper. Spoon into tomato shells and place in a baking dish coated with cooking spray. Bake covered in a preheated 350 degree oven for 25 minutes. Sprinkle with cheese and broil 3 minutes or until golden brown. Serves 4.

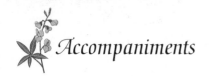

Apple-Cranberry Bake

3 cups peeled and chopped apples	8 tablespoons butter, melted
2 cups fresh cranberries	⅓ cup chopped pecans
1 cup sugar	½ teaspoon ground cinnamon
1½ cups quick oats	⅓ cup flour
½ cup packed brown sugar	

Combine apples, cranberries and sugar in a small bowl. Spread mixture evenly in a 13x9x2-inch baking dish. Combine oats, brown sugar, butter, pecans, cinnamon and flour in a small bowl. Spread evenly over the top of the fruit. Bake in a preheated oven at 325 degrees for 60 minutes or until brown and bubbly.

Baked Apricots

Cooking spray	⅔ cup packed dark brown sugar
4 (15-ounce) cans apricots halves in heavy syrup, drained	2 sleeves Ritz crackers, crushed by hand
⅔ cup packed light brown sugar	1½ cups butter

Spray a 13x9x2-inch baking dish lightly with cooking spray. Layer apricots in dish, fitting close together. Mix sugars together. Sprinkle sugar mixture and then crushed crackers evenly over the apricots. Melt butter and pour over all. Bake in a preheated oven at 300 degrees for 45 minutes or until bubbly and browned. Serves 12 to 15.

Recipe can be halved. Bake in a 8x8x2-inch square baking dish for 30 to 35 minutes.

Variation: Peaches may be substituted for apricots.

Curried Fruit

1 (15-ounce) can pineapple, drained and liquid reserved

1 (15-ounce) can peaches, drained and liquid reserved

1 (15-ounce) can pears, drained and liquid reserved

3 bananas, sliced lengthwise

1 cup packed brown sugar

Pinch salt

1 teaspoon lemon juice

2 teaspoons curry powder

8 tablespoons cup butter

Mix all liquid reserved from the fruit. Set aside. Put fruit in a 13x9x2-inch baking dish. Sprinkle with brown sugar. In a small bowl, mix together the salt, lemon juice, curry and ½ cup of the mixed fruit juice. Pour over the fruit. Dot with butter and bake in a preheated oven at 325 degrees for 60 minutes.

Hint: Peel banana and put your finger into the top of the banana and push all the way down. Your banana will split into 3 equal pieces.

Pineapple Supreme

¼-½ cup sugar

3 tablespoons flour

½ teaspoon salt

1 (29½-ounce) can crushed pineapple

¼-½ pound grated sharp Cheddar cheese

8 tablespoons butter

1 sleeve Ritz crackers, crushed by hand

Mix sugar, flour and salt together in a small bowl. Add pineapple and cheese and mix well. Place in a 1½-quart baking dish. Melt butter; add crackers and toss to coat. Spread evenly over pineapple mixture. Bake in a preheated oven at 350 degrees for 30 to 40 minutes or until bubbly and browned.

Especially good with ham.

Poncho's Baked Papaya

¼ cup sugar	½ cup thinly sliced water chestnuts
1½ teaspoons ground cinnamon	2 tablespoons golden seedless raisins
1½ cups cottage cheese	
11 ounces cream cheese	3 ripe papayas, halved and seeded
2 tablespoons chutney	⅓ cup butter, melted
1 teaspoon curry powder	

Mix together sugar and cinnamon in a small bowl. Set aside. In another bowl, combine cottage cheese, cream cheese, chutney and curry. Stir in water chestnuts and raisins. Place papayas in a baking dish. Spoon cheese mixture into cavities. Pour melted butter over the top and sprinkle with the sugar mixture. Bake in a preheated 450 degree oven for 15 minutes. Can be served warm, cold or at room temperature. Serves 8 to 12.

Variation: The cheese filling could be used on sweet crackers or gingersnaps as an appetizer.

Sherried Fruit

Must Be Made Ahead

1 (15-ounce) can pineapple chunks, drained	1 (15-ounce) can Bing cherries, drained
1 (15-ounce) can peach halves, drained	4 tablespoons butter
	½ cup sugar
1 (15-ounce) can apricot halves, drained	2 tablespoons flour
	2 tablespoons lemon juice
1 (15-ounce) can pear halves, drained	1 cup sherry
1 (15-ounce) can red apple rings, drained	

Place fruit in a 13x9x2-inch baking dish. Melt butter in a small saucepan. Add sugar, flour, lemon juice and sherry. Cook over low heat until thickened. Pour over drained fruit and refrigerate overnight. Bake in a preheated 350 degree oven for 45 minutes.

Stuffed Strawberries
Must Be Made Ahead

20 large strawberries, divided
1 (3-ounce) package cream cheese, softened
2 tablespoons finely chopped pecans or walnuts

1½ tablespoons powdered sugar
1 teaspoon orange or raspberry liqueur, optional

Dice 2 strawberries and set aside. Cut a thin slice from stem end of each of the remaining strawberries. Cut each strawberry into 4 wedges, starting at the pointed ends and cutting to, but not through the stem ends. Beat cream cheese until fluffy. Stir in diced strawberries, nuts, sugar and liqueur. Spoon or pipe about 1 teaspoon mixture into each strawberry. Makes 18 strawberries.

Great for teas and showers.

Padre's Macaroni

1 (8-ounce) package dry macaroni
1 (14½-ounce) can Mexican-style tomatoes, chopped
1 (10¾-ounce) can cream of mushroom soup, undiluted
1 (8-ounce) container sour cream

1 (4½-ounce) can chopped green chiles
1 cup shredded Monterey Jack cheese, divided
1 cup shredded Cheddar cheese, divided

Cook macaroni according to package directions and drain. Combine macaroni, tomatoes, mushroom soup, sour cream and chiles. Stir in ½ of each of the cheeses. Pour into a lightly greased 13x9x2-inch baking dish. Top with a mixture of the remaining cheeses. Bake in a preheated oven at 350 degrees for 30 minutes or until bubbly. Serves 6.

Not Your Same Old Macaroni

Yummy!

1½ cups dry macaroni
1 tablespoon margarine
1 medium onion, chopped
2 garlic cloves, minced
1 (14½-ounce) can diced tomatoes and liquid
1 tablespoon dried parsley
2 teaspoons instant chicken bouillon

½ teaspoon salt
½ teaspoon dried oregano, crumbled
½ teaspoon dried basil, crumbled
1 cup grated Cheddar cheese, divided
1 (16-ounce) package frozen chopped broccoli, thawed

In a large pot cook macaroni according to package directions; drain and reserve. In the same pot melt margarine and cook onions until translucent. Add garlic, tomatoes and liquid, parsley, bouillon, salt, oregano and basil. Bring to a boil and simmer for 3 minutes. Add macaroni, ½ cup cheese and broccoli. Pour into a 13x9x2-inch baking dish. Bake in a preheated 375 degree oven for 15 minutes. Uncover and top with remaining cheese. Bake 5 minutes longer or until the cheese is melted. Serves 4 to 6.

Linguine à la Checca

4 ounces dry linguine
Olive oil
1 garlic clove, sliced

3-4 Roma tomatoes, chopped
2 fresh basil leaves, snipped
Garlic salt to taste

Cook linguine according to package directions. Heat a small amount of oil in a saucepan. Add garlic and sauté for 1 minute. Add tomatoes and basil and sauté for 1 to 2 minutes. Add garlic salt to taste. Pour over pasta. Serves 2.

Parmesan Party Noodles

1 (10-ounce) package narrow egg noodles
2 cups small curd cottage cheese
2-3 cups sour cream
2 garlic cloves, minced
1 medium onion, finely minced
2-3 tablespoons Worcestershire sauce

2 dashes Tabasco sauce
2-3 cups grated Parmesan cheese, plus more for topping
Salt and pepper to taste
Grated Parmesan cheese for topping

Cook noodles according to package directions and drain. Place in a large bowl and add cottage cheese, sour cream, garlic, onions, Worcestershire sauce, Tabasco sauce, cheese, salt and pepper. Place in a greased 13x9x2-inch baking dish. Sprinkle with additional cheese, cover and bake in a preheated 350 degree oven for 45 minutes. Serves 4 to 6.

This recipe was given to me as a recipe shower gift when I was married in 1964. It has been served to rave reviews ever since.

Wild Rice and Mushroom Stuffing

1 cup wild rice
2-3 cups chicken broth
1 medium onion, chopped
4 tablespoons butter, divided

1 cup sliced mushrooms
¼ pound sausage, crumbled
Salt and pepper to taste

Cook wild rice in 2 to 3 cups chicken broth until tender. Sauté onions in 2 tablespoons of butter in a medium skillet for 5 minutes or until lightly browned. Remove onions from skillet and set aside. Add the remaining 2 tablespoons butter to skillet; add mushrooms and cook for 5 minutes. Fry sausage in a large skillet until lightly browned, stirring constantly; remove from heat and stir in onion and mushrooms. Add wild rice, salt and pepper to taste. Mix lightly. To make a more moist stuffing, add more chicken broth. Bake in a preheated oven at 350 degrees for 30 to 40 minutes. Serves 4.

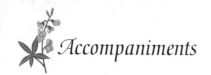

Southern Cornbread Dressing

1 celery rib, finely chopped	4 eggs, beaten
2 bunches green onions, finely chopped	1 (5-ounce) can evaporated milk
2 large green bell peppers, finely chopped	1 (10¾-ounce) can cream of mushroom soup, undiluted
1 bunch parsley, chopped	4 cups finely crumbled cornbread
2 large onions, finely chopped	5 slices dried white bread, finely crumbled
1 tablespoon poultry seasoning	½ sleeve saltine crackers, crumbled
Salt and pepper to taste	2 cups canned chicken broth
8 tablespoons margarine	

Sauté in a large skillet the celery, green onions, green pepper, parsley, onions, poultry seasoning, salt and pepper to taste in margarine. Combine eggs, evaporated milk and mushroom soup in a small bowl. Add cornbread, breadcrumbs and crackers alternately with egg mixture and broth. Add sautéed vegetables and mix well. Stuff turkey or chicken and place the remaining dressing in a 13x9x2-inch baking dish. Bake in a preheated 350 degree oven for 45 to 60 minutes.

Hint: If you are stuffing a turkey make broth from boiled turkey giblets and neck.

Cocktail Sauce

Must Be Chilled

1 cup ketchup	1 teaspoon Worcestershire sauce
1 teaspoon lemon juice	1 teaspoon Tabasco sauce
¼ cup prepared horseradish	Salt to taste
1 tablespoon prepared mustard	

Combine all ingredients and stir well. Store in a covered jar. Chill before serving.

You'll never want bottled again!

Unforgettable Grits Soufflé

1	cup white quick grits	4	eggs, slightly beaten
4	cups water	8	ounces grated sharp Cheddar cheese
1	teaspoon salt		
¾	cup margarine	11	drops Tabasco sauce
			Cooking spray

Cook grits in water with salt as directed on package for 2 to 5 minutes in a large pot. Add margarine. Stir some of the hot grits into the beaten eggs to temper. Then add egg mixture to grits, stirring constantly. Remove from heat. Add cheese and Tabasco sauce. Mix well. Place in a 13x9x2-inch baking dish that has been sprayed with cooking spray. Bake in a preheated oven at 350 degrees for 60 minutes. Serves 4.

Great served with pork.

Favorite Barbecue Sauce

1	cup water	¾	cup vinegar
1	(6-ounce) can tomato paste	⅓	cup lemon juice
5	teaspoons chili powder	8	tablespoons margarine
1½	teaspoons pepper	¼	teaspoon cayenne pepper
½	cup plus 1 tablespoon ketchup	6	tablespoons honey
½	teaspoon garlic salt	6	tablespoons brown sugar
3	tablespoons Worcestershire sauce	½	teaspoon salt

Combine water, tomato paste and chili powder in a medium saucepan, mixing well. Add pepper and ketchup and simmer for 5 minutes. Add garlic salt, Worcestershire sauce, vinegar, lemon juice, margarine, cayenne, honey, brown sugar and salt. Bring to a boil; reduce heat and simmer at least 60 minutes. Serve over ribs, chicken or brisket. Refrigerate leftover unused sauce. Makes 4 cups.

Horseradish Sauce

Must Be Chilled

2 tablespoons prepared horseradish   Juice from ½ lemon
¼ cup mayonnaise   ½ teaspoon sugar
¼ cup sour cream

Mix well and refrigerate in a covered jar. Makes ½ cup.

Basil Pesto

¾ cup walnuts   1 cup grated Parmesan cheese
3 cups packed fresh basil, stemmed   4 medium garlic cloves
1½ cups olive oil

Combine all ingredients in a food processor or blender. Turning the machine on and off rapidly, pulse the mixture several times until coarsely chopped. Scrape down sides. Continue to pulse until mixture is smooth. Makes 3½ cups.

Use as a topping on fresh tomatoes, cheese slices or hot pasta.

Brown Butter Sauce

4 tablespoons butter   1 tablespoon cider vinegar
3 tablespoons flour   1 tablespoon vanilla extract
1 cup packed brown sugar   ¼ teaspoon lemon extract
1 cup water

In a saucepan, over low heat, heat butter until light brown. Blend in flour, then sugar. Gradually add water and cook until mixture thickens and loses its starchy taste. Add vinegar and lemon and almond extracts. Serve hot over puddings or cakes.

Avocado Cream

1	large avocado (about 11 ounces)	¼	teaspoon white pepper
1	tablespoon lime juice	½	cup picante sauce
½	cup mayonnaise	2	green onions, finely sliced
½	cup sour cream	1	large Roma tomato, seeded and chopped
½	teaspoon seasoned salt		

Peel and pit the avocado and pulse it 2 or 3 times with the lime juice. Add mayonnaise, sour cream, seasoned salt, white pepper and picante sauce. Process until well blended. Serve over grilled chicken. Garnish with green onions and tomatoes. To use as a dip, chill for 2 to 3 hours. Top with green onions and tomatoes.

Microwave Lemon Curd

8	tablespoons unsalted butter	Grated zest of 3 large lemons
3	large eggs	½ cup fresh lemon juice
1	cup sugar	

Microwave the butter until melted. Reserve. In another bowl, whisk together the eggs, sugar, lemon zest and juice until well blended. Whisk in the melted butter. Microwave on high for 1½ to 2 minutes, whisking often, until curd is smooth and thick enough to coat a wooden spoon. Remove from the microwave and pour into sterilized jelly jars. Cover and allow to cool at room temperature. Store in the refrigerator for up to 4 weeks. Makes 2 cups.

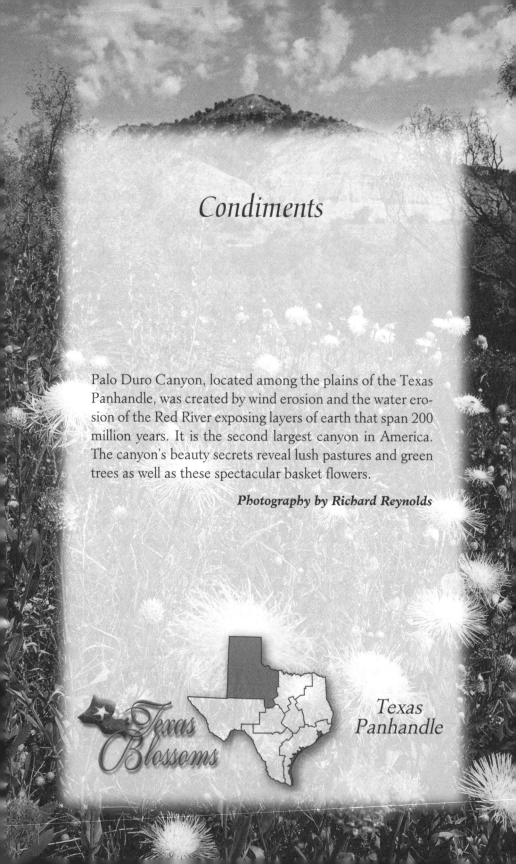

Condiments

Palo Duro Canyon, located among the plains of the Texas Panhandle, was created by wind erosion and the water erosion of the Red River exposing layers of earth that span 200 million years. It is the second largest canyon in America. The canyon's beauty secrets reveal lush pastures and green trees as well as these spectacular basket flowers.

Photography by Richard Reynolds

Texas
Blossoms

Texas
Panhandle

Texas
Blossoms

Richardson Woman's Club Pickles

We Started Selling These At Bake Sales In 1958!

1	gallon whole dill or sour pickles	3	tablespoons celery seed
5	pounds sugar	3	tablespoons whole cloves
3	tablespoons mustard seeds	8	garlic cloves
8	sticks cinnamon	4	jalapeños, optional
1	teaspoon allspice		

Drain and discard juice from pickles. Cut into ¾-inch thick slices and place in a 2-gallon crock. (Do not use aluminum!) Pour sugar and spices over pickles. After 24 hours, stir with wooden or stainless steel spoon. Then stir 2 to 3 times daily. They are ready to eat after the third day. Pack into four 1-quart jars and seal.

Hint: There will be lots of juice left when pickles are gone. Don't throw it away! It's wonderful for basting a baked ham. Also gives a delightful flavor to tuna or chicken salad. (Put some of the pickles in the salad too!)

An RWC Favorite from *The Texas Experience.*

Icy-Spicy Pickles

Must Be Chilled

2	(32-ounce) jars dill pickles	1	teaspoon hot red pepper flakes
4	cups sugar		Garlic cloves
2	tablespoons Tabasco sauce		

Drain pickles and cut into ¾-inch slices. Place in a large non-metal bowl. Add sugar, Tabasco sauce and pepper flakes. Keep at room temperature and stir frequently until juice forms, about 4 to 5 hours. Put pickles and juice into pint jars adding a garlic clove to each. Refrigerate for 1 week before serving.

Anytime Bean Relish

Must Be Made Ahead

2 (15-ounce) cans small kidney beans, drained and rinsed
¾ cup mayonnaise
½ medium onion, minced

1 large garlic clove, minced
2 tablespoons sweet relish
8 drops Worcestershire sauce
Salt and pepper to taste

Mix all ingredients together in a medium bowl. Cover and refrigerate for 2 days to enhance flavor.

Blue Ribbon Corn Relish

A Family Favorite

16-20 ears fresh corn
4 cups chopped celery
2 cups chopped red bell peppers
2 cups chopped green bell peppers
1 cup chopped onions
2 cups sugar

2 cups vinegar
2 teaspoons celery seed
2½ cups water, divided
2 tablespoons salt
¼ cup flour
2 tablespoons dry mustard
1 teaspoon ground turmeric

Husk and silk corn. Cook in boiling water 5 minutes; plunge into cold water. Drain. Cut corn from cobs, but do not scrape cobs. You will need 8 cups cut corn. In an 8 to 10-quart kettle or Dutch oven combine celery, bell peppers and onions. Add sugar, vinegar, celery seeds, 2 cups water and salt. Bring mixture to a boil. Boil, uncovered, 5 minutes, stirring occasionally. Blend flour, dry mustard and turmeric with ½ cup cold water. Add along with corn to boiling mixture. Return to a boil; cook and stir 5 minutes. Pack loosely in hot pint jars, leaving ½-inch headspace. Cover with lids. Process in boiling water bath canner for 15 minutes. When cool, adjust the jar rings. Makes 7 pints.

Fire and Ice Cranberries

1   (16-ounce) can whole-berry
    cranberry sauce
1   (10½-ounce) jar jalapeño pepper
    jelly

2   tablespoons fresh cilantro,
    chopped

Combine all ingredients in a small saucepan. Cook over low heat until jelly melts, stirring often. Cool and store in refrigerator. Makes 2½ cups.

Hint: Very good with ham and turkey.

This makes a very pretty appetizer poured over an (8-ounce) package of slightly softened cream cheese. Serve with crackers.

Wine Jelly

2   cups your favorite wine, sherry
    or port
3   cups sugar

1   bottle liquid fruit pectin
    Paraffin

Put wine and sugar in top of double boiler over boiling water. Stir until all sugar melts and mixture is hot. Add fruit pectin after removing from heat. Pour into sterilized jelly jars and seal with paraffin. If you use white wine, you can color it red or green. Beautiful jelly!

An RWC Favorite from *The Texas Experience.*

Jalapeño Jelly

½-¾ cup chopped jalapeño peppers
½-¾ cup seeded, chopped bell
     peppers
5 cups sugar

1-1¼ cups wine or white vinegar
½ cup water
1 bottle liquid fruit pectin
Paraffin

Place peppers in a large pot. Add sugar, vinegar and water. Bring to a boil for 5 minutes. Remove from heat and let cool for 20 minutes. Add fruit pectin; mix well and replace pot on heat. Allow jelly to come to a full boil; remove from heat. Stir well and pour into sterilized jelly jars. Seal with paraffin when jelly has cooled. Makes 5 to 6 pint jars.

Hint: Wear rubber gloves when working with jalapeños and other hot peppers and wash your hands when you're through.

This jelly makes an excellent and unusual appetizer. Spread crackers with cream cheese and top with small amounts of Jalapeño Jelly, or spread jelly over slightly softened cream cheese and serve with crackers on the side.

Variation:
¼ cup ground jalapeños with seeds
    (about 8 or 10)
¾ cup seeded, ground bell peppers
1½ cups white vinegar

6½ cups sugar
1 bottle liquid fruit pectin
Paraffin

Mix jalapeños, bell peppers, vinegar and sugar in large saucepan or kettle. Boil 8 to 10 minutes. Remove from heat; add liquid fruit pectin and stir well. Cool slightly and put in sterilized jelly jars. Seal with paraffin.

Hint: If you use red ripe bell peppers and red jalapeños, your jelly will be a beautiful red color. If you use green bell peppers and green jalapeños, you may wish to use green food coloring. Makes 6 to 8 pints jars.

These recipes are RWC Favorites from
The Texas Experience, our first cookbook.

Breads I

Wildseed Farms

For an explosion of color any time of the year, visit the Wildseed Farms, 7 miles from Fredericksburg on US Highway 290. They harvest up to 400,000 pounds of wildflower seeds annually. Visitors can see planting, harvesting and flowers in various stages of growth on the 600-acre farm.

Photograph provided by the Wildseed Farms

Texas Blossoms

Texas Hill Country

Texas Blossoms

Apple Festival Loaf

2 cups flour	2 large eggs
1 teaspoon baking soda	1 cup peeled, cored and chopped apples
1 teaspoon baking powder	
½ teaspoon salt	½ cup chopped dates
1 cup unsweetened applesauce	⅓ cup semi-sweet chocolate chips
½ cup sugar	¼ cup chopped walnuts, optional
3 tablespoons vegetable oil	Cooking spray

In a medium bowl, combine flour, baking soda, baking powder and salt. Mix well. In a large bowl, whisk together applesauce, sugar, oil and eggs. Add flour mixture, stirring until just moistened. Stir in apples, dates, chocolate chips and walnuts. Spoon batter into a 9x5x3-inch loaf pan that has been sprayed with cooking spray. Bake in a preheated 350 degree oven for about 1 hour or until top is golden brown and a toothpick comes out clean. Place pan on a wire rack and cool 10 minutes. Turn loaf out onto rack and cool completely. Makes 1 loaf.

Hint: To freeze, cool loaf completely and wrap in aluminum foil. Keeps up to 3 months.

An RWC Bake Sale Favorite.

The *"Apple Festival"* celebrates the apple crop during the last week of July in Medina. The Texas apple is called Elah, a type that originated in Israel.

Cranberry Surprise Loaf

2 (3-ounce) packages cream cheese, softened	½ teaspoon salt
2 eggs, divided	¾ cup apple juice
2 cups flour	4 tablespoons butter, melted
1 cup sugar	1½ cups coarsely chopped cranberries
1½ teaspoons baking powder	½ cup chopped pecans
½ teaspoon baking soda	

In small bowl, beat cream cheese until light and fluffy. Add 1 egg. Blend well. Set aside. In large bowl, combine flour, sugar, baking powder, baking soda and salt. Stir in apple juice, butter and the remaining egg, beaten. Fold in the cranberries and nuts. Grease and flour bottom only of a 9x5x3-inch loaf pan. Spoon half of batter into pan. Spoon cream cheese mixture over batter. Top with remaining batter. Bake in a preheated 350 degree oven for 65 to 75 minutes or until top springs back when lightly touched in center. Cool 15 minutes. Remove from pan. Cool completely and wrap in plastic wrap and store in refrigerator. Makes 1 loaf.

Hint: To chop cranberries in food processor, add about 2 cups fresh cranberries to food processor bowl with metal blade. Process with 10 on-off pulses or until all berries are coarsely chopped. If using frozen cranberries, chop them by hand while still frozen.

Always remove bread promptly from its pan to keep bottom and sides from becoming soggy. Wrap in or cover tightly with a towel until cool to prevent drying.

Double Good Lemon Bread

Bread:

½ cup vegetable shortening	½ teaspoon salt
1 cup sugar	½ cup milk
2 eggs	1 tablespoon finely grated lemon zest
1¼ cups flour	
1 teaspoon baking powder	½ cup chopped pecans

Lemon Syrup:

¼ cup sugar	3 tablespoons fresh lemon juice

Bread:

In a large bowl, combine shortening and sugar and beat well. Add eggs one at a time, beating after each addition. In a medium bowl, combine flour, baking powder and salt. Add to the shortening mixture with the milk and lemon zest. Stir until just blended. Fold in pecans. Spread evenly into a greased and floured 8x4x2-inch loaf pan. Bake in a preheated 350 degree oven for about 1 hour or until tester comes out clean. Makes 1 loaf.

Lemon Syrup:

While the bread bakes, make the syrup. In a small bowl, combine the sugar and lemon juice. Set aside, stirring occasionally. Don't worry if the sugar does not dissolve completely. Remove the bread from the oven, and using a fork, poke the top in several places. Stir the syrup, and then slowly drizzle it over the hot bread. Cool in the pan 15 minutes, then turn out onto a wire rack to cool completely.

Hint: Use a piece of spaghetti as a bread or cake tester. It goes all the way to the bottom of the pan.

Autumn Harvest Pumpkin Bread

1¼ cups vegetable oil
5 eggs, beaten
2 cups canned pumpkin
2 cups flour
2 cups sugar
2 (3-ounce) packages instant coconut pudding mix

1 teaspoon salt
1 teaspoon baking soda
1 teaspoon ground cinnamon
1 cup chopped nuts
1 cup coconut

In a large bowl, mix oil, eggs and pumpkin. Beat well. In a medium bowl, mix together the flour, sugar, pudding mix, salt, baking soda and cinnamon. Add nuts and coconut to dry ingredients and blend. Add dry ingredients to pumpkin mixture. Spread evenly into 2 greased and floured 9x5x3-inch loaf pans. Bake in a preheated 350 degree oven for 1 hour. Cool for 10 minutes and remove from pans. Makes 2 loaves.

Variation: Bake in mini-muffin pans in a preheated 350 degree oven for 20 minutes. (The muffins don't raise much so fill the tins almost full.) Makes 7 to 8 dozen.

An RWC Favorite, these muffins were served in the Tea Room.

The West Texas town of Floydada holds a *"Pumpkin Festival"* during the last weekend of October. The Indians loved pumpkins, squash and zucchini and introduced them to the Spanish when they came here.

Timeless Pineapple Nut Bread

1	(20-ounce) can crushed pineapple with liquid	4	cups flour
3	cups sugar, divided	½	teaspoon salt
1	cup butter	2	teaspoons baking powder
6	eggs, well beaten	1	cup pineapple juice
1	teaspoon vanilla extract	2	cups chopped pecans

Cook the crushed pineapple with 2 cups sugar until liquid is thick and syrupy and pineapple is almost candied. In a large bowl, cream together the remaining cup of sugar and butter. Add eggs and vanilla extract, mixing thoroughly. Sift together the flour, salt and baking powder and add alternately with the pineapple juice to the creamed mixture. Stir in the pineapple mixture and pecans. Spread evenly into 2 greased and floured 9x5x3-inch loaf pans. Bake in a preheated 350 degree oven for about 1 hour or until a toothpick inserted in loaf comes out clean. Cool for 10 minutes and remove from pans. Makes 2 loaves.

Date-Raisin Mini-Muffins

3	eggs, beaten	3	rounded tablespoons flour (yes, that's all)
¾	cup sugar		
1	teaspoon vanilla extract	4	ounces dates, chopped
1	cup chopped pecans	4	ounces golden raisins

In a small bowl, mix the beaten eggs, sugar and vanilla extract. Stir in pecans. In another bowl, mix together the flour, dates and raisins. Add to sugar mixture. Fill greased and floured mini-muffin tins ⅔ full. Bake in a preheated 350 degree oven for 10 to 12 minutes or until done. Makes 36 mini-muffins.

Hint: Stir batter just until all ingredients are moistened. The muffin batter should be lumpy.

Blueberry Tea Mini-Muffins

Mini-Muffins:

8 tablespoons butter, softened	¼ teaspoon salt
1 cup sugar	¼ teaspoon ground nutmeg
2 eggs	⅛ teaspoon ground cloves
1¾ cups flour	¾ cup buttermilk
1 teaspoon baking powder	1 (12-ounce) can blueberries, drained
¾ teaspoon baking soda	

Topping:

1 tablespoon grated orange zest	4 tablespoons butter, melted
⅓ cup sugar	

Mini-Muffins:

In a large mixer bowl, cream butter and sugar. Add eggs, one at a time, beating well after each addition. Sift together the flour, baking powder, baking soda, salt, nutmeg and cloves. Add to butter mixture alternately with buttermilk, beating well after each addition. Fold in blueberries. Line mini-muffin tin cups with paper liners and fill ⅔ full. Bake in a preheated 375 degree oven for 15 to 20 minutes or until done. Makes 4 dozen.

Topping:

In a small bowl, mix together the orange zest and sugar. Remove muffins from tins while hot and dip in melted butter and then in sugar mixture. May be made ahead and frozen.

An RWC Favorite served in the Tea Room.

Streusel Topped Strawberry Muffins

Muffins:

1½ cups fresh strawberries, coarsely chopped	¼ teaspoon freshly grated nutmeg
¾ cup sugar, divided	¼ teaspoon salt
1¾ cups flour	2 eggs, beaten
½ teaspoon baking soda	4 tablespoons butter, melted
	1 teaspoon vanilla extract

Streusel Topping:

½ cup chopped pecans	¼ cup flour
½ cup packed brown sugar	2 tablespoons butter, melted

Muffins:

In small bowl, combine strawberries and ½ cup sugar. Set aside for 1 to 2 hours. Drain and reserve liquid and strawberries separately. In small bowl, combine flour, baking soda, nutmeg and salt and set aside. In medium bowl, mix eggs, butter, vanilla extract, the remaining ¼ cup sugar and liquid from strawberries. Add flour mixture and stir just until combined. Fold in reserved strawberries. Spoon into greased muffin tins.

Streusel Topping:

Mix together pecans, brown sugar, flour and butter. Sprinkle over each muffin. Bake in a preheated 425 degree oven for 10 to 12 minutes or until muffins test done.

Grease baking pans with solid shortening only unless otherwise specified.

Healthy Zucchini Muffins

2	cups grated zucchini	2	tablespoons ground cinnamon
1½	cups sugar	1	teaspoon ground nutmeg
2	eggs	1	teaspoon baking soda
¼	cup vegetable oil	½	teaspoon baking powder
3	cups flour	1	cup chopped nuts, optional

Beat together the zucchini, sugar and eggs in a large bowl. Add oil and mix. In a separate bowl, stir together the flour, cinnamon, nutmeg, baking soda, and baking powder. Stir into zucchini mixture. Fold in chopped nuts. Fill greased muffin tins ⅔ full. Bake in a preheated 350 degree oven for 15 to 25 minutes for large muffins and 12 to 15 minutes for mini-muffins. Do not overcook; check with toothpick at 15 minutes. Makes 18 to 24 large muffins or 60 mini-muffins.

Pecan Pie Mini-Muffins

1	cup packed brown sugar	⅔	cup butter, melted (do not substitute)
½	cup flour		
1	cup chopped pecans	2	eggs, beaten

Combine brown sugar, flour and pecans in a medium mixing bowl. Set aside. In a separate bowl, combine the melted butter and beaten eggs. Stir into flour mixture just until moistened. Fill greased and floured or paper lined mini-muffin tins ⅔ full. Bake in a preheated 350 degree oven for 20 to 25 minutes or until a toothpick comes out clean. Remove immediately to cool on wire racks. Makes about 2½ dozen.

When muffins are done, remove immediately from the pan.

Blue Cheese Muffins

Must Be Chilled

Crust:

1 cup butter	2 cups flour
2 (3-ounce) packages cream cheese	Cooking spray

Filling:

3 eggs	1 teaspoon flour
1⅓ cups milk	½ cup (about 5-ounces) blue cheese
¼ teaspoon salt	1 teaspoon onion juice

Crust:

Cream together all crust ingredients in a mixer bowl or food processor. Wrap in plastic wrap and chill in refrigerator for 30 to 40 minutes or until dough feels slightly firm, but not hard to the touch. When the mixture is ready, pinch the dough into 48 equal chunks. Spray mini-muffin tins with cooking spray. To fill each tin, shape dough by pressing across bottom and up the sides extending slightly above the flat surface of the muffin tin.

Filling:

Mix all filling ingredients together. Fill crusts ⅔ full. Bake in a preheated 350 degree oven for 20 minutes or until golden brown.

The muffins are especially nice for brunch or a tea.

The Queen's Scones
with Sweet Cream Cheese

Scones:

2	cups flour	4	tablespoons cold unsalted butter
¼	cup sugar	1	large egg
1	tablespoon baking powder	1¼	cups whipping cream
1	teaspoon salt		Additional cream for brushing

Sweet Cream Cheese:

1	(8-ounce) package cream cheese, softened	¼	cup sour cream at room temperature
1	teaspoon vanilla extract	¼	cup whipping cream at room temperature
3	tablespoons sugar		

Scones:

Sift together flour, sugar, baking powder and salt in a medium bowl. Cut in butter until mixture is the consistency of cornmeal. In a small bowl, combine egg and cream. Pour into dry ingredients and mix until well blended. The dough will be slightly wet. Turn out onto a well floured surface and pat dough to ¾-inch thickness. Cut out scones with a 2½-inch biscuit cutter and place on lightly greased baking sheet. Brush tops with additional cream. Bake in a preheated 350 degree oven for 25 minutes or until golden brown. Serve with sweet cream cheese.

Sweet Cream Cheese:

Beat cream cheese with an electric mixer until fluffy. Beat in vanilla extract, sugar, sour cream and whipping cream until well blended. Cover and refrigerate until serving time. Makes 2½ cups.

Hint: Handle dough as little as possible for tender scones.

Tea Scones with Strawberry Cream Cheese

Scones:

2	cups flour	½	cup golden raisins
2	teaspoons baking powder	½	cup buttermilk
½	teaspoon salt	1	large egg
¼	teaspoon baking soda	1	tablespoon milk
6	tablespoons butter	1	tablespoon sugar

Strawberry Cream Cheese:

1 (8-ounce) package cream cheese, softened

2 cups strawberries, washed and hulled

1 tablespoon powdered sugar

1 tablespoon frozen orange juice concentrate

Fresh sliced strawberries for garnish

Scones:

Combine the flour, baking powder, salt and baking soda in a large bowl. Cut in butter until the mixture resembles coarse crumbs. Mix in the raisins with a fork. Beat together the buttermilk and egg and then add them to flour mixture. Mix lightly with a fork until the mixture clings together and forms a ball of soft dough. Turn the dough onto a lightly floured surface and knead gently, turning 5 to 6 times. Roll the dough to ½-inch thickness. Cut out scones with a 2-inch biscuit cutter and place on a greased baking sheet. Lightly brush the tops of scones with milk and sprinkle with sugar. Bake in a preheated 425 degree oven for 10 to 12 minutes or until golden brown. Serve with strawberry cream cheese and fresh sliced strawberries.

Strawberry Cream Cheese:

Combine cream cheese, strawberries, powdered sugar and orange juice in a food processor until creamy and smooth. Place in a small bowl; cover and refrigerate until serving time. At serving time, spoon into a pretty bowl and garnish with sliced strawberries.

Hint: Always use very cold butter when making scones.

Cranberry-Orange Scones

2 cups flour	8 tablespoons butter, cut into 1-inch cubes
1 tablespoon baking powder	
½ teaspoon baking soda	⅔ cup buttermilk
¼ teaspoon salt	1 cup dried cranberries
3 tablespoons sugar, divided	1 tablespoon milk
1 tablespoon grated orange zest	

Combine flour, baking powder, baking soda, salt, 2 tablespoons sugar and orange zest. Cut in butter until mixture is crumbly. Add buttermilk and dried cranberries, stirring until just moistened. Turn dough out onto a lightly floured surface; knead gently 5 or 6 times. Pat into an 8-inch circle. Cut into 8 wedges, and place 1 inch apart on a lightly greased baking sheet. Brush with milk, and sprinkle with remaining 1 tablespoon sugar. Bake in a preheated 425 degree oven for 15 minutes or until scones are golden brown. Makes 8 servings.

Hint: Like biscuits, scones are best piping hot. Baked scones freeze well. Heat thawed scones in a preheated 400 degree oven for 5 to 7 minutes.

How To Eat A Scone

Split the scone in half with a knife across it's girth. Place a spoonful of jam, lemon curd and sweetened cream onto a small plate. On one small bite, spread a little jam or lemon curd on the scone's crumb face. Top this with sweetened cream and eat just that mouthful. For true English elegance, never spread the entire half at one time! This is considered inelegant tea-table etiquette!

Lemon Poppy Seed Scones

3	cups flour	8	tablespoons butter
¼	cup sugar	3	large eggs
1	tablespoon baking powder	½	cup buttermilk
1	teaspoon baking soda	2	tablespoons grated lemon zest
½	teaspoon ground cinnamon	2	tablespoons poppy seed
½	teaspoon salt		

Combine flour, sugar, baking powder, baking soda, cinnamon and salt in a large bowl. Cut in butter until mixture resembles coarse crumbs. In a small bowl, combine eggs, buttermilk, lemon zest and poppy seeds and beat well. Stir into flour mixture only until just blended. Pat dough into greased 8x8x2-inch baking pan. Bake in a preheated 450 degree oven for 10 to 15 minutes. Cool slightly and cut into small squares. Serve hot.

Fresh Apple Coffee Cake
Best Made Ahead

1	cup vegetable oil	1	teaspoon ground cinnamon
2	cups sugar	1	teaspoon baking powder
2	eggs	3	cups chopped apples
2½	scant cups flour	1	cup chopped walnuts
½	teaspoon salt	1	(6-ounce) package butterscotch chips
1	teaspoon baking soda		

Cream together oil, sugar and eggs in a large bowl. Add flour, salt, baking soda, cinnamon and baking powder to creamed mixture and mix thoroughly. Fold the apples and nuts into the batter. Pour evenly into a greased 13x9x2-inch pan and sprinkle butterscotch chips on top. Bake in a preheated 350 degree oven for 45 minutes. Serves 12 to 16.

This coffee cake is also wonderful served with ice cream for dessert!

Texas Peach-Blueberry Coffee Cake

Coffee Cake:

2 cups flour	1 cup milk
1 cup sugar	2 eggs, slightly beaten
2 teaspoons baking powder	1 teaspoon vanilla extract
1 teaspoon salt	1 cup fresh sliced peaches
1½ teaspoons grated orange zest	1 cup fresh blueberries
8 tablespoons butter, softened	

Icing:

1 cup powdered sugar	3-5 teaspoons milk
¼ teaspoon almond extract	

Coffee Cake:

Combine flour, sugar, baking powder, salt and orange zest in a large bowl. Cut butter into flour mixture until the consistency of coarse meal. Add milk, eggs and vanilla extract. Stir until well blended. Pour ¾ of batter into a greased 13x9x2-inch baking dish. Top evenly with peaches and blueberries. Spoon remaining batter over fruit. Bake in a preheated 350 degree oven for 35 to 45 minutes or until golden brown. Cool 30 minutes. Serves 12.

Icing:

In a small bowl, blend together the powdered sugar, almond extract and enough milk to be of the consistency to drizzle over the coffee cake.

Variation: Three cups pitted, halved Bing cherries can be substituted for the peaches and blueberries.

Quick Flaky Cream Cheese Coffee Cake

2 (8-ounce) cans refrigerated
  Crescent dinner rolls, divided
2 (8-ounce) packages cream
  cheese, softened

1 cup sugar, divided
1 egg, separated
1 teaspoon vanilla extract

Spread 1 can Crescent rolls into an ungreased 13x9x2-inch baking dish, pressing seams together. Beat together the cream cheese, ¾ cup sugar, egg yolk and vanilla extract in a small bowl. Spread this mixture over the rolls. Lay the other can of rolls on top. Brush with beaten egg white and sprinkle with the remaining ¼ cup of sugar. Bake in a preheated 350 degree oven for 30 minutes. Serves 12 to 16.

Easy Orange-Nut Bread

¾ cup sugar
½ cup chopped pecans
1 tablespoon grated orange zest
2 (11-ounce) cans refrigerated
  biscuits

1 (3-ounce) package cream
  cheese, cut into 20 squares
8 tablespoons butter or margarine,
  melted
1 cup sifted powdered sugar
2 tablespoons orange juice

Mix sugar, pecans and orange zest together in a small bowl and reserve. Separate biscuits; then gently separate biscuits into halves. Place a cream cheese cube between 2 halves, pinching sides to seal. Dip in butter and dredge in reserved sugar mixture. Stand biscuits on edge in lightly greased 12-cup Bundt pan, spacing evenly. Drizzle with remaining butter and sprinkle with remaining sugar mixture. Bake in a preheated 350 degree oven for 45 minutes or until golden brown. Immediately invert onto serving plate. Combine powdered sugar and orange juice in a small bowl. Drizzle over warm bread. Serve immediately. Serves 8.

Lemon Coffee Cake

Coffee Cake:

1 cup vegetable shortening or margarine

2 cups sugar

4 eggs

1 teaspoon vanilla extract

½ teaspoon almond extract

1 teaspoon salt

3 cups flour

1 (21-ounce) can lemon pie filling

Glaze:

½ cup powdered sugar

¼ teaspoon vanilla extract

½ teaspoon almond extract

1 tablespoon milk

Coffee Cake:

In a large bowl, cream together the shortening with sugar. Add eggs (one at a time, beating after each), vanilla and almond extracts, salt and flour. Spread ¾ of batter on bottom of a greased 15x10x2-inch jelly-roll pan. Spread pie filling evenly over batter. Dot remaining ¼ batter on top. Bake in a preheated 350 degree oven for 30 minutes. Glaze while hot! Cool and serve.

Glaze:

Mix the powdered sugar, vanilla and almond extracts and milk in a small bowl. Drizzle over hot cake.

Variation: Other pie fillings can be used also.

Butterscotch Pecan Rolls

Must Be Made Ahead

½ cup chopped pecans	½ cup packed brown sugar
18 frozen Parker House dinner rolls	1 teaspoon ground cinnamon
8 tablespoons butter, melted	1 (3.5-ounce) package butterscotch pudding mix (not instant)

Sprinkle pecans in the bottom of a greased 10-inch tube pan. Arrange rolls in pan, spacing evenly. In a small bowl, mix the butter with brown sugar, cinnamon and pudding mix. Pour over the rolls. Lightly cover and let stand at room temperature overnight. Bake in a preheated 350 degree oven for 25 minutes. Cool for 10 minutes. Serves 8.

Babas Au Rhum

2 cups flour, divided	3 eggs, room temperature
1¼ cups sugar, divided	½ cup rum
1 (¼-ounce) envelope active dry yeast	½ cup water
½ cup milk	Whipped cream
4 tablespoons butter	Toasted almonds

In a large electric mixer bowl, combine ⅔ cup flour, ¼ cup sugar and the undissolved yeast. Heat the milk and butter over low heat in a small saucepan until very warm. Add to the dry ingredients and beat 2 minutes at medium speed. Add eggs and ⅓ cup flour. Beat at high speed 2 minutes. Stir in enough flour to make a stiff batter, about 1 cup. Cover and let rise in a warm place until double in bulk, about 1 hour. Bring the remaining 1 cup sugar, the rum and water to a full boil in a small saucepan, stirring constantly. Remove from heat and cool. Stir down the batter. Spoon into 12 greased muffin tins. Let rise until batter reaches top of cups, about 35 minutes. Bake in a preheated 375 degree oven for 15 minutes. Immediately prick with a fork. Spoon rum syrup over the cakes. Let cool on wire racks after the syrup is absorbed. Serve with whipped cream and toasted almonds crowning the tops. Serves 12.

French Doughnuts

1 cup boiling water	1 (¼-ounce) envelope active dry yeast
¼ cup vegetable shortening	
½ cup sugar	½ cup lukewarm water
1 teaspoon salt	2 eggs, well beaten
1 cup evaporated milk	7 cups flour, about
	Vegetable oil

In a large bowl, pour boiling water over shortening, sugar and salt. Stir well until shortening is dissolved. Add milk. Soften yeast in lukewarm water and add to mixture when mixture is lukewarm. Mix in beaten eggs. Stir in 4 cups flour and beat in well. Add enough flour (about 3 cups) to make a soft dough. Place in a large oiled bowl, turning to oil the top of dough. Cover and refrigerate until ready to use. On a lightly floured surface, roll dough to ¼-inch thickness. Cut with scalloped cookie cutter and fry in hot deep fat (360 degrees); brown on one side, turn and brown on other. Do not let dough rise before frying. Drain on paper towel. Cover with your favorite thin frosting. Makes 60 doughnuts.

Cinnamon Rolls

1 recipe French Doughnuts	1 cup sugar
6-8 tablespoons margarine, melted	3 teaspoons cinnamon

Cover and let dough rise in a large greased bowl until double in size. Divide dough into two parts and roll each into an 18x12-inch rectangle. Pour melted margarine evenly over dough, spreading with the back of a spoon. Mix together the sugar and cinnamon. Sprinkle mixture evenly over the margarine. Roll as for a jelly roll. Cut into 1½-inch slices. Place on lightly greased pans or baking sheet. Let double in size and bake in a preheated 350 degree oven for about 10 to 20 minutes or until browned. Cover with your favorite thin frosting. Makes 24 large rolls. Extras freeze well.

This is our family's favorite for Christmas morning. I always make them on Christmas Eve in the shape of a Christmas tree and warm them in the morning.

Kolaches

Kolaches:

2 (¼-ounce) envelopes active dry yeast

½ cup lukewarm water

4 tablespoons unsalted butter, softened

¼ cup vegetable shortening, preferably Crisco

¼ cup, plus 1 or 2 tablespoons sugar, divided

2 egg yolks

⅔ cup milk

1 teaspoon salt

4 cups flour

Melted butter, for topping

Creamy Peach Filling:

2 cups small-curd cottage cheese

½ cup peach butter

1 egg

1 tablespoon sugar

1 tablespoon unsalted butter, melted

½ teaspoon ground nutmeg

Prune Filling:

1 pound dried prunes

Water

1 teaspoon vanilla extract

1 cup sugar

1 teaspoon fresh lemon juice

1 teaspoon grated lemon zest

Poppy Seed Filling:

¾ cup sugar

2 teaspoons cornstarch

1½ cups poppy seed

¾ cup whole milk, divided use

¾ teaspoon almond extract

Kolaches:

In a small bowl, combine the yeast with the lukewarm water. Set aside. In a large bowl, cream together the butter, shortening and ¼ cup sugar until the mixture is light and fluffy. Mix in the egg yolks, milk and salt. Mix well. Stir in the dissolved yeast and the flour; mix until the ingredients are thoroughly blended into a soft dough. Cover the dough with a towel, and set the dough aside to rise to about double in size, approximately 1 to 1½ hours. Prepare fillings while dough rises. Grease a baking sheet. Pinch off pieces of dough about 1½ times the size of a

Kolaches continued

golf ball, flatten the balls slightly, and transfer them to the baking sheet. Place the balls at least 1 inch apart, and brush them liberally with the melted butter. Set them aside to double in size again, about 45 minutes. With your thumb, gently indent the top of the dough. Make the hole especially deep if you plan to use the poppy seed or peach filling. Spoon in a couple of teaspoons of filling and, with the poppy seed or creamy peach versions, coax the dough over the filling. Let the kolaches rest again for 15 to 20 minutes. Bake in a preheated 425 degree oven for 10 to 12 minutes or until golden brown. Remove from oven, immediately brush the kolaches with more butter and sprinkle with the remaining sugar. Transfer to a rack and cool. They are best eaten the day they are made.

Creamy Peach Filling:

Drain cottage cheese in a sieve for 30 to 45 minutes. Squeeze any remaining liquid from the cheese. In a small bowl, mix the cheese with the peach butter, egg, sugar, unsalted butter and nutmeg.

Prune Filling:

Put the prunes into a saucepan, and cover them with water. Add the vanilla extract and simmer until the prunes have softened, about 15 minutes. Drain and pit the prunes. Chop them in a food processor or by hand. In a small bowl, mix prunes together with the sugar, lemon juice and lemon zest.

Poppy Seed Filling:

Stir together the sugar and cornstarch in a small bowl. Set aside. Grind the poppy seeds in a blender with about ½ the milk. Place the poppy seed mixture and the remaining milk in a large heavy saucepan and bring the mixture to a boil over medium-high heat. Reduce the heat to simmer and stir in the reserved sugar and cornstarch mixture. Add the almond extract. Simmer, stirring often until very thick.

Kolaches are the national sweet of Czechoslovakia
and can be served any time of the day with almost anything.

Breads II

The East Texas Piney Woods seems like a different world compared to the rest of Texas. It's wonderfully green and contains four national forests rich in pines, cypress and hardwoods as well as shimmering lakes, the most spectacular of which is Caddo Lake. It is home to many cypress trees draped in a heavy curtain of Spanish moss and this lovely American lotus.

Photography by Richard Reynolds

East
Texas

Texas Blossoms

Never Fail Popovers

1 cup flour	1 cup milk
¼ teaspoon salt	1 teaspoon melted butter
2 eggs	

Sift the flour and salt together into a medium bowl. Beat eggs slightly in a small bowl and stir in milk and melted butter. Add liquid to the flour and salt. Stir until smooth. Fill cold, well greased custard cups a little more than ½ full of batter. Place cups on a baking sheet and place in a cold oven. Heat to 425 degrees and bake for about 1 hour. Watch closely. Check first at 35 to 40 minutes. You can use a popover pan. Makes 6 to 8 popovers.

Hint: The secret is to start in a cold oven.

Angel Biscuits

1 (¼-ounce) envelope active dry yeast	¼-½ cup sugar
½ cup water	½ cup vegetable oil
½ teaspoon baking soda	4½ cups flour
2 cups buttermilk	1 teaspoon salt
	4 teaspoons baking powder

Dissolve the yeast in warm water. Mix the baking soda into the buttermilk. In a large bowl, add the buttermilk mixture to the yeast. Then add sugar and oil, mixing well. Add flour, salt and baking powder and blend. Roll out on a lightly floured surface and cut with a small biscuit cutter. Place on a baking sheet and let rise about 45 minutes. Bake in a preheated 425 degree oven for 12 to 15 minutes. Makes 24 large or 48 small biscuits.

Hint: This dough will keep in the refrigerator for 4 to 5 days. If making half the recipe, use the whole package of yeast.

Variation: Whole wheat flour can be substituted for all-purpose flour.

Parmesan Popovers

Butter

9 tablespoons Parmesan cheese

3 eggs

1 cup milk

1 cup sifted flour

½ teaspoon salt

⅛ teaspoon cayenne pepper

Let all ingredients come to room temperature. Very generously butter the bottoms and sides of 9 (5-ounce) custard cups or muffin tins. Put 1 tablespoon Parmesan cheese in bottom of each cup. Set custard cups on a baking sheet. In a small bowl, beat eggs until well mixed. Add the milk, flour, salt and cayenne. Beat until just smooth. Fill cups half full. Bake without peeking in a preheated 425 degree oven for 35 minutes. Serves 9.

Pecan Buttermilk Biscuits

3½ cups flour

4 teaspoons baking powder

1 teaspoon baking soda

2 tablespoons sugar

¾ cup lard

1½ cups chopped pecans

1½ cups buttermilk

Butter, melted

Combine flour, baking powder, baking soda and sugar in a large bowl. Cut in lard until mixture resembles coarse crumbs. Add pecans and blend well. Pour in the buttermilk and stir until most of flour is moistened. Turn out on lightly floured surface and knead 4 to 6 times. Gently roll out to 1½-inch thickness. Cut with 2½-inch biscuit cutter. Place on lightly buttered baking sheet. Let rise for 30 minutes at room temperature. Brush tops with melted butter. Bake in a preheated 400 degree oven for 12 to 15 minutes. Delicious and you won't need to add additional butter.

Shortening can be substituted for lard, if you must!
Many cooks think lard is the secret to light fluffy biscuits and cakes.

Cheese Garlic Biscuits

2   cups buttermilk biscuit baking mix
⅔   cup milk
½   cup shredded Cheddar cheese

4   tablespoons butter or margarine, melted
¼   teaspoon garlic powder

In a medium bowl, stir together baking mix, milk and cheese to get a soft dough. Beat about 30 seconds. Drop by spoonfuls onto ungreased baking sheet. Bake in a preheated 450 degree oven for 8 to 10 minutes or until golden brown. Meanwhile, stir together melted butter and garlic powder. Brush over biscuits as soon as they are done. Serve warm. Makes about 1 dozen biscuits.

Pan de Elote

Means "Bread Of Corn" In Spanish

8   tablespoons margarine
¼   cup sugar
4   eggs
1   (15-ounce) can cream style corn
1   (4½-ounce) can chopped green chiles, drained
½   cup (about 2-ounces) shredded Monterey Jack cheese

½   cup (about 2-ounces) shredded Longhorn Cheddar cheese
1   cup flour
1   cup cornmeal
4   teaspoons baking powder
½   teaspoon salt

In a medium bowl, beat margarine and sugar until light and fluffy. Blend in eggs. Stir in corn, chiles, and cheeses. In a small bowl, combine flour, cornmeal, baking powder and salt. Add to mixture and mix just until moistened. Pour into greased and floured 12x8x2-inch baking dish. Bake in a preheated 325 degree oven for 50 to 55 minutes or until wooden toothpick inserted in center comes out clean. Serve warm.

State Fair Jalapeño Cornbread

They'll Want Seconds!

1	cup cornmeal	1	Texas-sized egg, slightly beaten
1	(15-ounce) can cream style corn	2	jalapeños seeded and chopped
¾	cup milk		or 1 (4½-ounce) can chopped green chiles
1	teaspoon salt	½	pound grated sharp Cheddar cheese
3	teaspoons baking powder		
⅓	cup vegetable shortening		

Mix together the cornmeal, corn, milk, salt, baking powder, shortening, egg and peppers in a medium bowl just until blended. Pour half the batter into a well greased hot iron skillet. Spread the cheese to within 1-inch of edges. Add remaining batter on top. Bake in a preheated 400 degree oven for 30 to 45 minutes. Serves 8.

Sopaipillas

2	cups flour	½	cup buttermilk
2	teaspoons baking powder	½	cup water
½	teaspoons salt		Fat for frying
2	tablespoons lard or vegetable shortening		

Stir flour, baking powder and salt together in a medium bowl. Cut in lard with a fork. Add buttermilk and water; mix well. Let stand for 30 minutes. Roll ⅛-inch thick on a lightly floured surface and cut into 2-inch squares. Fry in deep hot fat, being sure fat covers top of sopaipillas; use spoon to pour fat over surface, if necessary. Serve with honey and your favorite Mexican food dishes.

Richardson Woman's Club's Wildflower Fritters

1 cup buttermilk biscuit baking mix	¾ cup shelled sunflower seeds
1 teaspoon vegetable oil	2 eggs
¼ cup packed brown sugar	¼ cup milk
⅛ teaspoon garlic powder	Vegetable oil

In a small bowl, mix together biscuit mix, vegetable oil, brown sugar, garlic powder, sunflower seeds, eggs and milk. Heat 4-inches of vegetable oil to 375 degrees in a deep large pot. Drop batter 1 teaspoon at a time into oil. Cook until golden brown and floating on the top. Serve immediately.

This recipe was made for the city of Richardson's annual "Wildflower! Arts & Music Festival". Samples were given out to those attending the festival.

Longview Dinner Rolls

1 (25-ounce) package frozen Parker House dinner rolls	1 small bunch green onions, chopped
8 tablespoons butter	

Defrost rolls for 1 to 1½ hours. Put butter and onions in a microwave safe dish and microwave until onions are soft. Flatten each roll in palm of hand; place 1 teaspoon of onion mixture in each roll and pinch edges together. Place rolls on lightly greased baking sheet or cake pans approximately 1 to 3 inches apart. Let rise about 45 minutes or until double in size. Bake in a preheated 350 degree oven for 20 minutes or until golden brown. Makes 12 rolls.

Dona Maria's Cheese Bread

1	cup butter, softened	1	(4½-ounce) can chopped green chiles
1	cup mayonnaise		
8	ounces grated Monterey Jack cheese	1	teaspoon garlic salt
		1	loaf French bread, sliced

Mix butter, mayonnaise, cheese, green chiles and garlic salt in a medium bowl. Spread thickly on bread. Bake in a preheated 400 degree oven for 10 minutes or until melted and toasted.

Serve with Mexican food or cut into fourths and serve as an appetizer.

Over and Over Again Rolls

Must Be Made Ahead

½ cup vegetable shortening	4½ teaspoons active dry yeast
⅔ cup sugar	2¾ cups flour
1 teaspoon salt	Vegetable oil for container
1 cup boiling water	Butter, melted
1 egg, beaten	

Combine shortening, sugar and salt in a large bowl. Add boiling water and stir until shortening is melted. Cool slightly and beat in egg. In another bowl, mix yeast and flour. Add to shortening mixture. Knead well with hands. Store in an oiled, airtight container overnight in the refrigerator. (Be sure to turn the dough so all of it is lightly oiled.) When ready to use, roll out ¼-inch thick. Cut out with a 2-inch biscuit cutter and dip in melted butter. Fold in half and place on a baking sheet. Let rise about 2 hours or until double in size. Bake in a preheated 375 degree oven for 13 minutes or until golden brown. Makes 32 rolls.

This recipe changed me from a woman who
never made rolls to one who makes them over and over.

Twice Baked Bread

1	loaf French bread	¼	cup finely chopped onions
1	(8-ounce) package Swiss cheese slices, cut into triangles	1	tablespoon prepared mustard
8	tablespoons margarine, softened	4	slices uncooked bacon, cut into very small pieces

Partially slice the bread diagonally into 16 pieces, but do not cut through the bottom crust. Place a triangle of cheese in between each slice of bread. Place the bread on a foil covered baking sheet. Combine the margarine, onions and mustard in a small bowl and mix well. "Ice the bread" on top and sides. Place very small pieces of bacon on top. Bake in a preheated 400 degree oven for 20 minutes and serve hot.

Last Minute Rolls

2	(¼-ounce) envelopes active dry yeast	2	tablespoons butter
½	cup warm water	1½	teaspoons salt
1¼ cups milk		4½-5	cups flour
3	tablespoons sugar	Vegetable oil	

Combine yeast and warm water in a cup. Let stand for 5 minutes. In a small saucepan, combine milk, sugar and butter. Cook over medium heat, stirring constantly just until butter melts. Pour into a large bowl and cool to lukewarm. Stir in yeast mixture. Gradually stir in enough flour to make a soft dough. Turn dough out onto a floured surface. Knead until smooth and elastic, about 5 minutes. Place in a well oiled bowl, turning to oil the top. Cover and let rest in a warm place, free from drafts for 15 minutes. Divide dough in half. Shape each portion into 12 balls. Place in a greased 9-inch square pan 1 to 3 inches apart. Cover and let rise for 15 minutes. Bake in a preheated 425 degree oven for 11 to 12 minutes. Makes 2 dozen.

Focaccia

10	pieces dried tomatoes (about ⅓ cup)		2	teaspoons salt
½	cup boiling water		1	large egg
1	cup milk		3	tablespoons dried chives
3½-4 cups flour, divided			Vegetable or olive oil	
2	tablespoons butter or margarine		¼	cup olive oil, divided
2	(¼-ounce) envelopes active dry yeast		¼	teaspoon dried oregano, crumbled
2	tablespoons sugar		¼	teaspoon dried rosemary, crumbled

Combine tomatoes and boiling water in a small saucepan. Let stand for 30 minutes. Remove tomatoes from liquid, finely chop and set aside. To remaining liquid, add milk and butter and heat mixture to 120 to 130 degrees. In a large electric mixer bowl, combine 1½ cups flour, yeast, sugar and salt. Gradually add liquid mixture to flour mixture, beating at low speed until blended. Add egg and beat 3 minutes at medium speed. Stir in tomatoes, chives and enough remaining flour to make a soft dough. Turn dough out onto a lightly floured surface and knead for 5 minutes. Place in a large bowl oiled with vegetable or olive oil, turning to oil top. Cover and let rise for about 1 hour or until double in size. In a small bowl combine ¼ cup olive oil, oregano and rosemary. Punch dough down. Divide dough in ½ and shape each portion into a 10-inch round. Place on lightly greased baking sheets. Brush with ½ of olive oil mixture. Cover and let rest 10 minutes. Bake in a preheated 350 degree oven for 15 minutes. Brush with remaining olive oil mixture and bake 5 to 10 additional minutes or until lightly browned. Bread should sound hollow when tapped. Cool slightly on wire racks. Serve warm with olive oil for dipping.

Sandwiches

If you want to enjoy truly tranquil beauty, travel to the wide open spaces of South Texas. Long stretches of roads and ranch land impart picturesque views of fence posts and flowers like the bluebonnets, phlox and groundsel in Wilson County.

Photography by Richard Reynolds

Texas Blossoms

South Texas

Sandwiches

A Texas Blossoms Menu for a

Ladies Tea

Tea Scones with
Strawberry Cream Cheese
Chicken-Pecan Tea Sandwiches
Tuna Finger Sandwiches
Egg and Watercress Sandwiches
Olive Pinwheels
Apricot Sorpresa
Stuffed Strawberries
Chocolate Cherries
Chocolate Truffles
Richardson Woman's Club
Coffee Punch
Tea

Chicken-Pecan Tea Sandwiches

Must Be Chilled

2 cups minced cooked chicken	½ teaspoon seasoned salt
½ cup minced celery	¼ teaspoon pepper
1 cup finely chopped pecans	1 (1½-pound) loaf thin sliced white bread
½ cup mayonnaise	

Several hours before serving, mix chicken, celery, pecans, mayonnaise, seasoned salt and pepper together in a medium bowl. Cover and refrigerate. You may need to add extra mayonnaise for the filling to spread well. Makes 3½ cups of filling. Spread between 2 white bread slices. Remove crusts from each sandwich and cut into desired serving pieces.

Chicken and Pineapple Sandwiches

Cooked Salad Dressing:

1	tablespoon sugar	¾	cup vegetable oil
2	teaspoons dry mustard	1	egg
1	teaspoon salt	¼	cup vinegar
⅛	teaspoon cayenne pepper, optional	3	tablespoons cornstarch
		1	cup cold water

Sandwich:

1	(8-ounce) can crushed pineapple	2	cups English walnuts, chopped
1	cup chopped cooked chicken	½	cup cooked salad dressing
		24	slices white bread, buttered

Cooked Salad Dressing:

In a small bowl combine sugar, dry mustard, salt, cayenne, oil, egg and vinegar, but do not beat. Combine cornstarch and cold water in a saucepan and stir until thoroughly mixed. Cook over low heat stirring constantly, until mixture boils and becomes clear. Remove from heat and continue stirring for about 3 minutes. Pour hot mixture into oil mixture and beat vigorously until smooth.

Sandwich:

Combine pineapple, chicken, walnuts, and salad dressing. Spread between 2 buttered bread slices. Remove crusts from each sandwich and cut diagonally, into quarters. Makes 4 dozen small sandwiches.

*Bluebonnets are the state flower of Texas. They are treasured and admired, but are not to be picked. In the spring, you see dozens of children being photographed in lovely fields of bluebonnets. Burnet, located in the Texas Hill Country, is the Bluebonnet Capital of Texas and annually hosts the "**Bluebonnet Festival**" the second weekend in April.*

Tuna Finger Sandwiches

1	(8-ounce) package cream cheese, softened	1	teaspoon lemon juice
1	(6½-ounce) can white tuna, drained	1	(4-ounce) can chopped ripe olives
½	cup mayonnaise	1	teaspoon Worcestershire sauce
½	cup finely chopped pecans	1	(1½-pound) loaf thin sliced white bread

Blend together the cream cheese, tuna, mayonnaise, pecans, lemon juice, olives, and Worcestershire sauce in a medium bowl. Remove crusts from bread. Divide the spread equally by spoonfuls on ½ the bread slices. Top with the remaining bread slices. Cut each sandwich into 3 finger sandwiches. Wrap or cover sandwiches and refrigerate until ready to serve.

Pimiento Cheese Sandwiches

2	pounds grated sharp Cheddar cheese at room temperature	Salt to taste
1	small coarsely grated onion	Pepper to taste
1	(7-ounce) jar pimientos	Onion salt to taste
1	pint mayonnaise	Garlic salt to taste
3	tablespoons prepared mustard	Celery salt to taste
3	tablespoons Worcestershire sauce	Paprika to taste
		Bread

Lightly mix ingredients in a large bowl and store in a covered container up to 3 weeks in the refrigerator. Serve on your favorite bread and cut into desired sandwich shapes. Makes 2 quarts.

Eggs and Watercress Sandwiches

1 small bunch watercress	2 tablespoons Dijon mustard
5 hard-cooked eggs, shelled	Salt and pepper to taste
3½ tablespoons mayonnaise	1 (1-pound) loaf thin sliced bread

Using a knife, coarsely chop ½ of watercress and set aside; you should have about ½ cup lightly packed. Reserve remaining watercress sprigs for garnish. Chop eggs, add mayonnaise, mustard and season with salt and pepper. Mash to a smooth paste with a fork. Stir in chopped watercress. Make sandwiches with egg mixture. Slice as desired. Arrange on a plate and garnish with remaining watercress sprigs.

Cucumber Finger Sandwiches
Must Be Made Ahead

3 cucumbers	¼ teaspoon Worcestershire sauce
2 (8-ounce) packages cream cheese, softened	½ cup mayonnaise
	½ cup chopped nuts
1 garlic clove, grated	Dash paprika
1 tablespoon onion juice	Dash celery salt
1 teaspoon sugar	48 slices thin sliced white bread, crusts trimmed
1 teaspoon salt	

Peel and grate cucumber; drain very well. Blend cream cheese, garlic, onion juice, sugar, salt, Worcestershire sauce and mayonnaise in a medium bowl. Add cucumbers and nuts. Refrigerate overnight or up to 24 hours. Spread between bread slices. Cut into your favorite shapes. Makes 24 sandwiches.

Carrot Tea Sandwiches

1 (8-ounce) package cream
  cheese, softened
2 tablespoons salad dressing
1 teaspoon lemon juice

¼ teaspoon seasoned salt
8 carrots, finely shredded
1 (1½-pound) loaf thin sliced
  sandwich bread, crusts
  trimmed

Blend cream cheese, salad dressing, lemon juice and seasoned salt in a medium bowl. Fold in carrots. Spread between 2 slices trimmed bread and cut into squares. If prepared ahead, cover well and refrigerate until ready to serve.

Special Spinach Sandwiches

Must Be Made Ahead

2 (10-ounce) packages frozen
  chopped spinach, defrosted
1 (1.4-ounce) package Knorr
  vegetable soup mix
½ cup mayonnaise

1 (8-ounce) carton plain yogurt
1 (8-ounce) can water chestnuts,
  finely chopped
1 (1½-pound) loaf thin sliced
  wheat bread, crusts trimmed

Squeeze all the water out of the spinach. Finely chop spinach. Combine spinach, soup mix, mayonnaise, yogurt and water chestnuts in a medium bowl. Cover and refrigerate overnight. Place 1 tablespoon spinach mixture on 1 bread slice and spread evenly. Top with another slice and cut into squares or triangles.

Olive Pinwheels

Must Be Chilled

1   (8-ounce) package cream cheese, softened
1   tablespoon mayonnaise
¾   tablespoon dry ranch dressing mix
½   teaspoon Worcestershire sauce

½   cup finely chopped pecans
2   tablespoons chopped ripe olives
1   (5-ounce) jar pimiento stuffed olives, drained
1   (1½-pound) loaf thin sliced white bread

Blend together the cream cheese, mayonnaise, dressing mix, Worcestershire sauce, pecans and ripe olives in a small bowl. Trim crusts from bread. Using 2 slices, overlap about 1 inch and roll flat. Spread filling on bread, place row of stuffed olives at one end and roll. Cover well and chill. When ready to serve, slice into ½-inch pieces.

Olive-Pecan Tea Sandwiches

1   cup chopped pimiento stuffed olives, drained and liquid reserved
1   (8-ounce) package cream cheese, softened

¼   cup mayonnaise
½   cup chopped pecans
Dash pepper
1   (1½-pound) loaf thin sliced white bread

Mix together cream cheese, mayonnaise and 2 tablespoons olive liquid in a small bowl. Fold in pecans and olives. Spread on sandwich bread and trim crusts. Cut as desired.

Muffuletta Loaf

Must Be Chilled

⅔ cup olive oil	2 teaspoons lemon juice
½ cup chopped pimiento stuffed olives	1 teaspoon minced garlic
½ cup chopped ripe olives	1 (20-ounce) round Italian bread loaf
¼ cup chopped fresh parsley	¼ pound sliced salami
1 teaspoon dried oregano, crumbled	¼ pound sliced mozzarella cheese
½ teaspoon pepper	¼ pound pepperoni, sliced

Combine olive oil, olives, parsley, oregano, pepper, lemon juice and garlic; stir well. Cover and chill at least 2 hours. Cut bread in half horizontally; scoop out bottom, leaving about a ½-inch thick shell. Drain olive mixture and spoon half of mixture into bread shell. Top with salami, cheese, pepperoni and remaining olive mixture. Cover with bread top. Wrap loaf tightly with plastic wrap, and chill 6 to 8 hours. Cut loaf into wedges. Makes 8 servings.

Open-Faced Tuna Sandwiches

1 (9¼-ounce) can albacore tuna	¼ cup chopped ripe olives
¾ cup sliced celery	2 teaspoons lemon juice
¾ cup mayonnaise or Miracle Whip	4 English muffins, split, buttered and lightly toasted
½ cup shredded Cheddar cheese	
⅓ cup slivered almonds, toasted	

Drain and flake tuna. Combine tuna, celery, mayonnaise, cheese, almonds, olives and lemon juice and toss lightly. Spread each muffin half with about ⅓ cup tuna mixture. Bake in a preheated oven at 350 degrees for 5 to 10 minutes or until lightly browned.

Chili Burgers

1-1½	pounds ground beef	¼	teaspoon dried oregano, crumbled
1	medium ripe tomato, seeded and chopped		Zest of 1 lemon, grated
½	cup pitted ripe olives, chopped	2	tablespoons chopped fresh dill or parsley
1	teaspoon finely minced garlic		Salt and pepper to taste
½	teaspoon Dijon mustard	4	hamburger buns, toasted
1	tablespoon chili powder	⅓	cup sour cream
¼	teaspoon dried basil, crumbled	3	green onions, chopped
		½	cup grated Monterey Jack cheese

Prepare hot coals for grilling. Mix beef, tomatoes, olives, garlic, mustard, chili powder, basil, oregano, lemon zest and parsley. Season with salt and pepper. Gently form the mixture into 4 patties. Grill the burgers over hot coals, 3-inches from the heat, for about 4 minutes per side for rare meat. Serve immediately on buns. Top with sour cream, green onions and cheese.

My Hero

8	slices sour dough bread	4	slices purple onion, chopped
	Mayonnaise	4	slices Monterey Jack cheese
2	avocados, peeled, pitted and mashed	8	slices bacon, cooked crisp
	Lemon juice to taste	8	lettuce leaves
	Garlic salt to taste	8	slices tomatoes
		8	slices roasted chicken breast

Spread each bread slice with mayonnaise. In a small bowl combine avocado with lemon juice and garlic salt. Add chopped onions and spread on bread. Top with cheese, bacon, lettuce, tomatoes and chicken. Serve immediately. Serves 8.

Sweet Endings

Wildseed Farms

Expansive fields of poppies against a typical Texas landscape charm the many visitors to the Wildseed Farms.

Photograph provided by the Wildseed Farms

Texas Hill
Country

Texas
Blossoms

Bread Pudding with Rum Sauce

Pudding:

6	eggs
1	(14½-ounce) can evaporated milk
1	cup whole milk
1½	cups sugar
1	teaspoon vanilla extract
1	teaspoon almond extract

Dash ground nutmeg, optional

Dash ground cinnamon, optional

6	tablespoons butter, melted
1	cup raisins
9-10	slices bread, torn in pieces
1	(21-ounce) can sliced peaches, drained, cut up

Rum Sauce:

1	cup sugar
8	tablespoons butter
½	cup light cream

5	tablespoons rum

Dash ground nutmeg

Cornstarch, optional

Pudding:

Combine eggs, milks, sugar, vanilla and almond extracts and spices in the large bowl of an electric mixer and beat until mixed. Add butter, raisins, bread and peaches. Mix again and pour into a lightly oiled 13x9x2-inch pan. Bake in a preheated 350 degree oven for 1 hour. Top with Rum Sauce. Serves 12 to 15.

Rum Sauce:

Over low heat blend sugar, butter, cream, rum and nutmeg until butter melts. If the sauce is too thin, thicken with cornstarch.

Chocolate Raspberry Bread Pudding with Cream

Pudding:

2 cups semi-sweet chocolate chips, divided

Cooking spray

4 large eggs

1 cup firmly packed light brown sugar

½ teaspoon ground cinnamon

¼ teaspoon ground nutmeg

1 teaspoon vanilla extract

¼ cup Chambord liqueur

2 cups half-and-half

1 loaf French bread, baked, crusts removed and cut into 1-inch cubes (about 4 cups)

Spiced Cream:

2 cups heavy cream

⅛ cup sugar

¼ teaspoon ground cinnamon

⅛ teaspoon ground nutmeg

Pudding:

Melt 1 cup chocolate chips. Cool. Spray 2-quart baking dish with cooking spray. Whisk together eggs, sugar, cinnamon, nutmeg, vanilla extract, the melted chocolate chips and liqueur in a large mixing bowl until very smooth. Add the half-and-half and mix well. Add the bread and let the mixture sit for 30 minutes, stirring occasionally. Pour half the mixture into the prepared dish. Sprinkle the top with the unmelted chocolate chips. Pour the remaining bread mixture over the chocolate chips. Bake in a preheated 350 degree oven until the pudding is set in the center, 55 to 60 minutes. Let cool for 5 minutes. To serve, place pudding in a dish and top with Spiced Cream. Serves 8 to 10.

Spiced Cream:

Beat cream with an electric mixer on high speed in a large mixing bowl for about 2 minutes. Add the sugar, cinnamon, and nutmeg and beat again until the mixture thickens and forms stiff peaks, another 1 to 2 minutes.

Dutch Apple Brandy Cheesecake

Cinnamon Crust:

1¼ cups graham cracker crumbs	⅓ cup melted butter
⅓ cup ground walnuts or pecans	½ teaspoon ground cinnamon

Cheesecake:

4 (8-ounce) packages cream cheese, softened	1 teaspoon vanilla extract
1 cup sugar	⅛ teaspoon ground nutmeg
3 tablespoons apple brandy	4 eggs
1 teaspoon ground cinnamon	1 cup chunky applesauce
	¼ cup heavy cream

Crumb Topping:

¾ cup packed brown sugar	½ heaping teaspoon ground cinnamon
¾ cup flour	
⅓ cup melted butter	¼ heaping teaspoon ground nutmeg

Cinnamon Crust:

Combine graham cracker crumbs, nuts, butter and cinnamon. Press on the bottom and 1½ inches up the sides of a 10-inch springform pan. Bake in a preheated 350 degree oven for 10 minutes or until golden brown. Cool.

Cheesecake:

Beat cream cheese until smooth. Gradually add sugar, beating well. Add brandy, cinnamon, vanilla extract and nutmeg and blend well. Add eggs one at a time, beating until combined. Stir in applesauce and cream. Pour into cooled crust and return to 350 degree oven for 50 minutes or until center is nearly set.

Crumb Topping:

Mix all topping ingredients until crumbly. Sprinkle over cheesecake and bake 10 minutes more. After cake has cooled 5 minutes on wire rack, loosen the sides of pan and cool 30 minutes longer before removing sides. Serves 12 to 15.

Dreamy Cheesecake

Must Be Chilled or Frozen

Graham Cracker Crumb Crust:

4   tablespoons butter, melted

¼   cup sugar

1½ cups graham cracker crumbs
(about 18 crackers)

Cheesecake:

3   (8-ounce) packages cream
cheese, at room temperature

1½ cups sugar

4   eggs

4   teaspoons vanilla extract

2   teaspoons lemon juice

2   teaspoons grated lemon zest

Sour Cream Topping:

1½ cups sour cream, at room
temperature

⅓   cup sugar

1   teaspoon vanilla extract

Additional fresh fruit or glaze,
optional

Graham Cracker Crumb Crust:

Blend crust ingredients. Press onto the bottom of a 9-inch springform pan. Bake in a preheated 300 degree oven for 10 minutes.

Cheesecake:

In a large bowl, beat cream cheese until smooth. Add sugar, eggs, vanilla extract, lemon juice and lemon zest; beat until well blended. Pour into crust and bake for 1 hour 15 minutes or until set and center is no longer wet. The filling may crack around the edge, but it should not brown. Remove from oven and cool 10 minutes.

Sour Cream Topping:

Blend topping ingredients together. Spread evenly over entire surface of cheese-cake. Return to oven for 5 minutes. Cool to room temperature and refrigerate at least 5 hours before serving. Top with any fruit filling or glaze. For freezing, place a layer of plastic wrap over sour cream topping. Wrap in heavy aluminum foil. Freeze. To thaw, let stand at room temperature about 3 hours. Serves 16 to 20.

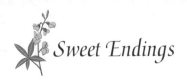

Low-Fat Cheesecake

Must Be Chilled

Crust:

1½ cups fine graham cracker crumbs

½ teaspoon ground cinnamon

⅓ cup margarine, melted

Filling:

2 eggs, beaten (or ½ cup egg substitute)

½ cup sugar

1½ cups creamed low-fat cottage cheese

1 (8-ounce) package low-fat cream cheese (not fat-free), softened

½ teaspoon vanilla extract

1 cup regular or fat-free sour cream

Pie filling, optional

Crust:

Mix all crust ingredients together and press evenly into an 8-inch springform pan. Set aside.

Filling:

Place eggs and sugar in blender. Blend until well mixed. Add cottage cheese and blend until smooth. Add cream cheese and vanilla extract. Blend all together. Pour into crust and bake in a preheated 350 degree oven for 35 minutes. Spread with sour cream while cheesecake is still warm. Cool and chill. Pieces may be topped with your favorite pie filling if desired. Serves 8 to 10.

French Mint Dessert

Must Be Chilled

18 large marshmallows

¼ cup milk

3 tablespoons crème de menthe

½ teaspoon peppermint extract

½ pint whipping cream, whipped

18 Oreo cookies, crushed

Melt marshmallows in milk; cool slightly and add cream de menthe and peppermint extract. Fold mixture into whipped cream. Pat half of the cookie crumbs into 9-inch pie pan. Slowly pour cream mixture over crumbs and top with remaining crumbs. Chill overnight. Serves 4 to 6.

Triple Chocolate Trifle

Must Be Chilled

1 (18¼-ounce) dark chocolate
   cake mix

4 (1.4-ounce) Heath toffee candy
   bars

2 (2.8-ounce) packages of Nestles
   chocolate mousse

1 (16-ounce) tub frozen whipped
   topping, thawed

Cook cake mix as package directs in 13x9x2-inch pan. Divide in half and save half in freezer for future use. Divide other half of the cake into three equal parts and crumble each part. Crush each candy bar in its own plastic bag. Prepare mousse as package directs and divide into thirds. In trifle bowl make three layers in this order: first layer-⅓ of crumbled cake; second layer-⅓ of chocolate mousse; third layer-1 crushed candy bar; fourth layer-⅓ of whipped topping. Repeat layers 2 more times. Sprinkle fourth candy bar on top layer of whipped topping. Chill. Serves 10 to 14.

Angel Food Cake
with Heavenly Lemon Sauce

½ cup sugar

1½ teaspoons cornstarch

½ cup water

¼ cup egg substitute

3 tablespoons fresh lemon juice

8 slices angel food cake

4-6 cups assorted berries, kiwi and
   grapes

Mix sugar and cornstarch in a small saucepan. Combine water, egg substitute and lemon juice, gradually stirring into the cornstarch mixture. Cook until mixture boils and thickens. Cool. Top each slice of cake with at least ½ cup of fruit. Drizzle with lemon sauce. Serves 8.

I first tried this to serve to someone who is diabetic.
I keep making it because I like it.

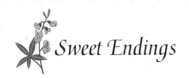

Bavarian Angel Dessert
Must Be Chilled

2 cups milk	½ cup cold water
4 eggs, separated	1 teaspoon vanilla extract
1 cup sugar	1 pint whipping cream, divided, sweetened if desired
2 tablespoons flour	
Dash salt	1 angel food cake
1 envelope unflavored gelatin	½ cup crushed black walnuts or pecans

Scald milk. Beat egg yolks and add to milk with sugar, flour and salt. Cook until custard coats a spoon. Dissolve gelatin in cold water. While the custard is hot, add vanilla extract and gelatin. Cool. Beat egg whites until stiff. Beat 1 cup whipping cream into stiff peaks. Fold egg whites and whipped cream into cooled custard. Break angel food cake into bite-size pieces and fold into custard. Put in 13x9x2-inch glass dish. Whip rest of whipping cream and frost the dessert. Top with crushed nuts and refrigerate. Serves 10 to 14.

Light and luscious ending for a heavy meal.

To make whipped cream hold up under refrigeration, as in icing for a cake: Soften 2 teaspoons unflavored gelatin in 2 tablespoons cold water for every 2 cups whipping cream. Heat gelatin over hot water to dissolve. Cool. As cream is whipped, blend in dissolved gelatin.

Double-Filled Lemon Dessert

Unusual Lemon Dessert

1½ cups sugar, divided	2 teaspoons grated lemon zest
½ cup flour	¼ cup lemon juice
½ teaspoon baking powder	2 tablespoons butter, melted
¼ teaspoon salt	1½ cups milk
3 eggs, separated	

Sift 1 cup sugar with flour, baking powder and salt. Beat egg yolks until light in color. Add lemon zest, lemon juice, butter and milk, mixing well. Stir in flour mixture until smooth. Beat egg whites until stiff, slowly adding remaining ½ cup sugar; fold into mixture. Pour into buttered 2-quart round baking dish. Set in pan containing hot water ½-inch deep and bake in a preheated 350 degree oven for 40 to 45 minutes. Results will be a cake-like top, lightly brown, with lemon pudding on bottom. Do not overcook. Serves 6 to 8. Good hot or cold.

Boiled Custard

1 quart milk, whole or 2 percent	12 large marshmallows
¼ cup sugar	Dash salt
4 eggs, beaten	2 teaspoons vanilla extract

Cook milk, sugar, eggs, marshmallows and salt in the top of a double boiler until the marshmallows melt or a candy thermometer reaches 180 degrees. In spite of the name, never let this boil! Cool and add vanilla extract. If not completely smooth, pour through a strainer or blend in blender a few seconds. Serve cold with whipped cream or top with vanilla ice cream. Serves 4.

A touch of bourbon is a tasty addition!

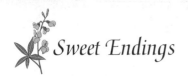

Apple Enchiladas

1   (20-ounce) can sliced pie apples
    (not pie filling) drained and
    liquid reserved
8   fresh flour tortillas at room
    temperature

1   tablespoon ground cinnamon
⅓   cup butter
½   cup sugar
½   cup packed light brown sugar
Water

Spoon fruit down the center of each tortilla; sprinkle with cinnamon. Roll and place seam-side down in a lightly greased 13x9x2-inch pan. Add enough water to reserved apple liquid to yield ½ cup. In a saucepan, bring butter, sugars and apple liquid to a boil. Reduce heat and simmer 3 minutes, stirring constantly. Pour butter mixture over enchiladas and let stand for 30 minutes. Bake in a preheated 350 degree oven for 20 minutes, uncovered. Serves 8.

Bunuelos

A Favorite From Mexico

1   teaspoon salt
1   teaspoon baking powder
2   tablespoons sugar
4   cups flour
2   eggs

1   cup milk
4   tablespoons butter, melted
Oil or fat for frying
Sugar and ground cinnamon
    mixture

Sift together the salt, baking powder, sugar and flour. Set aside. Beat the eggs thoroughly; then beat in the milk. Stir the dry mixture gradually into the egg-milk mixture. Add the butter and mix. Turn out onto a lightly floured board and knead very gently until the dough is smooth and elastic. Divide into about 40 small or 24 large balls. Roll these out to approximately 4 inches or 6 inches respectively. Fry in very hot, deep fat or oil (370 degrees) until delicately browned on both sides. Drain on paper towels, and sprinkle with the cinnamon and sugar mixture.

Cherry Berries on a Cloud

Must Be Chilled

Meringue Mixture:

6   egg whites
½   teaspoon cream of tartar
¼   teaspoon salt
2¾ cups sugar, divided
2   (3-ounce) packages cream
      cheese, softened

1   teaspoon vanilla extract
½   pint whipping cream, whipped
1   cup sour cream
2   cups miniature marshmallows

Cherry Berry Topping:

1   (21-ounce) can cherry pie filling

1   teaspoon lemon juice

Meringue Mixture:

Grease a 13x9x2-inch pan. Beat egg whites, cream of tartar and salt until frothy. Gradually beat in 1¾ cups sugar. Beat until very stiff and glossy, approximately 15 minutes. Spread in prepared pan and bake in a preheated 275 degree oven for 1 hour. Turn off oven and leave meringue in oven until cool. Mix cream cheese with the remaining cup of sugar and vanilla extract. Gently fold in whipped cream, sour cream and marshmallows. Spread over meringue; refrigerate overnight. Cut into serving pieces and top with Cherry Berry Topping.

Cherry Berry Topping:

Combine cherry pie filling and lemon juice. Serves 12 to 15.

Raw eggs separate more easily while still cold, but let egg
whites reach room temperature in order to get maximum
volume before beating. Egg whites that have been refrigerated
for up to 2 weeks produce a better meringue than do fresh ones.

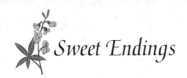

Blarney Stones

Must Be Made Ahead

Sponge Cake:

6 eggs, separated	1½ cups sifted cake flour
½ cup cold water	¼ teaspoon salt
1½ cups sugar	¾ teaspoon cream of tartar
½ teaspoon vanilla extract	

Icing:

1 cup butter, softened, do not substitute	Unsalted peanuts, freshly ground, lightly toasted
2½ cups powdered sugar, sifted	Maraschino cherries, optional
1 teaspoon vanilla extract	Whipped cream, optional
	Chocolate sauce, optional

Sponge Cake:

Beat egg yolks until thick and a light lemon color; add water and continue beating until very thick. Gradually beat in sugar and vanilla extract. Sift flour with salt and fold into the egg yolk mixture, a little at a time. Beat egg whites with cream of tartar until stiff peaks form. Fold egg whites into the other mixture, turning the bowl slowly as you fold in the egg whites. Pour into ungreased 13x9x2-inch cake pan, filling about ½ to ¾ full. If any batter is left over, put it into an 8x8x2-inch pan. Fill ½ full and use more pans if necessary. Bake in a preheated 325 degree oven for about 40 minutes. When the cake is done the top should be puffed and golden in color. As soon as you take the cake out of the oven, rest the edges of the pan on any raised surface and invert the cake. (This prevents the cake from falling.) Cool the cake. It is easier to work with the cake if it is either refrigerated or frozen first. Cut into desired size, either bite-size pieces, or larger, for plate service. They will be covered with icing and nuts so they will end up much larger in size.

Icing:

Beat butter, sugar and vanilla extract until creamy and ice the cake pieces. Top iced cake pieces with cooled peanuts. Top each piece with a cherry or whipped cream, if desired. If you have chocolate lovers, chocolate sauce can be drizzled over the cake pieces.

Creamy Flan

Must Be Made Ahead

Caramel:
¼ cup sugar

Custard:

1 (14-ounce) can sweetened
    condensed milk

1¾ cups milk

1 (3-ounce) package cream cheese,
    softened

4 eggs

2 egg yolks

1½ teaspoons vanilla extract

Caramel:

Set eight individual custard cups or an 8-cup soufflé dish within easy reach of the stove. Spoon sugar into a heavy 1-quart saucepan or skillet. Cook over low heat, watching carefully as the sugar melts into a golden-brown caramel syrup. There is no need to stir unless the sugar is melting unevenly. When the syrup reaches a rich medium-brown, remove the pan from the heat. Immediately pour about a teaspoon of caramel into the bottom of each custard cup, or pour all of it evenly into the soufflé dish. Tip the dishes if needed to distribute the caramel. The hot syrup will harden almost immediately.

Custard:

Put all the custard ingredients in a blender and blend briefly until the mixture is smooth. Pour the mixture into the top of a double boiler. Heat the mixture over low heat until it is warm throughout. Do not let the custard boil. Pour the custard into the cups or dish, and place them in a baking pan large enough to accommodate all of the cups with a little room for air circulation. Add enough warm water to the pan to cover the bottom third of the cups. Bake in a preheated 325 degree oven for 70 to 75 minutes for the small cups, and 80 to 85 minutes for the large dish, or until the custard is firm and light brown on top. Remove the flan from the oven and let it cool 15 to 20 minutes at room temperature. Cover the flan and refrigerate at least 4 hours or overnight. Remove flan from the refrigerator just before serving and unmold by running a knife between the custard and the dish. Cover each cup or dish with a plate and invert giving a brief shake. The custard should drop to the plate. Serve the flan immediately. In the unlikely event you have leftovers, they can be kept for up to 2 days. Serves 8.

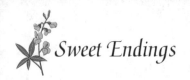

Delicious Chocolate Indulgence

Must Be Frozen

Pâté:

12	ounces bittersweet chocolate	5	eggs, separated
¾	cup unsalted butter	1	cup heavy cream
2	tablespoons cocoa	⅓	cup sugar

Ganache:

9	ounces bittersweet chocolate	¾	cup unsalted butter
½	cup, plus 1 tablespoon heavy cream		

Crème Anglaise:

1	cup milk	1	cup sugar
1	cup cream	1½	teaspoons vanilla extract
6	egg yolks		

Garnish:

Strawberry slices   Fresh mint

Pâté:

Grease a 9x5-inch loaf pan and line with parchment paper. In top of double boiler over hot water, melt chocolate, butter and cocoa. Do not boil. Remove from heat when chocolate has completely melted. Allow chocolate to cool, but not harden. Beat egg yolks until frothy, and then beat them into cooled chocolate. Beat heavy cream until it forms stiff peaks. Beat egg whites to soft peak stage and then gradually add sugar until stiff peaks are formed. Fold whipped cream into egg yolk-chocolate mixture, and then gradually fold in beaten egg whites. Pour mixture into prepared loaf pan. Tap pan to settle surface. Chill in refrigerator for 4 hours before transferring to freezer. Freeze for at least 3 hours.

Ganache:

Place all the ingredients for the Ganache in the top of a double boiler and melt over hot water, stirring until smooth. Cool slightly. Remove loaf pan from the freezer and pour a ⅛-inch layer of the Ganache on top of the frozen mixture

Delicious Chocolate Indulgence continued

without removing from the pan. Return pan to the freezer for 30 minutes, then remove again and dip into warm water. Unmold from pan, iced side down, onto a baking sheet lined with parchment paper; return to freezer for an additional 30 minutes. Remove from freezer and pour remaining Ganache (reheat if necessary) over Pâté so it coats all sides. Smooth with a spatula, if necessary. Freeze for at least 30 minutes more. (Prepared Pâté may be frozen for up to 2 weeks if wrapped well in freezer paper.)

Crème Anglaise:

Pour milk and cream in a small saucepan and scald over medium heat. Using a wire whisk beat the egg yolks with the sugar until thick and light in color. Gradually whisk milk-cream mixture into the egg yolks, then place mixture in the top of a double boiler and cook until mixture is thick enough to coat the back of a wooden spoon. (You should be able to trace a line with your finger through the back of the spoon without the two sides running together.) Fill a large stainless steel bowl with ice and water and place pan with cream mixture over the ice water. Stir until cool and then stir in vanilla extract. Refrigerate until well chilled. Makes 2½ cups. About 2 to 3 hours before serving, use a warm, dry knife to cut the Pâté into 3/8-inch slices. Spoon Crème Anglaise onto serving plates and place a slice of Pâté in the center of each plate. Cover with plastic wrap and refrigerate to allow filling to soften. Just before serving, garnish with a sliced strawberry and a fresh mint. Serves 24.

The directions are long, but the steps are easy.
It's well worth your time to make this.

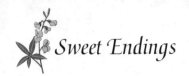
Chocolate Grasshopper Crêpes

Must Be Chilled

Chocolate Crêpes:

3	eggs	2	tablespoons cocoa
1	cup flour	1¼	cups buttermilk
2	tablespoons sugar	1	tablespoon butter, melted

Filling:

2	cups miniature marshmallows	1	cup heavy cream, whipped
⅓	cup milk	12	cooked chocolate crêpes
2	tablespoons crème de cacao		Whipped cream, optional
3	tablespoons crème de menthe		Shaved chocolate, optional
	Green food coloring, optional		

Chocolate Crêpes:

Place eggs in a medium bowl and beat with an electric mixer. Add flour, sugar and cocoa alternately with buttermilk. Stir in butter. Refrigerate batter about 1 hour. Cook on upside down crêpe pan or in traditional pan. Makes 12 to 14 crêpes.

Filling:

Heat marshmallows and milk in a saucepan over low heat, stirring constantly, until marshmallows just melt. Refrigerate, stirring occasionally, until mixture mounds slightly when dropped from spoon (about ½ hour). Stir crème de cacao, crème de menthe and several drops of green food coloring into marshmallow mixture. Beat heavy cream until stiff. Fold green mixture into whipped cream. Fill cooked crêpes. Fold over. Chill until firm. Top with extra whipped cream, if desired. May top with shaved chocolate.

Poteet Strawberry-Rhubarb Crisp

½ cup sugar	½ cup water
1¼ cups flour, divided	½ cup rolled oats
½ teaspoon ground cinnamon	1 cup packed brown sugar
2 cups sliced fresh rhubarb	8 tablespoons margarine, softened
2 cups sliced fresh strawberries	

Combine sugar, ¼ cup flour and cinnamon. Sprinkle over rhubarb and strawberries. Add water and pour into a 9-inch microwave cake pan. Cover with plastic wrap and cook on high for 3 minutes. Meanwhile, mix the remaining 1 cup flour, oats and brown sugar. Cut in margarine. Add topping to the strawberry mixture and cook uncovered in microwave on high for 8 minutes. Serves 6.

This is my husband's favorite dessert.

A Torte for Santa

2 cups cranberries, washed	1 cup flour
½ cup chopped walnuts	1 teaspoon almond extract
¾ cup butter, melted	2 eggs, well beaten
1 cup sugar	1 cup heavy cream, whipped

Butter a 10-inch pie pan. Sprinkle cranberries and nuts over the bottom of the pan. Mix butter, sugar, flour, almond extract and eggs together until well blended. Pour mixture over the cranberries and nuts. Bake in a preheated 325 degree oven for 35 to 40 minutes. Serve topped with whipped cream. Serves 1 Santa and 7 elves.

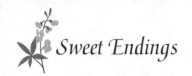

Pumpkin Custard Squares

Cake:

1   (18¼-ounce) package yellow
      cake mix
¾   cup butter or margarine,
      softened, divided
3   eggs, divided
Cooking spray
1   (29-ounce) can pumpkin
⅔   cup milk
½   teaspoon ground allspice
½   teaspoon ground cloves

½   teaspoon ground ginger
½   teaspoon salt
¼   teaspoon ground nutmeg
1   teaspoon ground cinnamon,
      divided
½   cup packed brown sugar,
      divided
1   cup chopped pecans or walnuts
Pecan or walnut halves

Spiced Whipped Cream:

1   cup whipping cream, whipped
1   teaspoon vanilla extract
½   teaspoon ground cinnamon

1   teaspoon grated orange zest
2   teaspoons sugar
Nut halves, optional

Cake:

Cut ½ cup butter into cake mix until you have moist even crumbs. Reserve 1 cup crumb mixture for topping. To remaining crumbs add 1 egg and stir until blended. Spoon into 13x9x2-inch pan that has been lightly sprayed with cooking spray and press lightly. Bake in a preheated 350 degree oven for 10 minutes until puffy. Beat 2 eggs, gradually adding pumpkin and milk. Add allspice, cloves, ginger, salt, nutmeg, ½ teaspoon cinnamon, and ¼ cup brown sugar to mixture and blend well. Pour over cake. Combine reserved crumbs with the remaining ½ teaspoon cinnamon and ¼ cup brown sugar. Add the remaining ¼ cup butter and stir until blended. Stir in nuts. Drop by spoonfuls to form an even layer of crumbs over the batter. Bake in a preheated 350 degree oven until custard is slightly set, 30 to 50 minutes. Cool completely. Top with Spiced Whipped Cream and nut halves.

Spiced Whipped Cream:

Combine whipped cream, vanilla extract, cinnamon, orange zest and sugar. Serves 12 to 15.

An RWC Favorite served at the Tea Room.

Dessert Tacos

Dessert for Mexican Fiesta!

1 tablespoon sugar	2 kiwi, peeled, cut into strips
¼ teaspoon ground cinnamon	1 pint strawberries, sliced and
4 (8-inch) flour tortillas	tops removed
1 tablespoon butter, melted	1 cup frozen whipped topping,
2 cups chocolate ice cream	thawed

Combine sugar and cinnamon. Brush tortillas with melted butter and sprinkle evenly with sugar mixture. Shape 4 sheets of aluminum foil into 4-inch balls on a baking sheet. Place tortillas, butter side down, on foil. Shape to resemble taco shell used to serve taco salad. Bake in a preheated 350 degree oven for 10 minutes or until crisp. Cool completely on foil. Remove tortilla shells; fill evenly with ice cream, kiwi and strawberries. Top with a dollop of whipped topping. Serves 4.

Kids Can Do It
Ice Cream Sandwich Dessert

Must Be Frozen

12 ice cream sandwiches	1 (7.25-ounce) bottle Magic Shell
1 (12-ounce) tub frozen whipped	topping
topping, thawed, divided	

Layer 6 sandwiches in an 11x7x2-inch dish and cover with ½ whipped topping. Place remaining sandwiches in dish and cover with remaining whipped topping. Drizzle Magic Shell on top and freeze. Serves 6 to 12.

Easy and yummy!

Fudge Sundae Pie
Must Be Frozen

Chocolate Sauce:

1 cup evaporated milk	1 cup miniature marshmallows
6 ounces chocolate chips	Dash salt

Dessert:

Vanilla wafers	1 (8-ounce) tub frozen whipped topping, thawed
1-1½ quarts vanilla ice cream, softened	Chopped pecans
	Maraschino cherries

Chocolate Sauce:

Put milk, chocolate chips, marshmallows and salt into a heavy 1-quart saucepan. Stir over medium heat until chocolate and marshmallows completely melt and mixture thickens. Remove from heat and cool to room temperature.

Dessert:

Line bottom and sides of a 9 or 10-inch pie plate with vanilla wafers. Spoon half of the vanilla ice cream over the vanilla wafers. Cover with half of the Chocolate Sauce. Repeat with the rest of the ice cream and sauce. Freeze until firm, about 5 hours. Garnish with whipped topping, pecans and cherries. The Chocolate Sauce can be made ahead of time and refrigerated. Reheated in the microwave, it can be served over ice cream as hot fudge sauce. Serves 8 to 10.

**This dessert is especially good when made with
Blue Bell ice cream, which has been a Texas favorite since 1911,
from the Blue Bell creamery in Brenham. Texas ranks third among
states in the production of commercial ice cream.**

Mary Todd Lincoln's White Cake

1	cup butter	1	teaspoon vanilla extract
2	cups sugar	1	teaspoon almond extract
3	cups flour	1	cup blanched almonds
2	teaspoons baking powder	6	egg whites
1	cup milk	¼	teaspoon salt

Cream butter and sugar until light and fluffy in a large bowl. Sift together the flour and baking powder; remove 2 tablespoons and set aside. Add sifted ingredients alternating with milk, to the creamed mixture. Stir in vanilla and almond extracts. Combine almonds with reserved flour mixture and add to batter. Beat egg whites until stiff. Add salt and fold egg white mixture into batter. Pour into greased and floured 10-inch Bundt pan. Bake in a preheated 375 degree oven for 50 to 55 minutes or until a cake tester comes out clean. Cool 5 to 10 minutes; remove from pan and cool on rack.

This recipe was created by M. Giron, a famous Lexington, Kentucky, baker on the occasion of Lafayette's visit to that city in 1825. The Todd family received the recipe from M. Giron and treasured it ever since. It was served on special occasions in Springfield, Illinois, and at the White House. Legend has it that Mary Todd Lincoln often made this cake for the president, and he always commented, "Mary's White Cake is the best I have ever eaten." This recipe has been passed down to the William Dale Nix family of Canadian, Texas, a descendant of the Todd family.

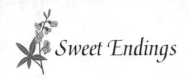

Apple Dapple Cake

Rich and Wonderful!

Cake:

2	cups sugar	1	teaspoon salt
1½	cups corn oil	1	teaspoon ground mace
3	eggs	3	cups finely diced peeled apples
3	cups flour	2	cups chopped pecans
1	teaspoon baking soda	2	teaspoons vanilla extract

Glaze:

2	cups packed dark brown sugar	1	cup butter
1	cup heavy cream		

Cake:

Combine sugar and oil. Beat well. Add eggs one at a time, beating after each addition. Sift flour, baking soda, salt and mace together and stir into egg mixture. Beat in apples, nuts and vanilla extract. Pour into buttered 9-inch tube pan or spray pan with cooking spray. Bake in a preheated 325 degree oven for 1 hour or until toothpick comes out clean. Cool and remove from pan.

Glaze:

Combine glaze ingredients and boil for 3 minutes. Reserve ⅓ cup of glaze. Pour remainder over hot cake. Cool and remove from pan. Put reserved glaze in a pitcher and let each one pour some over their own cake.

Hint: A 9-inch angel cake pan and a 10-inch Bundt pan each hold about 12 cups.

Special Harvest Cake

Diabetic Cake

2 cups flour	1 cup chopped dates or prunes
2 teaspoons baking soda	1½ cups unsweetened applesauce
8 tablespoons butter or margarine	1 cup chopped pecans
1 tablespoon Sweet'n Low	1 teaspoon ground cinnamon
1 teaspoon vanilla extract	¼ teaspoon ground cloves
1 egg	

Sift flour and baking soda; set aside. Cream butter, Sweet'n Low and vanilla extract. Add egg and beat well. Add dates, applesauce and pecans. Mix well. Add flour mixture, cinnamon and cloves and beat with electric mixer at medium speed until blended. Pour into greased 10-inch Bundt pan. Bake in a preheated 350 degree oven for 45 to 60 minutes or until done.

The Cake That Won't Last

1½ cups vegetable oil	3 bananas, chopped
3 cups flour	1 teaspoon baking soda
3 cups sugar	1 teaspoon vanilla extract
2 eggs	1 teaspoon ground cinnamon
1 (8-ounce) can crushed pineapple, drained	1 teaspoon salt
	1 cup chopped pecans

Mix all ingredients together and bake in greased and floured 10 to 12 cup Bundt pan for 60 to 75 minutes in a preheated 350 degree oven. Serves 12 to 16.

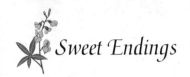

Apricot Layer Cake

Cake:

1	(18¼-ounce) package white cake mix
1¼	cups water
3	egg whites

⅓	cup vegetable oil
1	tablespoon grated orange zest
1	teaspoon orange or lemon extract
⅔	cup apricot preserves

Brown Butter Frosting:

8	tablespoons butter (do not substitute)
3½-4	cups powdered sugar, sifted

⅓	cup orange juice
¼	cup chopped pecans

Cake:

In a mixing bowl combine the cake mix, water, egg whites, oil, orange zest and orange extract. Beat on low speed for 30 seconds or until moistened. Beat on high for 2 minutes. Pour into 2 greased and floured 8-inch or 9-inch round cake pans. Bake in a preheated 350 degree oven for 30 to 35 minutes or until a toothpick inserted near the center comes out clean. Cool in pans 10 minutes before removing to wire rack; cool completely. Using a serrated knife split each layer in half horizontally. Spread the cut side of each bottom layer with ⅓ cup of apricot preserves. Replace tops and set aside.

Brown Butter Frosting:

In a heavy saucepan cook butter over medium heat for 7 to 8 minutes or until golden brown, stirring constantly. Pour into a mixing bowl. Add 3 cups powdered sugar and orange juice. Beat until smooth. Add enough of the remaining sugar to reach spreading consistency. Spread frosting between layers; frost top and sides of cake. Sprinkle with nuts. Store in refrigerator. Serves 12.

Hint: To divide layers evenly, measure the height of the layer and put toothpicks in the side of the layer at ½ the thickness all the way around the cake. Let the toothpicks guide your knife. (Some people think it is easier to use waxed dental floss rather than a knife.)

You'll have lots of requests for this recipe.

Butter Brickle Cake

Cake:

1 cup chopped pecans, plus additional for garnish

1 (18¼-ounce) package yellow cake mix

1 (3.4-ounce) package vanilla instant pudding

4 large eggs

¾ cup water

½ cup vegetable oil

½ teaspoon butter flavoring

1 cup almond brickle chips

Chopped pecans, optional

Brown Sugar Frosting:

8 tablespoons butter

1 cup packed brown sugar

¼ cup milk

2 cups powdered sugar, sifted

Cake:

Toast pecans. Set aside. Beat cake mix, pudding, eggs, water, oil and butter flavoring at medium speed with an electric mixer. Stir in almond brickle chips and pecans just until blended. Bake in 2 greased and floured 9-inch round cake pans in a preheated 350 degree oven for 30 to 35 minutes or until done. Cool in pans on wire racks for 10 minutes. Remove from pans, and cool completely on wire racks. Frost between layers, on top and sides. Serves 8.

Brown Sugar Frosting:

Melt butter in a small pan. Add brown sugar. Boil over low heat for 2 minutes, stirring constantly. Add milk and bring to a boil. Cool to lukewarm and gradually add powdered sugar. Place pan in ice water and stir until it reaches spreading consistency. Sprinkle with additional chopped nuts, if desired.

Hint: For easy frosting cover the edges of the cake plate with 3 to 4-inch strips of wax paper. Remove paper when finished and your cake plate will still be clean.

An RWC Favorite served at the Bridge Festival.

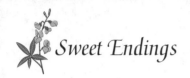

Better and Better Carrot Cake

Cake:

1½ cups unsalted butter, softened

1 cup firmly packed light brown sugar

1 cup sugar

2 teaspoons vanilla extract

3 large eggs, at room temperature

2½ cups flour

1 teaspoon baking soda

1 teaspoon baking powder

1 teaspoon ground cinnamon

¼ teaspoon salt

½ cup apple juice

1½ cups peeled grated carrots (about 3 or 4)

1 cup peeled, shredded sweet potato (about 1 large)

1 large Granny Smith apple, peeled and chopped

½ cup drained crushed pineapple

1 cup coarsely chopped pecans, toasted

3 tablespoons heavy cream

Cream Cheese Frosting:

2 (8-ounce) packages cream cheese, softened

8 tablespoons unsalted butter, softened

2 teaspoons vanilla extract

1 tablespoon fresh lemon juice

2 (1-pound) boxes powdered sugar, sifted

Cake:

Put the butter and the sugars in a large bowl and cream together until fluffy, 4 or 5 minutes, using the electric mixer on medium speed. Beat in the vanilla extract. Add the eggs one at a time, beating 20 seconds after each addition. In another bowl, stir together the flour, baking soda, baking powder, cinnamon and salt. Add dry ingredients by thirds to the butter mixture, alternating with apple juice. Beat for 45 seconds after each addition beginning and ending with flour mixture. Stir in the carrots, sweet potatoes, apples, pineapple and pecans and blend thoroughly. Divide the batter among 3 (9-inch) greased and floured cake pans. Bake on the middle rack of a preheated 350 degree oven for 25 to 30 minutes or until a toothpick inserted in the center comes out clean. Remove cakes to wire racks to cool for 10 minutes; turn them out onto the wire racks to cool. While the layers are still warm brush each with 1 tablespoon of heavy cream.

Better and Better Carrot Cake continued

Cream Cheese Frosting:

Put the cream cheese and the butter in a bowl and beat until smooth using the electric mixer on medium speed. Add the vanilla extract and the lemon juice and beat until combined. Gradually beat in the sugar on low speed until well blended and smooth. Place a cake layer on a cake plate and spread the top with a layer of frosting. Note: If the frosting is too warm you may need to put this first layer in the refrigerator 5 to 10 minutes. This will keep the frosting firm. Frost the other 2 layers and the top and sides of the cake. Garnish the sides of the cake with chopped pecans, pressing them gently on with your hands. Refrigerate.

This cake can be prepared ahead. It just gets better and better.

Cock-Eyed Cake

Try This When Camping

3	cups flour	10	tablespoons vegetable oil
6	tablespoons cocoa	2	tablespoons vinegar
2	teaspoons baking soda	2	teaspoons vanilla extract
2	cups sugar	2	cups water
1	teaspoon salt		

To Make at Home:

Mix flour, cocoa, baking soda, sugar and salt in a large bowl. Make three wells in dry ingredients. In each well, put oil, vinegar and vanilla extract. Pour water over top. Stir until nearly smooth and you can't see the flour. A few lumps are fine. Pour into a greased 13x9x2-inch pan and bake in a preheated 350 degree oven for 35 to 45 minutes or until done. Serves 18.

For Campfire Cooking:

Mix the dry ingredients at the ranch and divide in half. Place half the ingredients in a plastic bag and take camping. Reserve the rest of the ingredients for the next trip. At the campsite add half the wet ingredients and mix as directed. Put an 8-inch Dutch oven on hot coals and put additional hot coals on the top of the oven and bake for about 30 minutes. Serves 9.

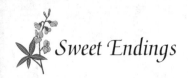

Creole Fudge Cake

Cake:

4	ounces unsweetened chocolate	3	eggs
1	cup firmly packed light brown sugar	2½	cups sifted cake flour
½	cup water	2	teaspoons baking powder
1	tablespoon instant coffee granules	½	teaspoon baking soda
1	cup sugar	¼	teaspoon salt
8	tablespoons butter or margarine, softened	1	cup milk
			Cocoa

Coffee Buttercream Icing:

2	tablespoons instant coffee granules	2	egg yolks
¼	cup hot water	6	cups sifted powdered sugar
1	cup butter or margarine, softened		Chocolate shavings, optional

Cake:

Combine chocolate, brown sugar, water and coffee in top of double boiler. Heat over simmering water until well blended. Cool. Add sugar slowly to butter, beating at medium speed until well blended. Add eggs, one at a time, beating well after each addition; continue beating until mixture is light and fluffy. Beat in cooled chocolate mixture. Sift together cake flour, baking powder, baking soda and salt. Add alternately with milk to creamed mixture. Divide batter among 3 (8-inch) round cake pans that have been greased and dusted with cocoa. Stagger pans in oven: bake in a preheated 350 degree oven for 25 to 30 minutes. Cool 10 minutes in pan. Turn onto racks; refrigerate until cold. Frost between layers, on sides and top with Coffee Butter Cream Icing. Sprinkle with chocolate shavings.

Coffee Buttercream Icing:

Dissolve coffee in hot water. Cool. Blend butter and egg yolks at medium speed of electric mixer. Add powdered sugar with coffee mixture; blend until smooth.

Hint: When alternating the addition of liquids and dry ingredients always begin and end with dry ingredients.

Easy Black Forest Cake

Best Made Ahead

Cake:

1 (18¼-ounce) package chocolate fudge cake mix

1 (21-ounce) can cherry pie filling
Cooking spray

Icing:

1 cup sugar
5 tablespoons margarine
⅓ cup milk

1 (6-ounce) package of semi-sweet chocolate chips
1 cup pecans, chopped
1½ teaspoons vanilla extract

Cake:

Mix cake according to package directions except use the can of cherry pie filling instead of water. Pour into 13x9x2-inch pan that has been sprayed with cooking spray and bake in a preheated 350 degree oven for 40 minutes. Ice while warm. Serves 12 to 16.

Icing:

Boil sugar, margarine and milk for 1 minute. Add chocolate chips, pecans and vanilla extract. Spread over warm cake. Best if made the day before.

Hint: If you're in a big hurry, use a can of fudge icing.

An RWC Favorite served at the Bridge Festival.

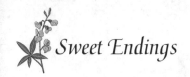

Hint of Mint Fudge Cake

Cake:

1	cup butter, softened	2	tablespoons water
2	cups sugar	2	teaspoons peppermint extract
4	eggs	2¼	cups flour
7	ounces semi-sweet chocolate, chopped, melted and cooled	½	teaspoon salt
		1	teaspoon baking soda
3	ounces unsweetened chocolate, chopped, melted and cooled	1¼	cups buttermilk
2	teaspoons vanilla extract		

Mint Glaze:

4	ounces semi-sweet chocolate, chopped	2	teaspoons light corn syrup
		¼-½	teaspoon peppermint extract
6	tablespoons butter	¾	teaspoon water

Cake:

Cream butter and sugar until fluffy. Add eggs 1 at a time, beating well. Add chocolates, vanilla extract, water and peppermint extract. Stir flour, salt and baking soda together. Add dry ingredients alternating with buttermilk. Pour into a well greased 10-inch Bundt pan or 9-inch tube pan. Bake in the center of a preheated 350 degree oven for 45 to 60 minutes or until a toothpick comes out clean. Cool 10 minutes on a wire rack. Take cake out of pan and cool another 20 minutes. This cake freezes well for 2 to 3 weeks. Serves 12.

Mint Glaze:

Melt chocolate and butter. Stir in corn syrup, peppermint extract and water. Pour over cake.

Super Chocolate Pound Cake

Awesome!

Cake:

6	ounces semi-sweet chocolate	1	tablespoon brandy
4	ounces milk chocolate	2¼	cups flour
2	tablespoons water	½	teaspoon salt
1	cup butter, softened	¼	teaspoon baking soda
2	cups sugar	1	cup buttermilk
4	eggs	½	cup chopped nuts, optional
2	teaspoons vanilla extract		Fresh strawberries, optional

Dark Chocolate Pour Frosting:

1	(6-ounce) package semi-sweet chocolate chips	2	tablespoons light corn syrup
2	tablespoons butter	3	tablespoons milk

Cake:

In medium saucepan melt together chocolates and water over very low heat and set aside to cool. In large bowl cream together butter and sugar until light and fluffy. Add eggs one at a time, beating after each addition. Blend in melted chocolate, vanilla extract and brandy. Sift together the flour, salt and baking soda. Add flour mixture alternately with buttermilk to chocolate mixture, beginning and ending with flour, blending after each addition. Fold in nuts. Pour batter into well greased and floured 10-inch tube pan or 12-cup Bundt pan. Bake in preheated 325 degree oven for 1 hour and 20 to 35 minutes or until a toothpick inserted in center comes out clean. Watch carefully. Cool in pan 10 minutes, then turn out on a rack and continue cooling for 20 minutes more. Place cake on platter and pour frosting over cake while cake is still slightly warm.

Dark Chocolate Pour Frosting:

Melt chocolate and butter in top of double boiler over simmering water, stirring often. Stir in corn syrup and milk and beat until smooth. Decorate with fresh strawberries.

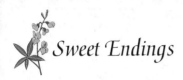

The Best Chocolate Cake in Texas

Cake:

8	tablespoons margarine	½	cup buttermilk
½	cup vegetable shortening	2	eggs, beaten
¼	cup cocoa	1	teaspoon baking soda
1	cup water	1	teaspoon ground cinnamon
2	cups flour	1	teaspoon vanilla extract
2	cups sugar		

Chocolate Icing:

8	tablespoons margarine	1	(1-pound) box powdered sugar, sifted
4	tablespoons cocoa		
6	tablespoons milk	1	teaspoon vanilla extract
		1	cup chopped pecans

Cake:

Place the margarine, shortening, cocoa and water in a small saucepan. Bring to a low boil and remove from heat. Cool. Sift together flour and sugar in a large mixing bowl. Pour cocoa mixture over the flour and sugar. Mix well. Add the buttermilk, eggs, baking soda, cinnamon and vanilla extract. Mix well and pour into a greased and floured 13x9x2-inch pan or a 15x10x1-inch pan. If using a 13x9x2-inch pan bake in a preheated 350 degree oven for 20 to 30 minutes. If using a 15x10x1-inch pan bake at 400 degrees for 20 minutes. Cake should pop back up when pressed lightly with finger.

Chocolate Icing:

Five minutes before cake is done; melt together margarine, cocoa and milk. Remove from heat as soon as mixture comes to a boil. Pour mixture over powdered sugar, and beat well. Add vanilla extract and chopped pecans. Spread on cake as soon as it is taken from oven. Cool and cover.

An RWC Favorite discovered during our testing.

Texas Twister Cake

1 cup flaked coconut	3 eggs
1 cup chopped pecans	1 (1-pound) box powdered sugar, sifted
1 (18¼-ounce) package German chocolate cake mix	½ cup margarine or butter, softened
1¼ cups water	1 (8-ounce) package cream cheese, softened
⅓ cup vegetable oil	

Grease and flour a 13x9x2-inch pan. Sprinkle coconut and pecans evenly over bottom of greased pan. In a large bowl, combine cake mix, water, oil and eggs at low speed until moistened and beat 2 minutes at high speed. Spoon batter evenly over coconut and pecans. In another large bowl, combine powdered sugar, margarine and cream cheese; beat until smooth and creamy. Spoon evenly over batter to within 1-inch of edges. Bake in a preheated 350 degree oven for 45 to 50 minutes, or until tester inserted in center comes out clean. Cool completely. Cut into squares and invert each square onto individual plate. Serve warm or cool; store in refrigerator. Serves 12 to 16.

San Saba, the pecan capital of the world, is host to the *"Pecan Festival"* on the first weekend of December.

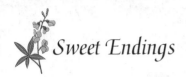

Mexican Wedding Cake

Cake:

2	cups sugar	1	(20-ounce) can crushed pineapple and liquid
2	cups flour		
½	teaspoon salt	1	cup shredded coconut
2	teaspoons baking soda	1	cup chopped pecans
2	beaten eggs	2	teaspoons vanilla extract

Frosting:

1	(8-ounce) package cream cheese, softened	8	tablespoons butter, softened
1	(1-pound) box powdered sugar, sifted	1	teaspoon vanilla extract

Cake:

Mix all ingredients and pour into 13x9x2-inch greased and floured pan. Bake in a preheated 350 degree oven for 25 to 30 minutes or until done. While cake is hot pour frosting on cake.

Frosting:

Mix all ingredients in a large bowl until creamy. Frost hot cake. Cool and refrigerate.

Variation: Omit coconut and vanilla extract from cake. Add 1 additional teaspoon of vanilla extract to frosting.

An RWC Favorite. The variation is the
Pineapple Cake served at the Bridge Festival.

Swedish Pound Cake

Cake:

1 cup margarine
2 cups sugar
5 eggs
1 teaspoon vanilla extract
2 cups flour

1 (6-ounce) package chocolate chips
1 (3½-ounce) can flaked coconut
1 cup chopped pecans

Glaze:

¾ cup sugar
¾ cup water

4 tablespoons margarine
1 teaspoon almond extract

Cake:

Cream together margarine and sugar; add eggs one at a time. Add vanilla extract, flour, chocolate chips, coconut and pecans. Pour into greased and floured tube pan or 12-inch Bundt pan. Bake in preheated 350 degree oven for 1 hour.

Glaze:

Cook all ingredients for 3 to 5 minutes. Turn cake out on a plate. Pour hot glaze mixture over warm cake.

Hint: There will be some of the glaze in bottom of cake dish; it takes awhile for the cake to soak up the glaze. A rimmed plate is a good idea.

An RWC Favorite served at the Bridge Festival.

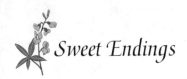

Gingerbread with Luscious Lemon Sauce

Gingerbread:

1 cup butter	Dash salt
2 cups sugar	2 teaspoons baking soda
4 tablespoons molasses	2 cups buttermilk
2 teaspoons ground ginger	2 eggs, well beaten
2 teaspoons ground cinnamon	3 cups flour
1 teaspoon ground cloves	Whipped cream, optional
1 teaspoon ground nutmeg	

Luscious Lemon Sauce:

1 cup sugar	1 egg, slightly beaten
8 tablespoons butter	¼ cup light corn syrup
Juice of 1 lemon	¼ cup boiling water
Grated lemon zest	

Gingerbread:

Melt butter, then add sugar, molasses, ginger, cinnamon, cloves, nutmeg and salt; mix well. Dissolve baking soda in the buttermilk and then add to butter mixture. Stir well. Add beaten eggs; stir in flour. Grease and flour 13x9x2-inch pan. Bake in a preheated 350 degree oven for 35 minutes. Serve hot or cold with whipped cream or lemon sauce.

Luscious Lemon Sauce:

Put all ingredients in top of a double boiler and stir until thick. May be served hot or cold. To microwave: mix all ingredients in a 2-cup measure. Cook 1 minute. Stir. Continue cooking in 4 (30 second) intervals, stirring between each one. Remember to adjust the cooking time according to the power of your microwave.

Orange-Zucchini Cake

Cake:

1	cup margarine	4	eggs
1	tablespoon grated orange zest	3	cups flour
1	teaspoon ground cinnamon	3	teaspoons baking powder
½	teaspoon ground nutmeg	½	teaspoon salt
¼	teaspoon ground cloves	⅓	cup fresh orange juice
2	cups packed light brown sugar	1	cup shredded zucchini

White Glaze:

1½ cups sifted powdered sugar	½	teaspoon vanilla extract
1 tablespoon margarine, softened	2-3 tablespoons milk	

Cake:

In large bowl cream margarine, orange zest, cinnamon, nutmeg, cloves and brown sugar until light and fluffy. Beat in eggs 1 at a time. Sift together flour, baking powder and salt. Blend into creamed mixture alternately with orange juice. Stir in zucchini. Turn into a 10-inch greased tube pan or Bundt pan and bake in preheated 350 degree oven for 55 minutes. If using a 13x9x2-inch pan bake at 350 degrees 30 to 35 minutes. Cool 10 minutes, remove from pan; cool completely. Ice the cake. Serves 12 to 16.

White Glaze:

Mix all ingredients and spread on cake.

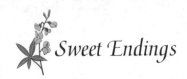

Toasty Oatmeal Cake

Cake:

1¼ cups water	1½ cups flour
8 tablespoons margarine	½ teaspoon salt
1 cup rolled oats	1 teaspoon baking soda
1 cup sugar	1 teaspoon ground nutmeg
1 cup packed brown sugar	1 teaspoon ground cinnamon
2 eggs	

Coconut-Pecan Frosting:

6 tablespoons margarine, softened	½ cup evaporated milk
½ cup sugar	1 teaspoon vanilla extract
1 cup coconut	¾ cup chopped pecans

Cake:

Bring water to a boil in a small pan. Add margarine and melt. Add oats and stir one or two times and set aside for 20 minutes. In a small bowl combine sugars and eggs. In a medium bowl combine flour, salt, baking soda, nutmeg and cinnamon. Pour oats mixture and sugar and egg mixture into dry mixture and stir well. Pour into a greased 13x9x2-inch pan and bake in a preheated 375 degree oven for 40 minutes.

Coconut-Pecan Frosting:

Cream together margarine and sugar; add coconut, milk, vanilla extract and pecans and spread over hot cake. Place under broiler until margarine melts and icing bubbles.

Totin' Cake

1	(18¼-ounce) butter recipe yellow cake mix	1	cup sour cream
¾	cup vegetable oil	½	cup sugar
4	eggs	¼	cup poppy seed
			Cooking spray

Mix all ingredients in an electric mixer and beat well. Put cake into a Bundt pan sprayed with cooking spray. Bake in a preheated 350 degree oven for 50 minutes.

A dear friend always called this cake her "totin' cake" because it is so quick and easy to make and great to take to friends, parties, etc.

Longneck Cake

1	cup vegetable shortening	½	teaspoon salt
2	cups packed dark brown sugar	1	teaspoon ground cinnamon
2	extra large eggs	½	teaspoon ground allspice
2	cups chopped dates	½	teaspoon ground cloves
1	cup chopped pecans, toasted	2	cups beer (let foam settle before measuring)
3	cups flour, sifted		
2	teaspoons baking soda		Powdered sugar

Cream shortening with brown sugar, add eggs and mix until fluffy. Stir in dates and nuts. Stir flour, baking soda, salt, cinnamon, allspice and cloves together and work into date-nut mixture (it will be stiff). Gradually stir in beer, mixing well. Pour into a greased and floured 12-inch Bundt pan. Bake 45 minutes in a preheated 350 degree oven, or until a toothpick inserted in the top comes out clean. Cool in pan on wire rack for 20 minutes. Remove from pan and cool right side up. Sprinkle with powdered sugar before serving. Serves 10 to 12.

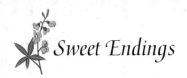

Surprise Nut Cake

Won Best of Show at Texas State Fair

Cake:

2 cups sugar	1 teaspoon baking soda
1 cup vegetable oil	½ teaspoon salt
3 eggs, well beaten	1 teaspoon ground cinnamon
1 cup buttermilk	1 teaspoon ground cloves
1 cup cut-up cooked unsweetened prunes	1 teaspoon ground nutmeg
	1 teaspoon vanilla extract
2 cups flour	1 cup chopped pecans

Buttermilk Glaze:

1 cup sugar	¼ teaspoon salt
½ cup buttermilk	1 teaspoon vanilla extract
1 tablespoon light corn syrup	1 tablespoon butter or margarine
¼ teaspoon baking soda	

Cake:

Mix sugar and oil together, add beaten eggs and mix well. Blend in buttermilk and prunes. Sift together flour, baking soda, salt, cinnamon, cloves and nutmeg. Stir into the above mixture and add vanilla extract and pecans. Bake in a greased and floured Bundt pan or 10-inch tube pan in a preheated 350 degree oven for 70 minutes.

Buttermilk Glaze:

Combine sugar, buttermilk, corn syrup, baking soda, salt, vanilla extract and butter. Bring to a boil over low heat. Continue cooking 4 to 5 minutes, stirring constantly. Spoon over hot cake.

This was one of our mother's favorite cake recipes, and my sister and I have continued to use it frequently. One or the other of us has contributed it to the Bake Sale during the annual Tour of Homes a number of times.

"Secret Ingredient" Cake

Cake:

¾ cup vegetable shortening	½ teaspoon grated nutmeg
1½ cups sugar	1 teaspoon ground cloves
2 large eggs	½ teaspoon ground allspice
2½ cups flour	1¼ cups tomato puree
1¼ teaspoons baking soda	1 cup chopped walnuts
½ teaspoon salt	1 cup raisins
2 teaspoons ground cinnamon	

Frosting:

8 tablespoons butter	3½ cups powdered sugar, sifted
1 (8-ounce) package cream cheese	1 teaspoon grated lemon zest
1 teaspoon vanilla extract	

Cake:

Cream together the shortening and sugar until light and fluffy in a large mixing bowl; then beat in eggs. In a separate bowl, sift together the flour, baking soda, salt, cinnamon, nutmeg, cloves and allspice. Stir the dry mixture alternately with the tomato puree into the wet mixture, stirring until smooth with each addition. Stir in the walnuts and raisins. Divide the batter between 2 (9-inch) greased round cake pans. Bake in a preheated 350 degree oven until the layers are nicely browned and cake tester comes out clean, about 30 minutes. Cool the layers completely and frost.

Frosting:

Beat the butter, cream cheese and vanilla extract together until smooth. Gradually beat in the powdered sugar, about ½ cup at a time, beating until smooth after each addition. Beat in the lemon zest.

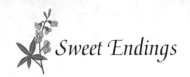

Sweetheart's Strawberry Cake

Cake:

1	(18¼-ounce) box yellow cake mix	½	cup boiling water
1	(3-ounce) box strawberry gelatin	4	eggs
⅓	cup vegetable oil	1	(10-ounce) box frozen strawberries, thawed, divided

Frosting:

4	tablespoons margarine	3	cups powdered sugar, sifted

Cake:

Blend together the cake mix and gelatin in a large mixing bowl. Add oil and water and mix well. Add eggs one at a time and beat well. Fold in ¾ box of strawberries until well blended. Pour into 3 (8-inch) greased and floured round cake pans. Bake in a preheated 325 degree oven for 40 to 45 minutes or until a toothpick inserted in middle comes out clean.

Frosting:

Beat together the margarine and powdered sugar. Add the remaining strawberries and stir well. Frost between each layer and then completely cover the outside of the cake. Serves 12.

Sugar-Free Apple Pie

1	(6-ounce) can frozen apple juice concentrate, thawed	1	teaspoon apple pie spice
4	tablespoons cornstarch		3-4 packets granulated sugar substitute
4	cups sliced Golden Delicious apples		Pastry for a 2 crust (8-inch) pie

Mix apple juice and cornstarch in saucepan over low heat until well dissolved. Stir in apples, spice and sugar substitute. Pour into unbaked pie crust and add top crust. Bake in a preheated 425 degree oven for 15 minutes; reduce heat to 350 degrees and bake another 30 to 35 minutes. Serves 6 to 8.

Apple Cobbler for Two

2	medium cooking apples, sliced	2	tablespoons flour, plus ⅓ cup, divided
1	teaspoon lemon juice		
3	tablespoons brown sugar		Cooking spray
¼	teaspoon ground cinnamon	2	tablespoons sugar
¼	teaspoon ground nutmeg	1	teaspoon baking powder
1	teaspoon vanilla extract	2	tablespoons milk
		1	tablespoon vegetable oil

Toss apples with lemon juice. Combine brown sugar, cinnamon, nutmeg, vanilla extract and 2 tablespoons flour. Add to apples and toss well to coat. Spoon mixture into an 8x8x2-inch baking dish that's been coated with cooking spray. Combine the remaining ⅓ cup flour, sugar and baking powder in a small bowl. Add milk and oil; stir until moistened. Drop dough by teaspoonfuls onto apple mixture. Bake in a preheated 375 degree oven for 15 to 20 minutes. Serve warm.

Apple Pie Alamo

1	cup sugar, plus ½ cup, divided	¼	teaspoon salt
2	tablespoons flour, plus 5 tablespoons, divided	5	cups peeled, cored and diced apples
1	egg, slightly beaten	1	(9-inch) unbaked pie crust
1	cup sour cream	¼	cup butter
1	teaspoon vanilla extract		

Mix 1 cup sugar and 2 tablespoons flour. Add the egg, sour cream, vanilla extract and salt. Beat until smooth. Add the diced apples and pour into the pie crust. Bake in a preheated 350 degree oven for 30 minutes. Mix the remaining ½ cup sugar, the remaining 5 tablespoons flour and butter to resemble crumbs. Cover the pie with crumbs and bake for 15 minutes longer. Top with ice cream. Serves 6 happy apple pie lovers.

Not your everyday apple pie!

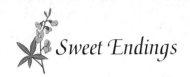

Sawdust Pie

Must Be Chilled

1½ cups sugar
1½ cups sweetened flaked coconut
1½ cups chopped pecans
1½ cups graham cracker crumbs
7   egg whites
1   teaspoon vanilla extract

1   (10-inch) unbaked pie crust
1   large banana, peeled and thinly sliced

Whipped cream, sweetened to taste

Chopped pecans

In a large mixing bowl combine sugar, coconut, pecans, graham cracker crumbs, egg whites and vanilla extract. Stir until blended. Pour mixture into pie crust and bake in a preheated 350 degree oven for 30 to 35 minutes. Cool to room temperature. Arrange banana slices over top of pie and cover with whipped cream and sprinkle with pecans. Refrigerate until ready to serve. Serves 8.

Million Dollar Pie

Must Be Chilled

1   (16-ounce) can sliced peaches, drained and cut up
1   (8-ounce) can crushed pineapple, drained
1   (6-ounce) jar maraschino cherries, drained and cut up
¼   cup lemon juice

1   (14-ounce) can sweetened condensed milk
1   cup whipping cream, whipped, or 1 (8-ounce) tub frozen whipped topping, thawed
2   baked (9-inch) graham cracker pie crusts

Combine peaches, pineapple, cherries, lemon juice, milk and whipping cream or whipped topping. Mix well and refrigerate for 3 to 4 hours. Pour into the 2 pie crusts. Serves 12 to 16.

Bumbleberry Pie

Wonderful Hot Weather Pie!

2	large cooking apples, peeled and chopped	1	cup fresh raspberries
1	cup chopped fresh rhubarb	1	cup sugar
1	cup fresh strawberries halves	½	cup flour
1	cup fresh blueberries	1	tablespoon fresh lemon juice
			Refrigerated pastry for 2 (9-inch) pie crusts

Combine apples, rhubarb, strawberries, blueberries, raspberries, sugar, flour and lemon juice in a large bowl, stirring gently. Fit one pie crust into a 9-inch pie plate according to package directions; spoon fruit mixture into crust. Roll remaining pie crust to press out fold lines. Cut into ½-inch strips and arrange in a lattice design over filling. Fold edges under and crimp. Place pie on a baking sheet. Bake in a preheated 400 degree oven for 25 minutes; reduce heat to 350 degrees, and bake 25 to 30 minutes longer, shielding edges with strips of aluminum foil to prevent excessive browning if necessary. Serves 8.

Hint: Frozen rhubarb and berries, thawed and drained, may be substituted for fresh.

Plain and Simple Cherry Cheesecake Pie

Must Be Chilled

1	(8-ounce) package cream cheese, softened	¼	teaspoon almond extract
1	cup sifted powdered sugar	1	(21-ounce) can cherry pie filling
1	teaspoon vanilla extract	1	baked (9 or 10-inch) graham cracker crust
1	cup whipping cream, whipped		

Beat together cream cheese, sugar and vanilla extract until smooth. Fold in whipped cream. Pour into graham cracker crust. Add almond extract to cherry pie filling and carefully spoon over cheese layer. Chill until set, at least 5 hours. Serves 8 to 10.

Mi Casa Caramel Pie

Must Be Frozen

4 tablespoons margarine	1 (16-ounce) tub frozen whipped topping, thawed
1 (7-ounce) package coconut, ¼ cup reserved	1 (12¼-ounce) jar caramel or butterscotch ice cream topping
½ cup chopped pecans	3 baked and cooled pie crusts
1 (8-ounce) package cream cheese	
1 (14-ounce) can sweetened condensed milk	

In a small saucepan, melt margarine and add coconut and pecans. Cook over medium heat until coconut is toasted. In separate bowl, mix cream cheese and sweetened condensed milk until smooth. Fold in whipped topping. Divide the mixture into thirds, layer into the pie crusts, starting with the cream cheese mixture, then top with the caramel topping. Repeat layers ending with the caramel topping and then sprinkle with the remaining coconut. Freeze. Thaw 10 minutes before serving. Very rich! Makes 3 pies. Serves 18 to 24.

Hint: Try to buy frozen pie crusts with plastic domes.

Avoid using too much flour when rolling pastry, as it results in a tough crust.

German Sweet Chocolate Pie

A Forties Recipe

1 (4-ounce) package German sweet chocolate	2 eggs
4 tablespoons butter	1 teaspoon vanilla extract
1 (12-ounce) can evaporated milk	1 (10-inch) pie crust, unbaked
1½ cups sugar	1⅓ cups sweetened, flaked coconut
3 tablespoons cornstarch	½ cup chopped pecans
⅛ teaspoon salt	Whipped cream or whipped topping, optional

Melt chocolate with butter over low heat, stirring until blended. Remove from heat; gradually blend in evaporated milk. Mix sugar, cornstarch and salt thoroughly. In a separate bowl, beat eggs and vanilla extract. Gradually blend egg mixture into chocolate mixture; then add sugar and cornstarch. Pour into pie crust. Combine coconut and nuts, sprinkle over filling. Bake in a preheated 375 degree oven for 45 minutes. Filling will be soft, but will set while cooling. Cool at least 4 hours before cutting. Serve with a dollop of whipped cream or topping. Serves 8 to 10.

Hint: Cut a foil collar to lay over pie crust edge while baking or your crust will be too brown before the pie is done.

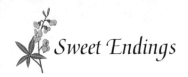

Mexican Soufflé Pie

Must Be Chilled

Chocolate-Kahlúa Crust:

30 chocolate wafers
¼ cup butter, melted

2 tablespoons Kahlúa

Filling:

⅓ cup Kahlúa
2 envelopes unflavored gelatin
½ cup milk, heated to boiling
2 eggs

½ cup sugar
⅔ cup vodka
1½ cups whipping cream

Chocolate-Kahlúa Crust:

Blend chocolate wafers in blender until crumbled. Combine with melted butter and Kahlúa, mixing well. Press in bottom and up sides of a 9-inch pie plate. Bake in preheated oven at 350 degrees about 10 minutes. Cool at least 1 hour before adding filling.

Filling:

Put Kahlúa, gelatin and milk into blender until gelatin is dissolved. Add eggs, sugar and vodka and blend. Pour into bowl and chill 15 minutes, stirring occasionally to keep smooth. Whip cream until thick. Fold gelatin mixture and cream together. Pour into crust and chill until set, about 1 hour. Serves 8.

The *"Citrus Fiesta"* is held during the last two weeks of January in Mission. Orange seeds were brought to Texas from Florida by a Spanish priest. Over time growing oranges developed into a thriving business in the Rio Grande Valley. In addition to oranges, the area produces large amounts of Texas Ruby Red Grapefruits that are shipped all over the world.

South Texas Grapefruit Pie
Must Be Chilled

3 grapefruits
1 cup sugar
1¼ cups water
2 tablespoons cornstarch
⅛ teaspoon salt

1 (3-ounce) package strawberry or raspberry gelatin
½ cup frozen whipped topping, thawed
2 baked 9-inch pie crusts

Peel, seed and section grapefruit over a bowl and reserve any juice. Combine sugar, water, reserved grapefruit juice, cornstarch and salt in a saucepan. Simmer until thick and clear. Add gelatin and stir until dissolved. Chill until it begins to set. Add whipped topping and mix well. Stir in grapefruit sections and pour into baked pie crust. Serves 16.

This is good pie to make when grapefruit is in season.
It is refreshing and you'll get many requests for the recipe.

Fluffy Peanut Butter Pie
Must Be Chilled

3½ cups Oreo cookie crumbs
10 tablespoons melted butter
2 baked (9-inch) pie crusts
2 (8-ounce) packages cream cheese

2 cups peanut butter
1½ cups sugar
3½ cups whipping cream, divided
1 (6-ounce) package semi-sweet chocolate chips

Blend cookie crumbs and butter. Press into pie crusts. Bake for 10 minutes in a preheated 350 degree oven. Let cool. Beat cream cheese and peanut butter together until smooth. Add sugar. In a separate bowl, whip 3 cups cream until it forms soft peaks. Add peanut butter mixture gradually. Pour into cooled crusts and refrigerate for 30 minutes. Combine the remaining ½ cup cream and chocolate chips in sauce pan. Heat on medium heat just until mixture boils. Immediately remove from heat and pour over cooled pies in a thin layer. Refrigerate until ready to serve. Serves 16.

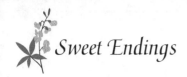

Old-Fashioned Lemon Chiffon Pie

Must Be Chilled

Graham Cracker Crust:

2   cups graham cracker crumbs   2   tablespoons sugar

¼   cup butter or margarine, melted

Filling:

1   (3-ounce) package lemon gelatin   1   cup evaporated milk

⅓   cup sugar   3   tablespoons fresh lemon juice

1   cup orange juice, heated   Pinch salt

1   tablespoon grated lemon zest

Graham Cracker Crust:

Combine graham cracker crumbs, butter and sugar and pat into 9-inch pie plate. Bake in a preheated 350 degree oven for about 8 minutes or until lightly browned. Cool.

Filling:

Dissolve gelatin and sugar in hot orange juice and chill until it's like a thick syrup, about 30 minutes. Chill lemon zest and milk in ice cube trays or other shallow tray in freezer until ice crystals form around the edge, about 15 or 20 minutes. Whip evaporated milk until stiff; then add lemon juice and whip until very stiff. Fold into gelatin mixture and spoon into crust. Chill at least 2 hours. Serves 8.

To prevent soggy crusts in custard-type pies, brush the unbaked pie crust with egg white. Bake at 425 degrees for 5 to 10 minutes before adding filling.

Divine Lime Pie

Delicious!

1 envelope unflavored gelatin	¼ cup grated lime zest, divided
1 cup sugar, divided	2 small drops green food coloring
¼ teaspoon salt	1 cup heavy cream, whipped, divided
4 eggs, separated	
½ cup lime juice	2 baked (8-inch) pie crusts
¼ cup water	Pistachio nuts, optional

Thoroughly mix gelatin, ½ cup sugar and salt in sauce pan. Beat together egg yolks, lime juice and water; stir into gelatin mixture. Cook over medium heat stirring constantly until mixture just comes to a boil. Remove from heat, stir in 3 tablespoons zest. Add food color sparingly to give a pale green color. Chill, stirring occasionally until the mixture mounds slightly when dropped from a spoon. Beat egg whites to soft peaks. Gradually add the remaining ½ cup sugar, beating until stiff peaks form. Fold gelatin mixture into egg whites. Fold in whipped cream. Spoon into cooled, baked pie crusts. Chill until firm. Edge with whipped cream and reserved lime zest or garnish with grated pistachio nuts.

Autumn Pear Pie

Easy, Unusual and Delicious!

2½-3 pounds assorted pears such as Bartlett, Bosc or Anjou	2 tablespoons honey
	1 teaspoon ground cinnamon
Pastry for a double crust (9-inch) pie	

Peel and core each pear and cut into eighths. Fit half of pastry into the bottom of the pie plate. Combine pears, honey and cinnamon. Pour into pie plate. Brush the edges of the pastry with water. Top with remaining pastry and crimp edges. Bake in a preheated 425 degree oven 40 to 45 minutes or until crust begins to brown. This pie is suitable for most diabetics. Serves 8.

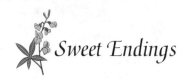

Trail Drive Peach Cobbler

Fruit Mixture:

6 tablespoons tapioca

6-7 cups fresh sliced peaches, peeled

1 cup sugar

¼ teaspoon ground cinnamon

¼ teaspoon ground nutmeg

Cobbler Dough:

8 tablespoons butter, softened

1 cup sugar

2 cups flour

1½ cups milk

2 teaspoons baking powder

1 teaspoon salt

Cobbler Topping:

1½ cups sugar

2 tablespoons cornstarch

⅛ teaspoon ground cinnamon

⅛ teaspoon ground nutmeg

½ cup boiling water

Fruit Mixture:

In a mixing bowl, combine tapioca, peaches, sugar, cinnamon and nutmeg. Mix thoroughly. Pour the mixture into a buttered 13x9x2-inch baking dish.

Cobbler Dough:

In a small bowl, mix thoroughly butter, sugar, flour, milk, baking powder and salt. Spread over fruit mixture.

Cobbler Topping:

In a medium mixing bowl, stir together sugar, cornstarch, cinnamon and nutmeg. Sprinkle evenly over the cobbler dough layer. Pour boiling water evenly over the cobbler. Bake in a preheated 375 degree oven for 1 hour and 20 minutes or until inserted knife comes out clean and the top has a golden crust. Serves 15.

Canned peaches were a staple of the chuck wagon cook.
He probably topped his cobbler with biscuits.

Casa Grande Fudge Pecan Pie

1	(6-ounce) package semi-sweet chocolate chips	2	tablespoons flour
8	tablespoons unsalted butter	1	cup light corn syrup
⅓	cup brandy	¼	teaspoon salt
3	eggs	1	cup chopped pecans
½	cup packed brown sugar	1	(9-inch) pie crust, unbaked

Combine chocolate, butter and brandy in a pan, heat and stir until butter melts and mixture is smooth. Cool. Beat together eggs, brown sugar, flour, syrup and salt until well mixed; then slowly beat in chocolate. Add pecans. Pour mixture into pie crust. Bake in a preheated 350 degree oven for 45 to 50 minutes. Cool slightly before cutting. Serves 6 to 8.

San Saba Pecan Pie

Must Be Chilled

First Layer:

1	(8-ounce) package cream cheese, softened	1	teaspoon vanilla extract
		¼	teaspoon salt
1	egg, beaten	1	(9-inch) pie crust, unbaked
⅓	cup sugar	1½	cups pecans

Second Layer:

3	eggs, beaten	1	cup light corn syrup
¼	cup sugar	1	teaspoon vanilla extract

First Layer:

Mix cream cheese, egg, sugar, vanilla extract and salt and spread over the bottom of the pie crust. Sprinkle with pecans.

Second Layer:

Combine eggs with sugar, corn syrup and vanilla extract and pour into pie crust. Bake in a preheated 375 degree oven for 35 to 40 minutes. After 15 to 20 minutes, cover with foil. Cool completely and refrigerate.

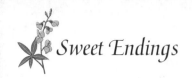

Sugar-Free Pecan Pie

⅓ cup water	¾ cup evaporated skim milk
⅔ cup fructose	2 extra large eggs
2 (1-ounce) packages sugar-free vanilla pudding, not instant	1 (9-inch) pie crust, unbaked
	¾ cup chopped pecans

Combine water and fructose and simmer over low heat for 5 minutes. Cool. Mix dry pudding into fructose mixture. Add skim milk and eggs and blend well. Pour into pie crust and sprinkle pecans on top. Bake in a preheated 350 degree oven for 30 minutes or until the top is firm. Cool 3 hours before slicing. Makes 8 servings.

Double Layer Pumpkin Pie

Must Be Chilled

1 (4-ounce) package cream cheese, softened	1 (16-ounce) can pumpkin
1 tablespoon, plus 1 cup milk or half-and-half, divided	2 (3.3-ounce) packages vanilla instant pudding
1 tablespoon sugar	1 teaspoon ground cinnamon
1½ cups frozen whipped topping, thawed	½ teaspoon ground ginger
1 baked (9-inch) graham cracker crumb crust	¼ teaspoon ground cloves

Mix cream cheese, 1 tablespoon milk and sugar in large bowl with wire whisk until smooth. Gently stir in whipped topping. Spread on bottom of crust. In a large mixing bowl, pour the remaining 1 cup of milk. Add pumpkin, pudding, cinnamon, ginger and cloves. Whisk for 2 minutes. (Mixture will be thick.) Spread over cream cheese layer. Refrigerate 4 hours or until set. Garnish with additional whipped topping. Store leftover pie covered in the refrigerator.

Easy Sugar-Free Pumpkin Pie

2	eggs, slightly beaten	1	teaspoon ground cinnamon
1	(16-ounce) can pumpkin	1	teaspoon vanilla extract
	Sugar substitute to equal ½ cup sugar	1	(12-ounce) can evaporated milk
½	teaspoon salt	1	(9-inch) pie crust, unbaked
2	teaspoons pumpkin pie spice		

Combine eggs, pumpkin, sugar substitute, salt, pumpkin pie spice, cinnamon, vanilla extract and evaporated milk. Pour into pie crust. Bake in a preheated 400 degree oven for 15 minutes. Reduce temperature to 350 degrees and bake 45 minutes longer.

Sugar-Free Strawberry Pie

Must Be Chilled

1	(3-ounce) package sugar-free strawberry gelatin	¾	(8-ounce) tub frozen whipped topping, thawed
1	cup boiling water	1	cup chopped fresh strawberries
½	cup cold water	1	baked (9-inch) pie crust
1	tablespoon lemon juice		

Dissolve gelatin in boiling water. Add cold water and lemon juice. Chill until slightly thickened. Fold together whipped topping and gelatin, blending well. Fold in strawberries. Pour into pie crust and chill about 3 hours.

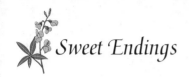

Glazed Almond Sugar Cookies

Cookies:

1 cup unsalted butter, softened

¾ cup sugar, plus sugar for forming cookies

1 teaspoon almond extract

2 cups flour

½ teaspoon baking powder

¼ teaspoon salt

Glaze:

1½ cups powdered sugar, sifted

1 teaspoon almond extract

4-5 teaspoons water

Sliced almonds

Cookies:

Combine butter, sugar and almond extract in large mixer bowl. Beat at medium speed 1 to 2 minutes until creamy, scraping bowl often. Reduce speed to low; add flour, baking powder and salt. Beat until well mixed, about 2 minutes. Roll dough into 1-inch balls; place 2 inches apart on cookie sheet. Flatten balls to ¼-inch thickness with the bottom of a buttered glass dipped in sugar. Bake in a preheated 400 degree oven for 7 to 9 minutes or until edges are lightly browned. Cool 1 minute then remove from cookie sheets. Cool completely.

Glaze:

Stir together powdered sugar, almond extract and water in small bowl with wire whisk. Decorate cooled cookies with glaze and sliced almonds. Makes 3½ dozen.

Almond Crunch Cookies

1 cup sugar	1 teaspoon cream of tartar
1 cup powdered sugar, sifted	1 cup butter, softened
1 cup whole wheat flour	1 cup vegetable oil
3½ cups flour, plus flour for forming cookies	2 eggs
	2 teaspoons almond extract
1 teaspoon baking soda	2 cups toasted chopped almonds
1 teaspoon salt	1 (12-ounce) package brickle bits

Sift together sugars, flours, baking soda, salt and cream of tartar. In the large bowl of an electric mixer beat together butter, oil, eggs and almond extract. Add dry ingredients a little at a time. Stir in the almonds and brickle bits. Shape into ¾-inch balls and place on an ungreased cookie sheet. Flatten with fork dipped in flour. Bake in preheated 350 degree oven for 14 to 15 minutes. When cool store in an airtight container. Makes 6 to 8 dozen.

Texas Two-Step Cookies

2¼ cups flour	¾ cup packed light brown sugar
⅓ cup cocoa	1 teaspoon vanilla extract
1 teaspoon baking soda	2 eggs
½ teaspoon salt	1 (12-ounce) package semi-sweet chocolate chips
1 cup butter or margarine, softened	
¾ cup sugar	1 cup chopped nuts, optional

In a small bowl stir together flour, cocoa, baking soda and salt. In a large bowl beat butter, sugar, brown sugar and vanilla extract until creamy. Add eggs and beat well. Gradually add flour mixture. Beat well. Stir in the chocolate chips and nuts. Drop by teaspoonfuls onto ungreased cookie sheet. Bake in a preheated 375 degree oven 8 to 10 minutes or until lightly browned. Cool, remove to a wire rack. Makes about 5 dozen.

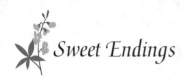

Chocolate Whirls

Must Be Made Ahead

Crust:

1 cup butter	1 teaspoon salt
1 (4-ounce) package cream cheese (do not use low-fat)	1 tablespoon orange juice
	1 teaspoon almond extract
1 cup sugar	3½ cups flour
1 egg, beaten	

Filling:

1 (6-ounce) package chocolate chips	4 ounces cream cheese, softened
½ cup powdered sugar	1 cup finely chopped walnuts
¼ cup orange juice	

Crust:

Cream butter and cream cheese. Gradually add sugar; add egg and beat well. Stir in salt, orange juice and almond extract. Add flour a little at a time. Form dough into 2 balls and refrigerate 4 hours.

Filling:

Combine chocolate chips, powdered sugar and orange juice. Cook in the top of a double boiler over simmering water until the mixture is smooth. Remove from heat. Stir in cream cheese and walnuts.

Assembly:

Remove half of dough from the refrigerator and roll into a 14x10-inch rectangle on a sheet of wax paper. Spread filling along one long side (you'll start rolling from here). Spread half the filling to within ½-inch of both short sides and within 1½-inches of the other long side. Roll rectangle like a jelly roll using the wax paper to help you. Roll the finished roll in another sheet of wax paper, twisting the ends. Refrigerate overnight. Repeat with the remaining dough and filling. The next day slice cookie rolls into ¼-inch slices. Keep unused dough in the refrigerator. Bake cookies on a greased cookie sheet in a preheated 350 degree oven until barely brown, about 15 minutes. Cool on racks. Makes 7 to 8 dozen.

**These cookies keep very well. They are better the day after they are made.
Wonderful for a care package for a college student.**

Easy Triple Chocolate Cookies

1   (18¼-ounce) package chocolate fudge cake mix

1   (12-ounce) package semi-sweet chocolate chips

2   (5-ounce) packages chocolate pudding

1½ cups chopped walnuts

1½ cups Hellmann's mayonnaise

Combine cake mix, pudding, chocolate chips and walnuts in large mixing bowl. Stir gently. Mix in mayonnaise. (Work slowly since the mix is powdery.) Shape dough by heaping teaspoonfuls into balls. Place on ungreased cookie sheet 2-inches apart. Bake in a preheated 350 degree oven about 15 minutes, or until tester inserted into center comes out clean. Cool about 3 minutes before transferring to cooling rack. The cookies will be very soft when they come out of the oven. They become very crisp on the cooling rack. Store in airtight container. Makes 5 to 6 dozen.

Always Good Currant Cookies

2   cups boiling water

1   cup dried currants

1   cup butter

1   cup sugar

3   eggs

2   cups flour

½   teaspoon salt

½   teaspoon baking soda

1   teaspoon ground cinnamon

2   cups rolled oats

1   cup chopped walnuts

Cover currants with boiling water. Simmer 3 to 4 minutes or until the currants are plump. Let cool. Reserve 6 tablespoons of currant liquid. Cream butter and sugar. Add eggs one at a time and beat until blended. Mix flour with salt, baking soda and cinnamon. Add flour mixture alternately with the 6 tablespoons of currant liquid. Blend in oats, walnuts and drained currants. Drop by tablespoonfuls onto greased cookie sheets. Bake in a preheated 350 degree oven about 12 minutes or until lightly browned. Makes 4 to 5 dozen.

This recipe is at least 85 years old.

Chocolate Luckies

4	tablespoons butter, softened	1	egg
1	(6-ounce) package chocolate chips	1	(18¼-ounce) package chocolate cake mix
⅓	cup milk	½	cup pecans, chopped

Combine butter and chocolate chips. Stir in milk and egg. Add cake mix and combine thoroughly. Stir in pecans. Drop by spoonfuls onto lightly greased cookie sheet. Bake in a preheated 350 degree oven for 10 minutes. Makes about 5 dozen.

Killer Ginger Cookies
Must Be Chilled

4½ cups flour	¼	teaspoon salt
2 teaspoons ground ginger	¾	cup butter or margarine
1½ teaspoons ground cinnamon	1	cup packed brown sugar
1½ teaspoons baking soda	1	large egg, lightly beaten
½ teaspoon ground cloves	¾	cup light molasses

Combine flour, ginger, cinnamon, baking soda, cloves and salt in bowl. Beat butter and sugar in large mixer bowl until light and fluffy. Beat in egg and molasses. Gradually beat in dry ingredients just until blended. Divide dough into 4 parts and flatten into disks. Wrap and refrigerate 4 hours or longer. Roll out 1 disk at a time on a lightly floured surface. Cut into cookie cutter shapes or shape into walnut-size balls and place on cookie sheets. If you want a crisper cookie, flatten the balls slightly. Bake in a preheated 350 degree oven for 8 to 12 minutes until edges are lightly browned. Cool one minute, then transfer to cooling rack. Makes about 4 dozen.

Candied Fruit Slices
Must Be Chilled

1 cup butter	2¼ cups sifted flour
1 cup powdered sugar, sifted	1 cup pecan halves
1 egg, beaten	2 cups soft candied cherries, cut in halves
1 teaspoon vanilla extract	

Cream butter and sugar. Add egg and vanilla extract. Stir in flour, pecans and cherries. Chill dough 1 hour. Divide dough in 3 parts, shape into 12-inch long rolls. Wrap in wax paper. Chill at least 3 hours longer. Cut into ⅛-inch slices, and place on ungreased cookie sheet. Bake in a preheated 350 degree oven for 13 to 15 minutes, until delicately browned on edges. Makes about 7 dozen.

Best "Fridge" Cookies
Must Be Chilled

1 cup packed brown sugar	3 cups flour
1 cup sugar	1 teaspoon baking soda
1 cup vegetable shortening	1 teaspoon salt
2 eggs	1 cup finely chopped pecans
5 teaspoons vanilla extract	

Cream sugars and shortening. Stir in eggs and vanilla extract. Mix flour, baking soda and salt and add to sugar mixture. Stir in pecans. Divide into 3 rolls and wrap in wax paper. Chill for several hours. Cut into ⅛-inch slices. Bake in a preheated 350 degree oven on greased cookie sheets for 12 to 14 minutes or until lightly browned. Makes 8 dozen.

Hint: After every slice turn the cookie roll ¼ turn so the roll doesn't get out of shape.

Rolls of cookies may be frozen and cooked later.

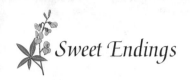

Golden Nuggets

Cookies:

1 cup sugar	1 cup cooked carrots, mashed
¾ cup vegetable shortening	2 cups sifted flour
1 egg	2 teaspoons baking powder
1½ teaspoons vanilla extract	¼ teaspoon salt
1 teaspoon lemon extract	

Orange Icing:

1 teaspoon grated orange zest	Powdered sugar
Juice of ½ orange	

Cookies:

Cream sugar and shortening. Add egg and extracts; mix well. Add carrots, mixing well. Mix flour, baking powder and salt and add slowly. Blend thoroughly. Drop by teaspoonfuls onto greased cookie sheet. Bake in a preheated 350 degree oven for 12 to 15 minutes. Do not let cookies brown. Cool completely. Frost with orange icing. Makes 5 dozen.

Orange Icing:

Combine all ingredients.

This was my daughter's favorite cookie and she took it to
Bible School when she was 5. When I arrived after Bible School to pick
her up, the teacher walked her to the door. One look at the little girl with red
swollen eyes was a sure heart stopper. When she had proudly announced her
offering of "carrot cookies" to the class, each child suddenly became not
hungry. True, it gave the teacher a great opportunity the next day
to talk of feelings, not refusing a gift so willingly given etc.,
but the cookies got a new name.

Stuffed Date Drops

1	pound whole pitted dates	1¼	cups flour
1	cup pecan halves	½	teaspoon baking powder
4	tablespoons butter or margarine	½	teaspoon baking soda
¾	cup packed brown sugar	¼	teaspoon salt
1	egg	½	cup sour cream

Stuff dates with pecans and set aside. Cream butter and sugar and beat in egg. Sift together flour, baking powder, baking soda and salt. Alternately add flour mixture and sour cream. Carefully stir in dates. Drop by teaspoonfuls onto greased cookie sheet. Bake in a preheated 350 degree oven for 8 to 10 minutes. Frost with any creamy frosting. May be made ahead and frozen.

These make a great holiday cookie with red and green frosting.

Sugar-Free Oatmeal Cookies

1	cup raisins	2	cups flour
Water		1	teaspoon baking soda
1	cup margarine or butter	1	teaspoon baking powder
2	eggs, lightly beaten	½	teaspoon salt
1	teaspoon vanilla extract	1	teaspoon ground cinnamon
4	teaspoons liquid artificial sweetener	½	teaspoon grated nutmeg
		1	cup rolled oats

Cover raisins with water in a small saucepan. Bring to boil and simmer 10 minutes. Set aside. In large bowl of electric mixer cream margarine, eggs, vanilla extract and sweetener. Into another bowl sift flour, baking soda, baking powder, salt, cinnamon and nutmeg. Drain raisins and reserve 8 tablespoons of the liquid. Stir oats and raisins into flour mixture. Add flour mixture to mixer alternately with liquid from the raisins, mixing on lowest speed until all ingredients are moist and well mixed. Drop by teaspoonfuls onto cookie sheet. Bake in a preheated 350 degree oven for 10 to 12 minutes. Makes 4 to 5 dozen.

Summer Lemonade Cookies

1 cup butter or margarine, softened	3 cups flour
	1 teaspoon baking soda
1 cup sugar, plus sugar for sprinkling cookies	1 (6-ounce) can frozen lemonade concentrate, thawed, divided
2 eggs	

In a mixing bowl, cream butter and sugar; add eggs. Combine flour and baking soda; add to the creamed mixture alternately with ⅓ cup of lemonade concentrate. Mix well. Drop by rounded teaspoonfuls onto ungreased baking sheets. Bake in a preheated 400 degree oven for 8 minutes. Remove to wire racks. Brush with remaining lemonade concentrate; sprinkle with sugar. Cool. Makes 6 dozen.

Cowboy Cookies

3 cups flour	1½ cups packed light brown sugar
1 tablespoon baking powder	3 eggs
1 tablespoon baking soda	1 tablespoon vanilla extract
1 tablespoon ground cinnamon	3 cups semi-sweet chocolate chips
1 teaspoon salt	3 cups rolled oats
1½ cups butter, softened	2 cups angel flake coconut
1½ cups sugar	2 cups chopped pecans

Mix flour, baking powder, baking soda, cinnamon and salt in bowl. In a large bowl beat butter on medium speed until smooth and creamy, about 1 minute. Gradually beat in sugars. Add eggs, 1 at a time, beating after each. Beat in vanilla extract. Stir in flour mixture until just mixed. Add chocolate chips, oats, coconut and pecans. For each cookie, drop ¼ cup of dough onto ungreased cookie sheet about 3 inches apart. Bake in a preheated 350 degree oven for 17 to 20 minutes until edges are lightly browned. Remove to rack to cool. Makes 3 dozen large cookies.

Cookies-in-a-Jar

Great For Gift Giving!

Cookie Mix:

½ cup cinnamon or butterscotch chips

½ cup packed dark brown sugar

1 cup rolled oats

1 cup buttermilk biscuit baking mix, divided

½ cup packed light brown sugar

To Make Cookies:

1 jar of cookie mix

8 tablespoons butter, melted

1 egg

1 teaspoon vanilla extract

Cooking spray

Cookie Mix:

Layer ingredients into a 4-cup airtight jar in the following order: cinnamon chips, dark brown sugar, oats, 1 cup buttermilk baking mix, light brown sugar and the remaining cup of baking mix. If you still have room, add more chips. Decorate the jar as desired and give as a gift with instructions on how to make the cookies.

To Make Cookies:

Empty the contents of jar into a medium bowl and blend well. Stir in butter, egg and vanilla extract and blend well. Shape into 1-inch balls. Place on a baking sheet coated with cooking spray. Bake in a preheated 350 degree oven for 10 to 12 minutes or until the cookies are light golden brown. Makes 2½ dozen.

Cool cookies completely before storing. Store chewy cookies in an airtight container and crisp cookies in a jar or cookie tin.

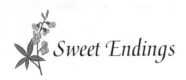

Peanut Blossoms

1	cup vegetable shortening	2	cups flour
1	cup packed brown sugar	½	teaspoon salt
1	cup sugar	2	teaspoons baking soda
2	eggs	1	(12-ounce) package semi-sweet chocolate chips
1	teaspoon vanilla extract		
1	cup peanut butter (crunchy is good)		

Cream shortening, sugars, eggs and vanilla extract. Stir in peanut butter. Add flour, salt and baking soda. Mix until mixture is creamy. Add chocolate chips. Drop by tablespoonfuls onto cookie sheet. Bake in a preheated 350 degree oven for 9 to 12 minutes until cookies are light brown. Makes about 6 dozen.

My husband hates peanut butter, but he likes these cookies!

Great Texas Pecan Cookies

1¾ cups butter (do not substitute)		1	teaspoon vanilla extract
1	cup sugar, plus sugar for forming cookies	3	cups sifted flour
		1½	cups chopped pecans

Cream butter and sugar; add vanilla extract and flour and mix well. Fold in pecans. Drop by teaspoonfuls onto ungreased cookie sheet. Mash down with fork dipped in sugar. Bake in a preheated 350 degree oven for 12 to 15 minutes or until lightly browned. Makes about 4 dozen cookies.

Applesauce Bars with Praline Topping

Bars:

4	tablespoons butter, softened	1	teaspoon baking soda
½	cup packed light brown sugar	¼	teaspoon salt
1	large egg	1½	cups peeled, chopped Golden Delicious apples
1	teaspoon vanilla extract		
1	cup chunky applesauce	½	cup chopped pecans
1½	cups flour		

Topping:

⅔	cup packed light brown sugar	1	tablespoon flour
3	tablespoons butter, softened	1	cup chopped pecans

Bars:

Cream butter and sugar. Add egg and vanilla extract; beat until well blended. Stir in applesauce. (The mixture may look curdled.) Put flour, baking soda and salt into a small bowl and stir until blended. Combine with sugar mixture. Fold in apples and pecans. Spread in a lightly buttered 13x9x2-inch pan.

Topping:

Blend brown sugar, butter and flour with a fork. Add pecans. Crumble mixture over batter. Bake on the center rack of a preheated 350 degree oven for 30 to 35 minutes or until the edges pull away from the sides of the pan.

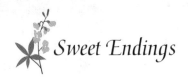

Apricot Almond Squares

Crust:

1 (18¼-ounce) package yellow or white cake mix

8 tablespoons margarine or butter, melted

½ cup finely chopped almonds

1 (14 to 16-ounce) jar apricot preserves, divided

Filling:

1 (8-ounce) package cream cheese, softened

¼ cup sugar

2 tablespoons flour

⅛ teaspoon salt

1 teaspoon vanilla extract

1 egg

Reserved apricot preserves

½ cup coconut

Crust:

In large bowl combine cake mix and margarine at low speed until crumbly. Stir in almonds. Reserve 1 cup of mixture for filling. Press remaining base mixture in bottom of well greased 13x9x2-inch pan. Carefully spread 1 cup preserves over base. (If the preserves are warmed, they will spread easier.)

Filling:

In same bowl, beat cream cheese, sugar, flour, salt, vanilla extract and egg until well mixed. Blend in remaining preserves at low speed. Carefully spread filling mixture over base. Combine reserved 1 cup base mixture and coconut. Sprinkle over filling. Bake in a preheated 350 degree oven for 30 to 40 minutes or until golden brown and center is set. Cool completely. Store in refrigerator. Makes 24 bars.

Special Coconut Bars

First Layer:

2   cups crushed graham crackers

8   tablespoons melted butter or
     margarine

2   tablespoons sugar

Second Layer:

1   cup coconut

1   (14-ounce) can sweetened
     condensed milk

½   cup chopped pecans

1   teaspoon vanilla extract

Third Layer

1   (12-ounce) package semi-sweet
     chocolate chips

½   (6-ounce) package butterscotch
     chips or a little less

1   heaping tablespoon peanut
     butter

First Layer:

Mix first layer ingredients and press in a lightly greased 13x9x2-inch pan. Bake in a preheated 350 degree oven for 8 minutes.

Second Layer:

Mix coconut, milk, pecans and vanilla extract and spread over first mixture. Bake 20 minutes more. Remove from oven.

Third Layer:

Melt chips together in double boiler. Add peanut butter to the melted chocolate mixture. Spread mixture over second layer while hot. Cool well before cutting. These freeze well.

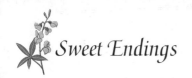

Lemon-Coconut Squares

Crust:

1½ cups sifted flour   ½ cup packed brown sugar
8 tablespoons butter, melted

Filling:

2 eggs, beaten   ¼ teaspoon salt
1 cup packed brown sugar   ½ teaspoon vanilla extract
2 tablespoons flour   1½ cups flaked coconut
½ teaspoon baking powder   1 cup chopped pecans

Frosting:

1 cup powdered sugar, sifted   Juice of 1 lemon
1 tablespoon butter, melted

Crust:

Mix crust ingredients and pat in buttered 13x9x2-inch pan. Bake in a preheated 275 degree oven for 10 minutes.

Filling:

Mix all filling ingredients thoroughly. Spread over baked crust. Bake in a preheated 350 degree oven for 20 minutes.

Frosting:

Mix all ingredients and spread over warm crust. Cut into squares. Makes 2 dozen.

Texas Gold Bars

1	(18¼-ounce) yellow cake mix without pudding	1	tablespoon vanilla extract
3	eggs, divided	1	(8-ounce) package cream cheese, softened
8	tablespoons margarine, melted	1	(1-pound) box powdered sugar, sifted

Combine cake mix, 1 slightly beaten egg and melted margarine. Press into a lightly greased 13x9x2-inch baking dish. Mix vanilla extract, cream cheese and powdered sugar. Beat the remaining 2 eggs slightly and add to mixture. Spread over top. Bake in a preheated 325 degree oven for 50 minutes. Let cool slightly before cutting into bars.

Hint: To "sift" powdered sugar, put it in a food processor and pulse 2 or 3 times.

Easy Fruit Squares

1	(18-ounce) package refrigerated sugar cookie dough	1	(11-ounce) can Mandarin oranges
1	(8-ounce) package cream cheese	1	jar salad cherries, cut in half
4	cups powdered sugar, sifted	2	kiwi, peeled, halved and sliced
1	tablespoon lemon juice		

Roll out cold cookie dough to 13x9-inch rectangle and place on cookie sheet. Bake in a preheated 350 degree oven for 8 to 9 minutes. Cool. Mix cream cheese, sugar and lemon juice and spread evenly over baked dough. Arrange fruit on top of cream cheese mixture. Cover with plastic wrap and refrigerate about 2 hours. Cut into squares.

Variation: You can substitute strawberries for the cherries and grapes for kiwi if you like.

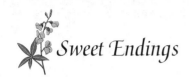

West Texas Pumpkin Bars

Bars:

4	eggs	2	teaspoons ground cinnamon
2	cups sugar	¾	teaspoon salt
1	cup vegetable oil	2	teaspoons baking powder
1	(16-ounce) can pumpkin	½	teaspoon ground ginger
2	cups flour	¼	teaspoon ground cloves
1	teaspoon baking soda	½	cup raisins

Pecan Cream Cheese Frosting:

1	(3-ounce) package cream cheese, softened	1	teaspoon vanilla extract
6	tablespoons margarine, softened	2	cups powdered sugar, sifted
		½	cup chopped pecans

Bars:

Mix eggs, sugar, oil and pumpkin in large mixing bowl. In a separate container, combine flour, baking soda, cinnamon, salt, baking powder, ginger and cloves. Add ⅓ dry ingredients to pumpkin mixture and mix well; then add another ⅓, and finally the remainder, mixing well after each addition. Stir in raisins. Pour into a greased 15x10x1-inch jelly-roll pan. Bake in a preheated 350 degree oven until light brown, 25 to 30 minutes. When cool, frost with cream cheese frosting.

Pecan Cream Cheese Frosting:

Mix cream cheese, margarine and vanilla extract. Gradually beat in powdered sugar. Spread on Pumpkin Bars and sprinkle with pecans.

These bars have been made at Thanksgiving by our family for many years. They can be frozen. Nice to have for entertaining and kids love them!

Crunchy Fudge Bars

1	(6-ounce) package butterscotch chips	1	(6-ounce) package chocolate chips
½	cup peanut butter	½	cup powdered sugar, sifted
4	cups crisp rice cereal	2	tablespoons butter
		1	tablespoon water

Melt the butterscotch chips with the peanut butter in a heavy saucepan over low heat, stirring until blended. Stir in the cereal. Press one-half of the mixture into a buttered 8x8x2-inch pan. Chill. Set remainder aside. In a double boiler, stir the chocolate chips, sugar, butter and water until the chocolate melts. Spread over the chilled mixture. Top with the reserved mixture. Cut into 1½-inch squares. Makes 25 squares.

Vienna Bars

1	cup butter	1	cup semi-sweet chocolate chips
2	egg yolks	4	egg whites
1½	cups sugar, divided	¼	teaspoon salt
2½	cups flour	2	cups finely chopped nuts
1	(10-ounce) jar raspberry or apricot preserves		

Cream butter with egg yolks and ½ cup sugar. Add flour and knead with fingers. Pat on greased cookie sheet about ⅜-inch thick. Bake in a preheated 350 degree oven for 15 to 20 minutes or until lightly browned. Remove from oven, spread with preserves and top with chocolate chips. Beat egg whites with salt until stiff. Fold in remaining 1 cup sugar and nuts. Gently spread on top of preserves and chocolate chips. Bake for another 25 minutes. Cut into squares or bars. Makes 2 dozen bars.

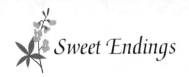

Brownie Mix-in-a-Jar

Great For Gift Giving!

Brownie Mix:

2	cups sugar	1	cup chopped pecans
1	cup cocoa	1	cup chocolate chips
1	cup flour		

To Make The Brownies:

1	cup butter or margarine, softened	4	eggs
		1	recipe brownie mix

Brownie Mix:

Layer ingredients into a 6-cup airtight jar in order given. Decorate the jar as desired and give as a gift with instructions on how to make the brownies.

To Make The Brownies:

In a large bowl of an electric mixer, cream the butter. Add the eggs, 1 at a time, beating well after each addition. Add the brownie mix and continue to beat until mixture is smooth. Spread the mixture into a greased 13x9x2-inch pan. Bake in a preheated 325 degree oven for 40 to 50 minutes. Makes 24 servings.

Tuxedo Brownies

Must Be Chilled

Brownies:

8	tablespoons butter	1	cup flour
4	ounces unsweetened chocolate	¼	teaspoon salt
4	eggs, beaten	½	teaspoon vanilla extract
2	cups sugar	1	cup chopped pecans

Filling:

4	tablespoons butter, softened	2	tablespoons milk
2	cups powdered sugar, sifted	1	teaspoon vanilla extract

Glaze:

6	ounces German sweet chocolate	6	tablespoons butter

Brownies:

In a medium saucepan, melt butter and chocolate over low heat. Add eggs, sugar, flour, salt, vanilla extract and pecans and stir until well blended. Pour brownie mixture into a lightly greased 13x9x2-inch pan. Bake in a preheated 350 degree oven for 25 minutes. Allow brownies to cool before spreading with filling. Makes 2 or 3 dozen.

Filling:

In a small bowl, blend filling ingredients. Spread evenly over brownie layer. Refrigerate until chilled.

Glaze:

In a small saucepan, melt together glaze ingredients. Cool slightly. Pour on top of brownies. Let harden. Cut into small squares or bars.

A chocolate lovers dream!

Chocolate Cherries

1	(7-ounce) package vanilla wafers, crushed
½	cup powdered sugar
½	cup finely chopped walnuts, lightly toasted
¼	cup boiling water
2	tablespoons light corn syrup

2	teaspoons brewed coffee
30	maraschino cherries with stems, chilled
18-24	ounces semi-sweet chocolate pieces
½-1	tablespoon vegetable shortening, optional

Mix together vanilla wafers, powdered sugar, walnuts, water, corn syrup and coffee and set aside. With lightly oiled or wet hands form the above mixture around the cherries and lightly freeze. Slowly melt 18 ounces chocolate in the top of a small deep double boiler. Do not let chocolate cool or reduce in temperature at any time or it will become too firm to dip. Before melting, you may add a little vegetable shortening (about ½ to 1 tablespoon) which will keep the chocolate thinner. Do not try to add anything to the chocolate later. This is tricky and you may need more chocolate to complete the recipe. Dip each cherry in melted chocolate, allowing the extra chocolate to drip back in the pan. Place on a rack or waxed paper to cool. Store in a cool dry place, in an airtight container. They will keep refrigerated for a long time. Makes 30.

Wonderful candy!

Big-Batch Fudge

4	cups sugar	2	cups semi-sweet chocolate chips
1	(12-ounce) can evaporated milk	1	pint marshmallow creme
	Butter or margarine to grease pan, plus 1 cup	1	teaspoon vanilla extract
		1	cup chopped pecans

Butter the sides, top to bottom, of a heavy, 3-quart saucepan with high sides. In it combine sugar, evaporated milk and 8 tablespoons butter. Cook over medium heat stirring frequently until it comes to a boil and all the grains of sugar are dissolved. Continue to stir frequently until reaching the soft ball stage, 235 degrees. Remove from heat; add chocolate chips and marshmallow creme. Beat until chocolate and marshmallows are melted and blended. Stir in vanilla extract and nuts. Cool to 110 degrees and then begin beating. Continue beating until fudge stiffens and loses it's gloss. Pour into a buttered 13x9x2-inch baking dish. Score fudge while warm for neater squares, using tip of a knife. When candy is cool and firm, cut along score marks.

Tumbleweeds

1	pound Almond Bark	1	(12½-ounce) can lightly salted peanuts
1	(12-ounce) package peanut butter chips	2	(1⅝-ounce) cans potato sticks

Melt Almond Bark and peanut butter chips in a medium bowl on high in microwave. Stir in peanuts and potato sticks and drop in desired size on waxed paper. Makes about 3 dozen.

Chocolate Truffles

Must Be Chilled

Truffles:

3   tablespoons unsalted butter

⅔   cup whipping cream

1   tablespoon sugar

6   ounces semi-sweet baking chocolate

1   tablespoon flavoring: vanilla extract, brandy, rum or bourbon

Coating:

Cocoa powder, optional

Chocolate sprinkles, optional

Powdered sugar, optional

Finely chopped nuts, optional

Truffles:

Heat butter, cream and sugar over almost boiling water until very hot; remove from heat and stir in chocolate until melted. Mix well; add flavoring and cool. Refrigerate until firm. Form into 1-inch balls. Place balls on wax paper lined cookie sheet. Refrigerate about 1 hour until firm.

Coating:

Roll truffles in desired coating and store in refrigerator. Bring to room temperature before serving.

Microwave Pralines

1½ cups firmly packed brown sugar
⅔ cup half-and-half
⅛ teaspoon salt

2 tablespoons butter or margarine
1½ cups pecan halves

Combine sugar, half-and-half and salt in a deep 3-quart casserole dish. Mix well. Stir in butter and microwave on high 7 to 9½ minutes or until mixture reaches soft ball stage, 235 degrees, stirring once. Stir in pecans, cool 1 minute. Beat by hand until mixture is creamy and begins to thicken, about 3 minutes. Drop by tablespoonfuls onto waxed paper. Makes 12 to 16 pralines.

Orange Pralines

2¼ cups small pecan halves
2 cups sugar
¾ cup half-and-half
¼ teaspoon salt

2½ tablespoons light corn syrup
Juice and grated zest of 1 orange
4 tablespoons butter
1 teaspoon vanilla extract

Lightly toast pecan halves in oven, set aside. Cook sugar, cream, salt and corn syrup in saucepan and stir constantly until mixture boils. Continue cooking and stirring until mixture reaches softball stage, 235 degrees, on candy thermometer. Add orange juice and zest and cook until it until it reaches 240 degrees. Add butter and vanilla extract. Cool. Beat until mixture holds shape. If it sets up too fast, add a few drops of half-and-half and warm on stove. Add pecans. Drop on waxed paper. Store in covered container. Makes 30 to 35 Pralines.

An RWC Favorite. We discovered this favorite during testing.

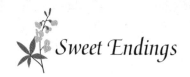

Candy Strawberries

Must Be Chilled

1 (2¼-ounce) package slivered almonds

Green food coloring

1 (7-ounce) package angel flake coconut

2 (3-ounce) packages strawberry gelatin

1 (14-ounce) can condensed milk

Red and green sugars

Toss almonds in small jar with a few drops of green food coloring. Set aside. Mix coconut, strawberry gelatin and milk well. Place in freezer or refrigerator until firm enough to handle. Shape into strawberries and roll in red sugar. Dip blossom end into green sugar. Stick green-colored almond into end for stem. Can be frozen. Makes 30 to 40 strawberries.

Quick Toffee Bars

Must Be Frozen

35 saltine crackers

½ pound butter (do not substitute)

1 cup packed dark brown sugar

1 (12-ounce) package chocolate chips

Cover jelly-roll pan with foil. Line with whole saltine crackers, pushed together. Melt butter over low heat; stir in brown sugar until thoroughly mixed. Pour mixture over crackers. Bake 350 degrees for 6 to 10 minutes or until lightly browned. Remove from oven, sprinkle top with chocolate chips and smooth over top of crackers, sealing edges. Freeze until hard. Remove from freezer; bring down on counter top with force so that it breaks into bite-size pieces. Good chilled or at room temperature. Makes 35 servings.

Variation: Reduce butter to ¼ pound. Reduce chocolate chips to 1 (6-ounce) package and add 1 cup chopped nuts.

Candy

'English 'Toffee

Candy:

1 cup butter (do not substitute)
1 cup sugar

1 tablespoon white corn syrup
1 cup chopped pecans

Topping:

1 cup pecans, divided
1 (6-ounce) package semi-sweet chocolate chips, divided

2 tablespoons vegetable shortening, divided

Candy:

Melt butter in a medium saucepan on medium high heat. Add sugar and corn syrup. Stirring constantly, cook on medium high until it reaches 290 degrees on a candy thermometer. Add pecans and cook 3 minutes more, stirring constantly. Pour into a greased 8x8x2-inch pan. Cool.

Topping:

Chop pecans in food processor until very fine like meal. Melt ½ cup chocolate chips and 1 tablespoon shortening in microwave on 50 per cent power 2 to 3 minutes until smooth. Spread on one side of candy and press ½ cup pecan meal evenly over chocolate. Cool. Turn candy on waxed paper and repeat on other side using the remaining chocolate chips, shortening and pecans. When cool break into bite-size pieces and store in a metal container. Candy will keep several weeks. Recipe may be doubled using a 15x11x1-inch jelly-roll pan.

This is our family's Christmas favorite.

Candy Dandies

2	cups sugar	½	cup peanut butter
4	tablespoons cocoa	1	teaspoon vanilla extract
½	cup milk	1¾	cups rolled oats
4	tablespoons butter	¾	cup nuts

Mix together sugar, cocoa, milk and butter in a small saucepan; bring to a boil for 1 minute. Remove from heat and add peanut butter and vanilla extract. Mix well. Quickly fold in oats and nuts and drop by teaspoonfuls onto waxed paper.

Texas Rangers

Must Be Made Ahead

70-80	pecan halves	8	(1-ounce) squares semi-sweet chocolate
½	cup bourbon		
4	cups powdered sugar, divided	1	square paraffin (about the size of 1 chocolate square), optional
¾	cup butter, softened		

Toast pecans lightly in 350 degree oven. Cool. Soak pecans in bourbon overnight. Drain pecans, reserving bourbon. Add bourbon to 2 cups powdered sugar, mixing well. Cream butter until smooth; add 2 cups powdered sugar and mix well. Combine bourbon mixture with butter mixture. Shape dough around pecan halves, forming into balls. Quick chill in freezer. Melt chocolate in double boiler. Use a wood skewer to dip chilled candy balls into chocolate and place on waxed paper to dry. (Paraffin is an option for a much firmer coating, adding more powdered sugar if needed in dough. Results will be good without the paraffin). Makes about 6 dozen candies.

Additional Contributors:

Doris Abernathy
Suzanne Adamson
Marge Alesch
Danna Almon
Connie Altemus
Phyllis Arnold
Novella Bailey
Lola Barnes
Dodie Barr
Mary Jon Bass
Brenda Beardsley
Ruth Becker
Jean Beler
Gail Bell
Jo Ann Gibson Bell
Joan Bell
Sandy Bell
Norma Bishop
Freeda Blount
Betty Blume
Mary Boyter
Betty Braham
Marvis Brock
Bernadette Brockman
Peggy Brooks
Sue Brooks
Kitty Brown
Susan Browning
Lori Brumley
Margret Bryant
Jo Buchwald
Pat Burbridge
Shannon Burton
Mary Jane Buscanics
Martha Buss
Ida Buys
Carrie Carello
Kathy Carter
Audrey Castleman
Betty Cearley
Popy Chaffee

Frank "Tiny" Chambers
Shirley Chambers
Elizabeth Chandler
Myrt Christenson
Nell Churchill
Martha Clem
Lonnie Collings
Sandy Cook
Frances Cordell
Naomi Cornman
Gloria Crouch
Alice Cunningham
Donna DeMoss
Teddy Denton
Linda Ditto
Betty Dodson
Emma Dooley
Betty Dryer
Joyce Duncan
Judy Duncan
Marilyn Duncan
Ida Dwight
Hazel Early
Velma Eden
Orene Edison
Leona Fay
Kenny Fields
Anne Fish
Allie Floyd
Mary Frost
Colleen Gardner
Carolyn Georges
Betsy Gibson
Patsy Gooding
Virginia Green
Jane Greer
Margie Griffin
Elaine Grimes
Virginia Gruben
Cindie Hackney
Joan Haefling

Wanda Hamby
Christine Hanna
Kellene Hardy
Colleen Hartley
Billye Hartman
Fern Hauck
Janice Havard
Virginia Head
Jackie Helmick
Brenda Hicks
Nancy Hicks
Gay Hilbert
Betty Hildebrand
Hazel Hill
Claire Hine
Rusty Hoffman
Betty Holcombe
Ruth Holzschuh
Raye Hoover
Jeanne Housley
Caren Houston
Jo Huffhines
Cynthia Hurley
Adele Hutton
Kathleen Jaroszewski
Marjo Jeanes
Joyce Jenkins
Mary Spain Jobe
Betty Johnson
Jean Johnson
Patricia Johnson
Peggy Jones
Carolyn Kaufman
Kellie Kauitzsch
Mary Kay
Sandy Keiser
Shady Kennedy
Ruth Kimberlin
Peggy King
Carolyn Kirklen
Doe Knower

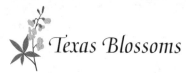

Texas Blossoms

Margaret Konings
Shirley Lake
Wilene Landfair
Mary Jo Lanford
Mary Lasiter
Betty LaVergne
Diana Leatherman
Doris Lee
Gerry Leftwich
Pearl Leino
Dorothy Levens
Ann Lewis
Linda Lewis
Imp Lightner
Deborah Lipscomb
Ann Long
Lorene Lotridge
Glenda Markwardt
Oma Ruth Massey
Susan Suttle Massey
Jan Matzdorf
Virginia Matzen
Virginia Maupin
Marjorie McBeath
Jeanne McCaleb
Dot McCalpin
Marion McDaniel
Margaret McDonald
Mary McDonald
Martha McDowell
Patsy McGuffey
Eloise McIntosh
Susan McLendon
Mary Ann McMullan
Amanda Miller
June Miller
Ann Mize
Betty Morrison
LaRuth Morrow
B. J. Mueller
Mary Ann Myers
Marie Myler
Vicky Nayes
Rhonda Neathery

Evelyn Nesselratte
Helen Newell
Ruth Newheiser
Pauline Nusser
Barbara O'Dell
Sharon Odell
Ethnye Olsen
Dorothy Ordonez
Carol Pack
Ila Parker
Pat Parker
Margene Parr
Jean Payne
Nancy Pedden
DeEtte Peters
Jo Philippi
Mildred Phillips
Patti Henry Pinch
Margaret Plugge
Carole Price
Caroline Prickett
Ruth Quance
Claire Rambin
Margaret Reaves
Helen Reed
Mary Jane Riedlinger
Shirley Rind
Kelly Ringham
Hope Rivier
Ann Robinson
Tempe Robinson
Mary Rode
Mary Ann Rumbo
Martha Schenken
Helen Schlueter
Charlotte Schubert
Catherine Schultz
Wendy Seldon
Dorsey Shaw
Shirley Shipman
Jan Shirley
Betty Shurtleff
Sheryl Skiles
Jeff Smith

Julia Sue Smith
Laura Snow
Marion Sowka
Ann Sparkman
Virginia Steenson
Dorothy Swanson
Nancy Swords
Jane Thomas
Winnie Thomas
Barbara Thompson
Carolyn Thompson
Zoe Thompson
Peggy Thorburn
Peggy Tipton
Peggy Uchman
Bonnie Valliant
Jerre Vaughn
Marjorie Veerman
Janice Vergez
Jere Wagenhals
Mary Frances Waggener
Mary Wagner
Susan Wagner
Laura Waguespack
Greta Wallace
Frances Warren
Mary Ann Webster
Yvonne Weinhardt
Pauline Welp
Patty Wierzowiecki
Gene Whitaker
Eddie Williams
June Williams
Pat Williams
Liz Willson
Alliene Wilson
Virginia Wimberly
Carolyn Wingo
Skip Winnette
Gayle Mendel Wisman
Loudell Wood
Enola Woolard
Annie Laurie Wright
Shirley Wright
Marion Young
Mae Zimmerman

Index

Index

Index

Index

Index

Index

Index

Index

O

Okra

Olives

Onions

Oranges and Orange Juice

P

Pancakes

Pasta

Index

Index

Index

Index

Index

Index

Index

Richardson Woman's Club
P.O. Box 831963
Richardson, Texas 75083-1963

Please send:

_____	copies of *Texas Blossoms*	@	$21.95 each	$ _____
	Postage & handling	@	$ 4.00 each	$ _____
	(Texas residents add tax)	@	$ 1.81 each	$ _____
			Total per Book	$ _____
_____	copies of *The Texas Experience*	@	$20.00 each	$ _____
	Postage & handling	@	$ 4.00 each	$ _____
	(Texas residents add tax)	@	$ 1.65 each	$ _____
			Total per Book	$ _____
			TOTAL ENCLOSED	$ _____

Please mail to:

Name _____

Address _____

City _____ State _____ Zip _____

Make checks payable to: *Richardson Woman's Club Texas Cookbooks*

- -

Richardson Woman's Club
P.O. Box 831963
Richardson, Texas 75083-1963

Please send:

_____	copies of *Texas Blossoms*	@	$21.95 each	$. _____
	Postage & handling	@	$ 4.00 each	$ _____
	(Texas residents add tax)	@	$ 1.81 each	$ _____
			Total per Book	$ _____
_____	copies of *The Texas Experience*	@	$20.00 each	$ _____
	Postage & handling	@	$ 4.00 each	$ _____
	(Texas residents add tax)	@	$ 1.65 each	$ _____
			Total per Book	$ _____
			TOTAL ENCLOSED	$ _____

Please mail to:

Name _____

Address _____

City _____ State _____ Zip _____

Make checks payable to: *Richardson Woman's Club Texas Cookbooks*

Please list names and addresses of your favorite stores
where you would like to see TEXAS BLOSSOMS sold.

_____

_____

_____

_____

_____

_____

_____

_____

_____

_____

_____

- -

Please list names and addresses of your favorite stores
where you would like to see TEXAS BLOSSOMS sold.

_____

_____

_____

_____

_____

_____

_____

_____

_____

_____

_____